江南大学中央高校基本科研业务费专项资金资助项目
"认知语言学视角下的外语习得研究"(2017JDZD08)

大数据时代的英语写作教学与研究

刘 梅 编著

苏州大学出版社
Soochow University Press

图书在版编目(CIP)数据

大数据时代的英语写作教学与研究/刘梅编著. —苏州：苏州大学出版社，2018.12(2019.11重印)
ISBN 978-7-5672-2679-1

Ⅰ.①大… Ⅱ.①刘… Ⅲ.①英语—写作—教学研究—高等学校 Ⅳ.①H319.36

中国版本图书馆 CIP 数据核字(2018)第 284817 号

书　　名：	大数据时代的英语写作教学与研究
编　　著：	刘　梅
责任编辑：	金莉莉
装帧设计：	刘　俊
出版发行：	苏州大学出版社(Soochow University Press)
社　　址：	苏州市十梓街1号　邮编：215006
印　　装：	虎彩印艺股份有限公司
网　　址：	www.sudapress.com
邮　　箱：	sdcbs@suda.edu.cn
邮购热线：	0512-67480030
销售热线：	0512-67481020
开　　本：	700mm×1000mm　1/16　印张：15　字数：262千
版　　次：	2018年12月第1版
印　　次：	2019年11月第3次印刷
书　　号：	ISBN 978-7-5672-2679-1
定　　价：	48.00元

凡购本社图书发现印装错误，请与本社联系调换。服务热线：0512-67481020

"Do you like writing?"
"Why do you write?"
"How often do you write?"

这是笔者每次在写作课伊始问学生的三个问题。

对第一个问题,学生的回答(每个班有一个或两个例外)基本都是"No"。

第二个问题的答案也大体一致,"因为老师要求""因为考试要求"。第三个问题,多久写一次?这个回答也可以归为几大类:"从不"(如无作业或考试要求);"偶尔";"一个月一次";"一周一次"已经是非常罕见的答案了。

当笔者明确这里的写作包括中英文,不论长短,不管正式与否,微博、QQ说说或微信朋友圈都算写作的时候,答案就不同了。写作的频率和欲望,在这个语境下,就有了非常不一样的答案。

所以,学生一直有写作、有用文字表达的欲望和能力,但是为什么具体到英语写作就变得困难了呢?进入大数据时代,多媒体和信息技术的发展日新月异,它们的到来,对于英语教学,尤其是英语写作教学的发展有什么样的意义呢?

长期以来,英语写作一直被认为是听、说、读、写、译英语几项基本技能里最难的一项。无论是在平时的学生写作练习中,还是在各种国内、国际标准化英语测试中,与其他英语技能发展相比,英语写作是学生的薄弱环节,跟英语听、读技能相比,更是远远落后。学生的雅思考试成绩单上也往往出现听力、阅读得高分甚至满分,而写作只有可怜的 6 分或 6.5 分的情况。写作能力发展滞后,一方面与写作技能本身的特点相关,另一方面也是由于我国现行的外语教学体制还是没能摆脱"应试教育"的枷锁,从小学到中学的英语教学仍然以应试为主,英语写作也是以中考和高考得高分为唯一导向。新的教学理论和方法难以进入写作课堂。其结果往往就是学生的英语作文基本上都是"洋八股"的套路,议论文写作套路更是重灾区。在这样的教学模式导向下,学生鲜有机会写出表达自我价值、反映时代脉搏、充满真情实意、语言鲜活灵动的好文章。在大学新生入学以后的写作中也往往发现,学生对议论文写作相对熟悉,各种模板、套路信手拈来。在课后的调查和访问中,学生也反映在高考应试阶段背诵过大量的范文,中学老师在课堂上强调的也是写作得分的套路。因此,大学英语写作教学课堂开始阶段的学生作业,陈词滥句屡见不鲜,而且积习难改。在这种情况下,传统的教法和写法无法激起学生进一步的学习兴趣和写作欲望。只有采用新颖的教学方法、多元的教学管理,加强师生互动和生生互动,融合数字化平台和大数据技术,才能提升学习者对英语写作教学的满意度和幸福感。

但是进入大数据时代,面对怎样切实提升学生英语写作能力的任务,大部分教师仍感力不从心:怎样设计适合时代特点的写作话题?怎么有效组织课堂教学?如何批改作文并给出反馈?如何运用大数据为教学服务?这些都是写作教学中的重要环节。即使写作教师认真地对待这些环节,也并不能保证学生的实际写作能力就会得到有效提升。同时,大学英语写作教学,即使是英语专业的写作课堂,也存在着教学课时不足的问题。写作教师一般至少担任两个班级的写作教学任务,大学英语的写作教师面临的是大班课教学,人数更多而课时更少。大量的写作批改任务也使得教师对学生习作的评改费时长、反馈慢、效率低。此外,学生写作动机缺乏,课后自主写作练习不够,等等,这些都导致现阶段英语写作教学效果不太令人满意,学生写作水平较低。

众所周知,写作能力是语言能力发展中十分重要的一环,也是构建思辨能力的有机组成部分。随着教育理念的发展更新和"互联网+"大数据时代的到来,现代教学中对多媒体和网络技术的运用日渐增多。大数据时代为大学英语写作教学提供了新的方式和资源,使写作教学可以不再局限于教材和课堂之中,也为学生写作能力的提升提供了契机。对于广大的英语写作教师而言,信息化和数据化的教学环境会给传统的写作课堂带来怎样的改变?应该怎么应对大数据时代带给英语写作教学的挑战?怎么抓住机遇全面提升写作教学和学生写作能力？这都是需要思考和解决的问题。目前有关写作的书籍很多，但是以写作教材为主，英语写作教学的研究理论类书籍甚少。将大数据技术与英语写作教学相结合，全方面分析、研究新时期英语写作教学新生态环境和发展的系统性著作更为鲜见。

　　本书就是基于这样的角度，将大数据时代的多媒体和网络技术与英语写作教学和研究相结合，探索大数据时代英语写作教学的改革与创新。它系统性地将大数据为外语教育，特别是英语写作教学发展带来的变化、挑战与机遇进行全方位地剖析，对大数据时代给英语写作带来的创新性的教与学的方式进行深度探讨，以期为大学英语写作教学与研究提供新的启示和途径，也为学生写作能力的提升提供参考和建议。

　　本书分为八个章节。第一章对英语写作教学研究进行梳理，回顾和评价了英语写作教学领域的研究主题、研究主体、研究方法、研究内容、研究手段及写作研究发展趋势。第二章从英语写作教学的角度详细探讨了大数据的时代特点，包括写作者身份和教学管理者身份的多重性，基于数字化平台的写作体验（如移动写作、协作写作、同题写作等）以及与英语写作课堂相结合的慕课、微课和翻转课堂等。第三章分析了大数据时代为英语写作教学带来的变化、挑战与机遇，以及如何结合大数据技术进行写作教学模式重构。第四章尝试性探讨了英语写作教学与研究中的热点和难点——大数据时代英语写作中的身份构建。从基于语料库的英语写作者身份建构，到英语写作教师的身份建构，并以国外两名写作教师的案例分析报告为例，探索写作中身份研究的意义。第五章对大数据时代的网络资源与数据库运用、自动写作评估系统实践与研究进行综合评测。第六章是本书的重点：大数据时代英语写作的评价与反馈。在对英语写作反馈的理论进行简要评介后，结合笔者教学实践中的大量案例分析和实例，详细地、系统性地分析教师反馈、同伴反馈、在线反馈、线上线下多稿评改的混合反馈方式的优势和劣势。笔者期待通过这些详尽的案例和评析，给写作教学同人们提供英语写作评价和反馈方式的一个最佳视角，并结合自己学生的特色和课程特点，经过不断尝试、反思和改进，发现属于自己的最优化教学途径。第七章从自己教学实践的经验出发，结合大数据的新生态环境，对新型的英语写作课程设计提供了一个示例和参考。课程设计难免不成熟，存在诸多不足。希望通过这个不太完善的课程设计,为写作教学提供一些启发。第八章基于笔者20年从事英语专业第一线教学工作,尤其中写作教学的经验,全面地总结、分析了在学生习作中常出现的错误,并与读者们分享优秀的学生习作。

真诚地希望这本将系统化的理论研究与大量的学生案例结合起来进行分析探讨的小书,能够给读者们带来一些启发和思考。最后,特别感谢江南大学朱敏华老师给本书提供的素材和帮助。感谢本书的策划编辑杨华为书稿付出的辛勤劳动。书中难免有不足之处,恳请读者们批评指正。

刘梅　江南大学
2018 年 7 月

目 录

第一章　英语写作教学研究梳理 / 1

　　第一节　写作研究主题分类 / 1

　　第二节　写作研究现状分析 / 5

　　第三节　写作研究发展趋势 / 7

第二章　大数据的时代特点——从英语写作教学的角度 / 9

　　第一节　写作者身份的多重性 / 10

　　第二节　教学管理者身份的多重性 / 11

　　第三节　基于数字化平台的写作体验 / 13

　　第四节　慕课、微课与翻转课堂 / 22

第三章　大数据时代英语写作教学的改革与创新 / 25

　　第一节　大数据为英语写作教学带来的变化、挑战与机遇 / 25

　　第二节　大数据时代英语写作教学模式重构 / 33

第四章　大数据时代英语写作中的身份建构 / 37

　　第一节　基于语料库的英语写作者身份研究 / 38

　　第二节　英语写作教师身份研究 / 40

　　第三节　写作中身份研究的意义 / 48

第五章　大数据时代英语写作的资源运用与评估　/ 49

　　第一节　网络资源与数据库　/ 49
　　第二节　自动写作评估系统　/ 53
　　第三节　自动写作评估系统研究与实践　/ 54
　　第四节　小结　/ 56

第六章　大数据时代英语写作的评价与反馈　/ 57

　　第一节　英语写作反馈的理论基础　/ 57
　　第二节　教师反馈与案例分析　/ 58
　　第三节　同伴反馈与案例分析　/ 77
　　第四节　在线反馈与案例分析　/ 96
　　第五节　线上线下多稿评改的混合反馈模式　/ 123

第七章　大数据时代英语写作的课程设计　/ 145

　　第一节　写作课程设计理论基础　/ 145
　　第二节　写作课程教学目标的重新定位　/ 148
　　第三节　英语写作课程设计示例　/ 150
　　第四节　写作课程评价与反馈　/ 154

第八章　学生习作与评析　/ 159

　　第一节　学生习作常见错误与分析　/ 159
　　第二节　学生习作与评析　/ 176

结语　/ 209

附录　/ 212

参考文献　/ 217

第一章 英语写作教学研究梳理

英语写作能力培养，作为听、说、读、写、译几项基本技能里最难培养也最难见成效的一项，一直以来都是国内英语教育工作者尤其是写作教学专家和学者研究和探讨的主题。过去30多年来，随着研究者对写作研究的重视，英语写作研究论文数量持续、稳步增长。研究内容越来越深入并细化到研究的每个层面；研究方法不断得到拓展；跨课程、跨学科的研究陆续涌现；研究成果越来越技术化和立体化。及时梳理和分析国内英语写作研究的历时性发展进程，有利于廓清问题，查漏补缺，看清今后英语写作研究的发展趋势和方向。

第一节 写作研究主题分类

总的说来，过去30多年来，国内对英语写作研究的兴趣持续增长，论文数量逐年增加。在研究方法上，非实证性研究比例逐渐下降，实证性研究比例上升并占据优势，实证性研究的数据收集方法更加多样化(朱岩岩，2011；赵俊峰、郝晶、高艳明，2010)；在研究内容上，涵盖英语写作的各个主要方面，如写作教学、写作结果、写作语境、读者反馈、写作过程、评估、评分与测试、研究回顾等(李志雪、李绍山，2003；秦朝霞，2009)。其中写作教学的研究比重最大，写作反馈、写作影响因素受到普遍的关注，写作结果的研究有所下降，写作过程得到一定程度的重视，而在写作教师、写作教材、跨学科研究方面尚需加强(张之材，2018)。此外，英语写作研究与多媒体网络教学平台、现代信息技术等结合更加紧密；尤其是在进入以用户创建内容和社交互动的 Web 2.0 的时代后，技术支持的社会交互在英语写作教学中的作用日益凸显。移动学习、数字化平台、大数据等新技术的涌现，为技术支持的英语写作教学与研究提供了新的方法和视野(罗凌，2017)。

李志雪、李绍山的研究以 1993—2002 年间 CNKI 所收录的国内 8 家外语类核心期刊上的写作文献(不包括各种书评和访谈)为源数据,秦朝霞的研究同样以这 8 家外语类核心期刊文章为基础,时间跨度为 2000 年至 2007 年。这 8 家外语类核心期刊分别是:《外语教学与研究》《现代外语》《解放军外国语学院学报》《外语界》《外语与外语教学》《外语研究》《外语学刊》《外语教学》。朱岩岩增加了《外语电化教学》和《外国语》两种外语类核心期刊。秦朝霞、李志雪、李绍山、赵俊峰、朱岩岩的数据截止到 2010 年,赵俊峰的研究梳理时间跨度最短(2005—2007),朱岩岩的研究时间跨度稍大(1980—2010);他们的数据都限定于外语类核心期刊(8 种或 10 种)。张之材的研究回顾时间截止到 2016 年,是英语写作研究综述类时间节点最新的。按照以往此类研究的文献来源以及期刊载文的实际情况,作为此类研究最新的综述,张之材选定的也是 8 家外语类核心期刊作为文献来源。通过比较各类核心期刊英语写作论文综述,笔者可以把这段时间与英语写作相关的研究主题归类如下。

表 1.1　国内英语写作研究论文综述

论文概况	文献选择	期刊选取范围	主题分类
李志雪,李绍山. 对国内英语写作研究现状的思考——对八种外语类核心期刊十年(1993—2002)的统计分析[J]. 外语界,2003(6).	1993—2002 年,127 篇	8 种:《现代外语》《外语教学与研究》《解放军外国语学院学报》《外语界》《外语与外语教学》《外语学刊》《外语研究》《外语教学》	写作教学、跨课程/跨学科研究、影响英语写作的因素、篇章结构、写作测试与评估、语言、写作中存在问题及其他
秦朝霞. 国内大学英语写作研究现状及发展趋势分析[J]. 现代外语,2009(2).	2000—2007 年,136 篇	8 种:同上述 8 种	写作教学、写作结果、写作语境因素、读者反馈、写作研究回顾、写作评估评分、测试过程、写作过程
赵俊峰,郝晶,高艳明. 大学英语写作研究现状调查[J]. 外语学刊,2010(6).	2005—2007 年,71 篇	8 种:同上述前 6 种及《外国语》《国外外语教学》	写作教学研究、写作文本研究、写作理论研究、语料库研究、写作研究综述、写作测试与评估、写作教材研究、影响外语写作的因素
朱岩岩. 对我国英语写作研究发展的调查和思考[J]. 外语界,2011(6).	1980—2010 年,426 篇	10 种:同李志雪、李绍山 8 种及《外国语》《外语电化教学》	学生策略因素、教师教学因素、写作语言因素、写作环境因素、反思与借鉴

(续表)

论文概况	文献选择	期刊选取范围	主题分类
张之材.2008—2016年国内大学英语写作研究述评——基于8种外语类核心期刊的统计分析[J].当代教育理论与实践,2018(1).	2008—2016年,189篇	8种:同李志雪、李绍山8种	写作理论与现状总结、写作过程、写作结果、写作影响因素、写作教学、写作反馈、写作教师、写作教材、写作测试与评估、跨课程/跨学科研究

表1.2 英语写作研究论文主题的数量与比例

研究主题	数据来源	数量/个	占比/%
写作教学研究	李志雪、李绍山文	37	29.31
	秦朝霞文	54	39.7
	朱岩岩文	66	15.49
	赵俊峰等文	28	39.4
	张之材文	55	29
写作影响因素	李志雪、李绍山文	17	13.39
	秦朝霞文	24	17.64
	朱岩岩文	57	13.38
	赵俊峰等文	13	18.3
	张之材文	27	14
反馈方式	朱岩岩文	37	8.69
	秦朝霞文	8	5.8
	张之材文	29	5
写作测试与评估	李志雪、李绍山文	8	6.3
	秦朝霞文	6	4.4
	朱岩岩文	31	7.2
	赵俊峰等文	13	18.3
	张之材文	19	10
跨课程/跨学科研究	李志雪、李绍山文	20	15.74
	朱岩岩文	27	6.34
	张之材文	4	2
	秦朝霞文	5	3.7
研究综述/回顾	朱岩岩文	13	3.05
	赵俊峰等文	2	2.8

可以看出,在本阶段涉及的各类英语写作研究论文主题里,写作教学研究一直占有重要的地位。究其原因,长期以来,被诟病"费时低效"的写作教学一直是研究者关注的焦点。比较各个时期的数据可以看出,各时期的具体比例虽

然有所不同,但写作教学在同时期所有研究主题里占比最大。写作教学的研究呈多角度趋势,所探讨的内容又可细分为三大板块:教学现状类(包括课程设置、教材、教学问题调研)、教学实践类(包括各类写作教学方法引介或试验、教学环节、教学课件和软件开发)和教学理论类(包括大学英语写作教学目标、途径与构想)。

写作影响因素方面的研究占比仅次于写作教学研究。写作过程可以受到非常复杂的因素影响,既有宏观的、外部的中西语言问题,又有微观的、内部的学习者个体因素,还有客观的任务布置,等等。宏观方面的研究多是关于母语思维、语言迁移等外部因素影响。学习者个体因素方面,研究者从认知心理、写作焦虑、写作动机、写作策略等方面进行研究。王立非(2005)从国内英语写作实证研究的文章中发现,在众多影响因素中,二语水平、母语写作能力、写作任务和条件、写作练习频率、元认知能力等对二语写作的质和量有不同程度的影响。数字化手段的运用、大数据时代的到来也为英语写作影响因素方面的研究提供了新的思路和途径。罗凌(2017)基于自建平台对大学生移动英语写作学习行为进行了调查与分析,并通过问卷和访谈了解学生对移动英语写作的效果评价。

自从过程写作法被引入二语教学以来,反馈随之成为写作教学的一个重要环节。写作的反馈形式和方法也逐渐成为近年来写作研究者关注的重点,反馈研究成为发展最快的主题之一,写作评估反馈的总数量逐年递增。反馈的形式主要有同伴反馈、教师反馈、在线反馈和多元反馈对比研究。在同伴反馈方面,研究者从同伴互评的有效性、反馈模式测量评价表、同伴的分组方式以及对写作能力发展的作用等角度展开研究。在教师反馈方面,有对教师书面反馈特征、反馈焦点和策略的研究,但更注重教师反馈对学生英语写作的影响研究(张之材,2018)。朱岩岩(2014)在2000—2013年国内二语写作评估反馈研究论文的调查中指出,虽然以经验式、总结式为主的非实证性研究的论文仍占多数,但以定量、定性研究为主的实证性研究在缓慢上升。英语写作评估反馈研究近年来开始借鉴多媒体技术、数字化平台、语料库等现代教学手段。研究内容上涵盖二语写作中的自我评估、教师反馈、同伴互评、计算机辅助评估、多级评估模式等诸多方面。杨晓琼、戴运财(2015)介绍了自动写作评分系统和批改网写作优势,采用问卷调查、半开放式访谈和对学生作文进行实验前测、后测的方法,对批改网在大学英语写作教学中的使用情况进行学生写作能力、写作学习动机和自我效能感的实证研究。研究结果表明,基于批改网的自主写作教学模式能够有效提高学生的英语写作总体水平,激发学生的英语写作学习动机和提高自我效能感。

此外,写作测试与评估、跨课程和跨学科研究的论文也都占有一定比例。写作教材、研究综述等方面的研究较少。近期的研究热点"二语写作中的身份"几乎很少涉及。

第二节 写作研究现状分析

一、研究主体

纵观 30 多年来的英语写作研究文献,过去对写作的研究以教学法、篇章结构、写作与相关学科的关系、写作错误分析等为主,研究主体为学生的研究相对较少。近年来的研究更关注学习者主体,研究学生写作心理、写作情感因素、写作策略运用等学习者影响因素的文章大量增加。研究对象绝大多数仍然是本科生,尤其是非英语专业本科生,其次是英语专业本科生,研究对象为硕士和博士的较少。

二、研究方法

从研究方法上来看,从以"非材料性方法为主,以实证性研究为辅"的研究(李志雪、李绍山,2003)逐渐发展到非实证性研究逐渐下降、实证性研究缓慢上升的阶段(朱岩岩,2011)。在 2010 年,实证性研究论文已经占到该年度英语写作研究论文总数的 94.87%。赵俊峰等(2010)也提出实证性研究已占据绝对优势。在 2005—2007 年间所选的 71 篇文献中,实证研究 63 篇,达到总数的 90.1%。从 2005 年的 83.3%,到 2006 年的 92.3%,再到 2007 年的 95%,实证研究数量一直在稳步攀升。相比之下,非实证研究所占比例呈逐年递减趋势。当然,赵俊峰等的研究时间跨度只有 3 年,所选文献相对有限。但结合朱岩岩的数据,可以确定的是,自 2005 年以后实证性研究就一直高于非实证性研究。

我国语言学研究统计方法还是比较单调的,定量研究方法应用水平有待提高。在采用实证性研究方法时,由于研究者对统计学研究方法掌握不够,在研究中会出现变量选取不足或不恰当等问题。技术手段的运用和网络平台评估方式丰富了研究手段和数据采集方法,但从效度和信度上如何加强研究方法的科学性仍然是今后实证研究要解决的问题。

三、研究内容

李志雪、李绍山(2003)曾指出,传统的写作研究重点多年不变,关于写作教学方面的研究一直占比很重,所以重复研究现象严重。如介绍"过程教学法"和"成品教学法"的文章早在1996年就已经出现,但到了2002年仍然有相同主题的文章,内容和研究方法大同小异。写作影响因素和写作中的语言问题等也存在同样的重复研究现象。但近年来写作教学研究主题的强势地位逐渐削弱,写作研究内容呈现多元化、多角度、更加细致深入的趋势。(秦朝霞,2009;赵俊峰等,2010;张之材,2018)

四、研究手段

技术的革新与发展给英语写作提供了丰富的资源和发展契机。越来越多的高校建立起数字化教学网络。这些现代化的多媒体教学设施和设备不仅为学生创设了自主学习、移动学习的资源环境,也为广大研究者提供了现代化的教学和研究平台,大大丰富了写作方式、教学方式和研究手段。网络反馈方式的研究以句酷批改网最具代表性。研究者认为批改网在大学英语写作教学中对于提高学生的自主写作能力、激发学生用英语写作的动机、提高学生对自身写作能力的自我效能感等方面有着积极意义,也有助于深化大学英语教学改革所倡导的培养学生自主学习能力的理念(杨晓琼、戴运财,2015),但是这种网络评估和反馈方式也存在明显不足。何旭良(2013)在关于批改网英语作文评分的信度和效度的研究中发现基于网络平台的评价和反馈具有其局限性:在词汇和语法层面给予学生的反馈较多,但在写作内容、篇章结构、语体修辞、内容逻辑性及连贯性方面尚不能给予学生足够的反馈。另外,和教师的人工评分相比,基于批改网的机器评分显著偏高。杨晓琼、戴运财(2015)也指出批改网对于内容切题、篇章结构、逻辑等方面无法全面评估;不能识别结构较复杂的句子;"低频警示"疑为中式英语,但未能给出参考用法;评语概括性强,未给予详细评价;等等。要充分利用批改网的优势,一方面要提高系统的智能性,丰富语料库;另一方面基于网络技术的写作评估与反馈方式,要和其他反馈手段相结合,以弥补其不足。只有在大学英语写作教学中结合运用批改网的在线即时反馈、同伴反馈和教师反馈时,学生的自主写作能力及写作教学质量才会得到有效提高。

此外,大数据、移动学习等关键词也进入研究者视野并成为新的研究手段。

大数据与外语教育的有机融合改变了新时期英语写作教学的生态环境,创新了英语写作教与学的方式,为我国外语教育提供了新的发展空间。王娜(2016)所在的北京科技大学基于数字化英语写作教学团队使用数字化平台开展写作教学与研究,探索数字化写作教学对学生写作能力与写作动机的影响,以及其对传统课堂结构变革的促进作用。优质平台的数字化学习资源能够有效地改善课堂教学结构,促进学生真实、自主、建构性地认知,从而提高文本的质量、流畅性、准确性和丰富性,并改善写作过程。多元化、开放式、微型化、数字化的学习资源,对学生英语写作能力的提高产生了积极且深远的影响。李书影(2017)介绍了大数据与英语写作智能平台的结合:从人机互动情况、数据维度变化、人工反馈与机器反馈数据对比、AI主题文艺作品等角度解读学习者的自主学习特点和语言产出能力,探究大数据生态环境下英语写作教学的新途径。

可以看出,随着现代教育技术、网络远程教学、翻转课堂等的进一步广泛开展,如何实现传统教学手段和大数据时代网络平台教学手段的融合互补,将是今后相当长一段时间内英语写作教学与研究的方向。

第三节　写作研究发展趋势

综上所述,国内英语写作研究处于平稳发展的状态,2000年以后英语写作研究论文数量更是经历了井喷式增长。英语写作的研究方法越来越科学,研究内容越来越细化,研究手段越来越多样化,研究结果越来越立体化,但在外语类核心期刊论文总量中所占比例仍然偏低,研究综述的比例仍然有待提高。在语料库应用、写作思辨能力培养、学术英语写作、在线评价与反馈等研究热点出现的同时,对于写作理论、写作教师、写作教材以及跨学科研究还可以进一步加强。

二语写作中的身份(identity)是目前英语写作研究中的热点与难点,它关系到写作的过程、结果、作者、教师和整个写作领域的方方面面。我国英语学习者的英语写作能力依然欠缺,如何运用语言构建作者身份,进一步有效参与国际社会文化交流,提升写作能力是广大研究者们要思考和探究的问题。关于英语写作者身份研究、英语写作教师身份研究、写作领域身份研究等都将为我国二语写作教学与研究的未来提供新的理论和视角。

随着现代教育技术的更新发展、数字化学习资源的建设和应用,信息技术与外语教育的融合将进一步加深。大数据时代将英语写作教学与信息技术整合在一起,为学生写作资料的收集、作业的提交、习作的修改和评阅、教师教学资料的呈现、课堂活动的组织、师生在线互动等提供支持,从而实现写作教学评估系统与写作教学的无缝对接。当今的大学英语写作教学具有文本、作者与读者三大基本取向(王海啸,2014),对于这三方面的研究可以反映出学生的技能与认识等因素,教师将大数据特点注入写作教学中,可以帮助学生更加全面地把握作者与文本之间的关系。通过积极构建写作教学评估系统,创建数字化英语写作资源平台,教育者和研究者们可以借助评估系统进行数据分析,及时了解学生的学习状态及他们在学习上存在的困难。比如,教师可以通过大数据查看学生的在线活动,了解他们在词汇、句型、语法方面的使用现状,进而调整教学方法。

毫无疑问,大数据环境赋予英语写作教学与研究更加丰厚的内涵。同时,大数据的时代特点也为大学英语写作教学,包括写作教学资源、写作目的、写作内容与组织、写作辅助手段与工具、写作评估及写作能力的内涵带来从观念到行为等多方面的变化。大学英语写作教学改革也面临着新的机遇和挑战(王海啸,2014)。英语教育者和研究者们在适应的同时,也在努力探索、改革和创新。

大数据时代的写作研究成果不局限于传统的研究论文、论著,还将涌现出更多新形式,比如英语写作软件、英语评估修改平台(软件)、英语写作教学网站、英语写作资源数据库等。积极探索和建设数字化学习资源,对促进教学内容和教学方法的改革、激发学生的学习兴趣、提高教学效果和教学质量均有着积极的意义。如何利用现代信息技术和资源设计出满足学生个性化学习需求的教学方案?如何利用用户所产生的数据开发出更加智能化、更有针对性的写作教学与评估系统?如何建设一支既精通教学又掌握技术的新型师资队伍?如何利用大数据更好地为英语写作教学和研究服务?这些都将是今后相当长时间内英语写作教学和研究者以及技术人员要面临的课题。

可以预见,英语写作教学与研究将朝着全方位、科学化、数据化和多元化的方向发展。

第二章 大数据的时代特点——从英语写作教学的角度

信息化时代为外语教学提供了全新的学习方式和前所未有的丰富资源。21世纪互联网技术的发展和普及及新媒体的出现又使人类社会从信息时代跨入一个全新的大数据时代。笔者以"大数据"为关键词在中国知网对2015年以来的论文进行了检索(时间跨度为2015年1月1日到2018年7月20日),共检索到论文95 876篇。显然大数据这一主题受到学者们的广泛关注。在"外国语言文字"分类下,检索到以"大数据"为关键词的论文484篇。可见,外语界的学者们也开始关注大数据时代对外语教学与研究的影响。再把"写作"的关键词添加进来和"大数据"一起在外国语言文字分类下检索,文献数量达到127篇,占了外语语言文字研究近1/3的量。可以看出,这3年来大数据时代的信息技术为传统的英语写作教学带来的变化和挑战已引起了英语写作教学研究者越来越多的关注。

"大数据"一词由英文"big data"(海量数据、巨量数据)翻译而来,是指由数量巨大、结构复杂、类型众多的数据构成的数据集合。大数据带来的信息风暴正在变革我们的生活、工作和思维方式,大数据开启了一次重大的时代转型。它给英语写作带来系统性的变革,对教师角色、学生角色、学习材料、写作环境以及写作的评估和测试等方面产生深远影响(刘润清,2014)。在大数据时代,学生可以利用网络输入作文关键词,轻松获取海量的话题资源和数据。强大的搜索引擎和数字化平台还能提供多样化的写作指导、测试与反馈。这也为英语写作教师带来新的机遇和挑战。外语教师开始关注大数据方法对外语教学创新的启示,思考大数据时代英语教师教学能力的提升,以及写作研究与改革的新途径。

麦肯锡全球研究所的报告《大数据:创新、竞争和生产力的下一个前沿领域》里首次提出大数据概念,把大数据定义为大小超出了传统数据库软件工具的抓取、存储、管理和分析能力的数据群。麦肯锡的报告指出,海量的数据规模、快速的数据流转、多样的数据类型和价值密度低是大数据的四大特征。维克托·迈尔-舍恩伯格及肯尼斯·库克耶编写的《大数据时代》(2013)认为大数据具有5V特点:Volume(大量)、Velocity(高速)、Variety(多样)、Value(低价值密度)、Veracity(真实性)。大数据时代对大学英语写作教学改革的推进意义深远,王海啸总结了大数据时代的特点及其对大学英语写作教学的启示。他把大数据的时代特点归纳为9大点:用户既是数据的使用者,也是数据的生产者;数据来源于合作,合作能够产生更多的数据;数据与产生数据者的意志和意识可以是无关的;数据产生同时也运用于社会的各行各业;对数据的评价与分享也是数据;公众对信息的甄别能力愈加重要;数据可以帮助预测,也可以提供建议;大数据带来全新的时间和空间概念;大数据带来新的行为和思维方式(王海啸,2014)。杨永林等(2014)则认为人们对大数据时代的理解有多面性,语言教学者与研究者们应该做的是针对不同的研究对象,采用功能化的分析,了解大数据开发与研究的意义。他进一步把大数据研究和英语写作结合起来,提出了12个方面的功能性特点:(1)量大面广:学生群体大,参与教师多,课程门类广。(2)过程真实:教学过程真实自然,动态扩展,管理便捷。(3)内容可比:教学内容多元实用,既可细化,又可参比。(4)管理可控:教学组织全程可控,教学活动记录完整、全面。(5)海量资源:教学资源海量储备,检索方便,一键调取。(6)自动分类:问题类型合理,海量数据真实,亦可自动分类。(7)多元反馈:反馈信息充分,知识点多,靶向性强,推送及时。(8)评测绿色:测验考试动态化、绿色化;作业批改自动化、智能化。(9)四化管理:成绩管理上,实现了参数化、自动化、常态化、便捷化。(10)数据友好:数据挖掘(data mining)、管理智能、提取便捷、分析简便。(11)诉求精确:提取的大数据无须筛选,可直接满足用户对当前任务的精确诉求。(12)靶向应用:提取的大数据无须二次加工,可以直接使用,省时省力,方便教学。

笔者将大数据背景和英语写作教学与研究相融合,总结特点如下。

第一节 写作者身份的多重性

近年来,英语写作领域身份的多重性已逐渐受到越来越多学者们的关注。写作者的身份(writer identity)研究对于英语写作教学与改革有着重要的意义。大数据又赋予了写作者身份更多的内涵。大数据时代,网络和数字化平台使写作前所未有地走近大众,极大地扩张了传统写作主体的内涵。写作者真正成了学习的中心,自主学习性大大增强;他/她可以自己决定怎么学、学什么、如何学、何时学、在哪里学、学快一点还是慢一点(刘润清,2014)。师生关系也发生了变化,大数据时代使得谁都可以成为信息和资源的拥有者,教师失去了绝对的权威,写作者也可以参与知识的协商和共建。写作者与读者的间隔被消解,写作者身份与读者身份融为一体。写作者本人既是作者又是读者。写作也不再是作者一个人的自言自语和独自狂欢,任何作品都可以由写作者传到面向公众的数字化平台,通过双向的反馈和对话,实现写作者、读者、评价者与反馈者之间的有效互动。写作者身份也随时可以转换为读者、评价者、反馈者。这种身份的互换无形中会增加写作者的写作兴趣,促使写作者更加注重提升自己的写作能力和思辨能力。

第二节 教学管理者身份的多重性

教师身份是教师这一特殊社会群体依据社会的客观期望并凭借自己的主观能力,为适应所处环境而表现出来的特定行为方式。在大数据时代背景下,教学内容、教学方法、教学手段、教学环境等的改变促使作为教学管理者的教师身份相应发生改变。传统的教师角色是传道、授业、解惑。传统的课堂里教师是讲授者、课堂活动组织者、信息资源提供者。大数据时代,教师身份更加多元化。

一、学习资源的管理者和数据的整合者

在教育的大数据背景下,学生能轻易获得丰富的英语写作学习资源与地道的英语学习材料。国内外大学开发的英语写作精品课和慕课等视频提供了无限的学习机会和信息来源。在这个前提下,英语写作教师已经不只是单纯的信息提供者,而是学习资源的管理者和大数据的整合者。在学生面对海量数据无所适从时对英语学习资源进行评估,帮助她们做出更好的选择,剔除糟粕,留下更有针对性的、有价值的内容。在此基础上再对学习材料进行有机整合,根据学生特点和需求,选定教学内容。这也需要教师具有大数据时代的信息技术应用能力,能熟练运用各种技术手段和数字平台为写作学习、教学服务。

二、知识的协商者和互动学习的指导者

丰富的网络资源和数据决定了学生和教师在知识信息的获取方面具有同

等身份。英语写作教师的权威身份被打破,变成知识的协商者和互动学习的指导者。英语写作教师与学生以文本为交流通道和信息载体,双方进行积极有效、多方位的动态交流。针对不同的写作任务,教师引导学生获取大数据下的有效信息,组织线上线下讨论,进行合作协商、意义协商,不断提高写作文本的输出质量。教师与学生在积极有效的动态交流中,借助于大数据背景下数字化资源平台的支持,组成学习团队,分享海量范文,实现互评互议,激发学生的写作兴趣,了解"对话"与"交流"对于语言表达的重要性,在自然真实的学习过程中,提高英语写作技能。(杨永林,2012)

三、写作过程的诊断者和写作成果的评估者

写作教学中的"师生交互",更为主要地体现在作业批改与反馈上。传统的写作教学模式为:学生写作—提交书面作业—教师评改、反馈—学生根据要求修改完善。有的写作教师会要求学生修改完善后进行二次反馈,甚至三次、四次等多次评改反馈。如此循环往复也是写作课教师工作量繁重、学生对写作缺乏兴趣的原因之一。作文评改与反馈作为英语写作教学的重要一环,对学生提高语言能力和写作能力有着不可低估的作用。在大数据背景下,借助于数字化和网络平台,一方面,学习者可以借助于学习语料库提供的海量优质资源,选择适合自己水平和进度的语言输入量,比如,选择自己感兴趣的话题进行写作;另一方面,写作者完成习作后,通过数字化平台的自动评分与评改系统,可以及时获得充分的反馈信息,根据评改建议修改完善。然后可以按照自己的需要多次提交,获得尽可能多的反馈建议,从而达到丰富写作者语言输出、提高写作能力的目的。教师作为评价者和反馈者的身份在这一过程中被削弱,但绝对不是可以被取代的。对于数字化平台写作的研究表明,自动评分与反馈系统还存在诸多不足,如不能识别结构较复杂的句子,不能评估学生作文的流畅性,对疑为中式英语的用法未能给出参考用法;评语概括性强、未给予详细评价从而不能切实提升写作者语言输出能力等(何旭良,2013;杨晓琼、戴运财,2015)。研究者把文中段落颠倒后进行评测,结果得到相同的分数。这就意味着自动评测系统对于最为重要的宏观评测方面,如内容是否切题、篇章结构是否合理、逻辑论证是否完善等方面无法全面评估。而这些方面对于英语写作能力都是至关重要的。缺乏这些方面的诊断和指导,学生无法真正获得写作能力的提升。这也正是为什么写作教师在学生的写作过程和习作评测反馈中还需要扮演诊断者和评估者的角色。教师评改和反馈更灵活,更全面,更有针对性,对全局的把握也

更强,也就具有更高的信度和效度。大数据时代英语写作教师的诊断和评估结合网络平台的技术手段,能弥补单一反馈模式的不足,切实提升学生的写作能力。

第三节 基于数字化平台的写作体验

数字化学习资源是信息技术与教育深度融合的落脚点之一,技术支持的英语写作教学近年来已引起众多外语教学研究者的关注。在进入用户创建内容、分享数据、使用数据进行社交互动的 Web 2.0 时代以来,技术支持的交互写作在教学中的重要作用逐渐凸显。大数据、数字化平台、移动学习等纷纷进入人们的视野,也为外语写作教学与研究提供了新的资源与途径。

基于优质平台的数字化写作教学能有效提高学生的英语写作能力(陈娟文、王娜,2016)。在大数据时代,英语写作资源发生了巨大的变化,多元化、多样化、极大丰富的数字学习资源改变了传统的、单一的写作课堂。自动写作评改系统(Automated Essay Scoring, AES)也应运而生。AES 利用专业化的计算机程序对作文文本进行评估、评分并提供修改反馈与建议,它的研究和开发是机辅语言测试走向智能化的具体体现。AES 系统的开发始于 1996 年,经过 40 多年的发展,自动写作评估系统采用统计、自然语言处理、人工智能等方面的最新成果,实用性和有效性日益提高,成为越来越多的英语写作学习者和写作教师的得力助手。

一、自动写作评改系统

国外研发成功并投入使用的自动评改系统有 10 余种,其中比较具有代表性的系统是 IEA(Intelligent Essay Assessor)、E-rater(Electronic Essay Rater)和 PEG(Project Essay Grader)(Ramineni & Williamson,2013:25-39)。IEA 重内容,轻形式。运用的是一种基于潜在语义分析的知识分析技术软件对作文文本意义进行自动评估,包括对文本的语法、词汇等内容质量做评估分析,但是不分析文本的语言质量和篇章结构。PEG 重形式,轻内容,更多关注作文的浅层特征,主要是根据作文质量尤其是其内在性和接近性对作文进行评分,注重语言质量分析,但不对内容做分析评估。与前两种系统相比,E-rater 则既重内容,又重形式。E-rater 结合统计技术、自然语言处理技术、信息检索技术对作文的语法、用词、写作机制、写作风格、组织结构等进行总体评分和实时诊断反馈。在评分过程中考虑到了作文内容、语言质量和篇章结构,更大程度地模拟了人工评分的过程,与 IEA 和 PEG 相比,评分信度和效度更高(梁茂成、文秋芳,2007)。这些 AES 系统各具优点,但它们主要针对以英语为母语的学习者,由于一语和二语学习者的作文在写作过程和写作文本特征方面存在显著差异,所以对以英语为外语或二语的学习者的英文写作适用性不是很强。

在这种前提下,针对英语非母语的英语学习者(EFL)特点的英语写作自动评改系统在国内投入研发,使用最为广泛的是句酷批改网(http://www.pigai.org)和极智批改网(http://www.smartpigai.com)。句酷批改网简称批改网,是目前国内高校教师与学生使用最广泛的在线自动作文批改系统,2010 年正式运营上线,目前作文批改篇次已达到 4.4 亿次(数据截止到 2018 年 7 月)。批改网以自然语言处理技术和语料库技术为基础,通过对比、分析学生习作和标准语料库文本的差距,对学生的英语书面作文进行即时评分、反馈内容分析结果,并提供修改建议。

图 2.1　句酷批改网个人网站图

批改网是大数据时代语言智能研究的产物,也是数字化平台写作教学与研究的促进者。与国外使用的自动写作评分系统相比,批改网作为一种本土化的在线自动作文批改系统,具有其优点。它从 192 个维度来审查和自动批改学生习作,给出评分,并就语法、词汇、表达规范性等给予反馈意见。批改网能够真实记录学生提交和修改作文的过程,保留所有的修改数据,从而形成个性化的学习者写作数据库。教师也可以随时调阅、人工批改作文,推荐作文和下载作文及相关数据,分析整理数据,等等。由于在线写作批改系统即时批改与反馈的特性,学生完成作文提交后会立刻得到评分与反馈。为了提高评分,学生会根据平台语料库对自己习作中的用词、句子结构等不足之处不断搜索、选择、反复修改。如图2.2所示的同学修改最多的一篇作文修改次数达到了80多次。经过反复修改,在写作评分由较低分数逐渐提升到较高分数的过程中,学生也更容易获得成就感和满足感。同时,在反复修改过程中,学生自然而然会更关注词汇、语法等语言细节,从而在一定程度上提高语言的表达能力,促进学生写作能力的提升。

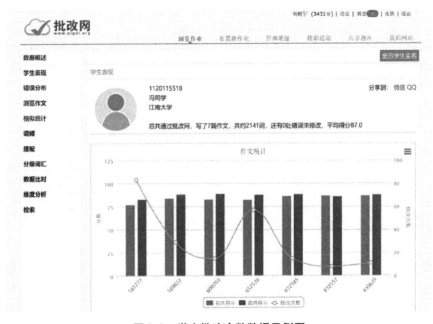

图2.2 学生批改次数数据示例图

当然,批改网作为自主研发的本土化自动写作批改系统,也存在诸多不完善的地方:如不能评估文章内容切题与否,不能识别结构复杂的句子,对文章修辞没有反馈,尤其对文章的内部逻辑和关联性、文章的流畅性无法给出反馈等(何旭良,2013;杨晓琼、戴运财,2015)。此外,与人工评分相比,批改网评分普遍偏高,评语建议趋于千篇一律,没有个性化特征。在这些年的发展中,批改网也在不停地吸收用户反馈,改善用户体验。如增加"互评"和"群批"功能(如图2.3)。生生互改、师生互改的上线也意味反馈方式的增加和完善,交互性增强,语料库进一步扩大,但是系统设置"在截止日期后生效"的学生互评功能并不能最大限度地帮助学生的协作学习。如改为在线互评,更能打破师生之间的界限,让写作者能随时在线转换身份,成为读者、评价者、反馈者、意义协商者等,共同创建、完善大数据时代的写作语料库。

图2.3 句酷批改网互评示例图

二、智能化写作平台

英语写作的研究,从"改不改"到"应当改",从"自动改"到"智能改",又从"智能改"到"社群改",发展速度日新月异。在全球化和大数据的推动之下,写作教学与研究的数字化平台也得到进一步发展和推广。目前高校自主研发使用的智能写作系统有清华大学和高等教育出版社联合开发出的体验英语写作教学资源平台、浙江大学开发的英语智能写作平台等。其中比较有代表性的是由清华大学体验英语教学团队主导开发的"体验英语——写作教学资源平台"(Teaching Resources Platform,TRP)。TRP从学生的学习需求和目标出发,利用写作过程的多元数字化学习资源,将数字化学习资源与优质数字化教学平台有效结合,创建真实、自主、交互的学习环境,以提升学生英语写作能力(杨永林等,2014)。TRP系统经过多年的数据收集、系统开发、教学实践、平台延伸等工作,已经成长为一个具有优质资源的数字化平台,历经了1.0版、2.0版……发展到目前的iSmart-TRP 3.2版。这个平台实现了在线学习与课堂教学的有机结合,为混合式学习和翻转课堂开辟了网络空间,既可降低写作教师的工作强度,又可提高作文评改的质量。以一篇200词左右的英语作文评改为例,TRP评改时间约为40秒,"抓错率"一般在38%左右,"正确率"在85%以上。然后,根据文章内容及水平,TRP 系统自动生成英语评语。评语涵盖作文的总体评价、是否跑题、拼写错误、语法错误、长度要求、是否迟交等多个方面的评定。最后,系统针对这篇文章提供一份详细的"体检报告",以激发学习者的纠错意识,使学习者最终能写出通顺、无语法错误的英语作文。

来自清华大学、北京科技大学、中国政法大学的教学实践表明,通过 TRP 平台的使用,大数据的理念与实践在多方面对于英语写作课教学有着积极的支撑作用。基于大数据的教学改革,更加有助于构建适合社会发展的新型教学模式。2012 年,北京科技大学数字化英语写作教学团队在写作教学中引入"体验英语——写作教学资源平台"进行数字化写作教学的实践与研究,探索数字化写作教学对学生写作能力及写作动机的影响以及对传统课堂结构变革的促进作用。借助于 TRP,这个团队构建了 300 余万字的中国学生英语写作语料库。通过对这些原汁原味的真实文本的分析,建立了基于海量数据的错误类型语料库。同时,通过人机互动、师生共同协作开发生成开放性资源,如教师评改的课堂范文、学生提交的多稿作文、同伴互评的批改妙语、平台自动评改系统的三级评议等都是语料库的来源。多元化学习资源与写作过程环环相扣,创造了真实且生动的学习环境,满足了不同情境的课堂教学需求,激发了学生的学习兴趣与热情。陈娟文和王娜于 2016 年开展的定性与定量实证研究表明,基于优质平台的数字化学习资源能够有效促进学生文本的质量、流畅性、准确性和丰富性的提高,在写作过程中发挥着重要的作用。

大数据支持下的智能化写作平台体现了 9 个方面的迅捷性(杨永林、丁韬,2017):自动评改的迅捷性、资源查询的迅捷性、资源分享的迅捷性、教师反馈的迅捷性、词汇记忆的迅捷性、分享交流的迅捷性、教师备课的迅捷性、试卷制作的迅捷性、练习测验的迅捷性。基于大数据技术和智能写作平台的数字化学习资源以提高写作能力为核心,为学生意义建构、学习写作提供多元化的信息输入。真实的体验式学习促成以"试听"导写、以"说"带写、以"读"促写、以"译"助写,全方位地激发学生的学习兴趣,拓展思维,解决英语写作中"写什么"和"如何写"的两大问题,切实有效地提高学生的写作能力。

三、移动写作

大数据、数字化资源、学习分析的新技术运用日益丰富,无处不在的移动通信技术及智能移动设备又为微型移动学习提供了载体。移动学习(M-learning)的概念最早由国际远程教育学家 Desmond Keegan 于 2000 年引入中国(刘豫钧、禹淑芳,2004)。移动学习基于移动计算设备的辅助,在任何时间、任何地点都能展开,有着自身的鲜明特点:其一是学习资源的数字化。拥有大数据支持的移动智能设备,在通信网络环境下能在智能手机、平板电脑等移动设备端自由灵活进行。其二是学习方式的泛在化。在移动学习模式下,学习者可根据自身的需要随时随地选择适合自己的学习内容及资源。其三是学习时间的碎片化。移动学习大多发生在正规的课堂教学之外,学习时间一般比较短。比如,学生用手机移动终端设备下载大学授课视频,安装学习软件就可以随时随地学习,很好地利用零散时间。用网络空间和碎片时间来置换课堂时间,是课堂教学的有益补充。其四是学习时效的及时性。学生通过移动设备及网络可以随时随地获取学习任务,获得资源信息,及时与教师、同学进行交流互动,及时解决学习问题,了解学习效果,这也是移动学习的最大特点和优势。在我国,大学英语移动学习应用模式研究大体可分为两类:一类是移动学习与其他教学手段相结合的模式研究,如移动学习与微课、翻转课堂等的结合研究;一类是探讨用不同移动终端技术构建的移动学习模式,如对微博、微信、英语学习公众号和移动学习平台的研究。大学英语移动学习设计研究目前的热点主要在于移动设备的情境感知和无缝学习空间的设计(翟芳、武永平,2015)。

移动智能技术的进一步发展,智能手机、平板、iPad、iPod 等便携式移动设备的普及、网络资费的下降和移动网络覆盖区域的扩大,使移动写作更广泛地进入人们的视野。智能移动设备越来越卓越的性能给移动写作提供了极大的便利:如大屏幕高分辨率,文本浏览,视频和音频文件,WiFi、蓝牙等连接方式,大容量存储卡,功能强大的内置操作系统,可以安装多种第三方应用软件等,都使得移动写作不仅成为可能,也成为一种必然。胡茶娟、张迎春(2014)对100名学生的调查表明,学生更关注当下流行的写作话题,更愿意尝试新技术形式的写作任务。他们喜欢尝试的新型移动写作方式排名前三位的有:网络日志(76.5%)、博客(70.4%)、BBS 发帖(66.3%)。刘奕、王小兰(2010)将博客引入写作教学,发现博客能为学生提供高效多元的写作反馈服务。翟芳、武永平(2015)的研究基于微信即时通信功能用于移动学习的特性,探讨通过微信群、朋友圈及公众平台实现移动写作的方法与途径,通过数据分析,验证微信移动写作的积极效果。微信是一款为智能终端提供即时通信服务的免费应用程序。它不受通信运营商及操作系统的限制,消耗流量少,传送文本、图片、音频和视频都非常快捷。2018 年 3 月,微信月活跃用户数超过了 10 亿人次。可以说,在国内,微信正成为大数据环境下获取信息、发挥交互作用的第一大平台,而年轻人是微信使用的一个重要群体。这也意味着微信在移动学习领域具有庞大的用户群体和便捷的传播平台,可以为移动写作者提供更多的学习选择和更丰富的互动合作方法。翟芳、武永平(2015)在经过合理的课前设计、了解学生特点的基础上搭建移动学习环境(建立微信群和创建公众号)、发布学习内容、布置写作任务、组织写作主题讨论,然后学生开始写作过程。教师还对习作开展形成性评价,要求写作者按要求在微信朋友圈发布初稿,提交习作后阅读至少5位同学的作文并评价,并选择性转发。写作者按照互评建议进行修改,以文档或图片形式将二稿发给写作教师。教师修改后使用网页版微信反馈给学生,对于共性问题或较为复杂的问题直接语音输入进行交流探讨。写作者再据此修改形成三稿,教师给出终极评价结果。最后教师推荐优秀习作作为范文发表在朋友圈。该研究证明基于微信的移动写作模式对学生的语言表达、英语思维方式产生了较为深刻的影响,使学生的写作能力有了可喜的变化。

罗凌(2017)对大学生移动英语写作行为做了调查研究,通过数据挖掘和问卷访谈发现,大学生在为期2个月的研究阶段一共有38种移动写作学习行为。其中6种对英语写作学习最为关键,分别是写前的小组审题、头脑风暴和语言准备,写后的小组互评、小组修改及发表后评价。学生移动英语写作时间呈现全天候分散式特点。写作学习最多的时段为晚上。移动写作最主要的场所是宿舍,其次是教室和图书馆,此外还有"路上"等非传统学习场所,表明移动技术使学生写作不受地点限制。

大数据支持下的移动写作多维交互模式能营建亲切友好的交流环境,使写作者在移动环境下灵活安排学习时间和地点,有效地延伸课堂教学的时间和空间。受信任的学习环境、无缝的学习空间、自主选择的灵活性和丰富的交互方式都体现了英语写作移动学习模式的优势。而高校大学生的智能设备持有率高,移动学习的意愿强,移动终端的选择丰富。短信、电邮、微博、QQ、微信及移动写作平台等都可以成为移动写作的载体。当然,因为移动学习的碎片化特性,也存在一些弊端,比如不易建立系统的知识体系,小组协作学习受限(每个人选择的学习时间不一致),学习过程监控不够,等等,但大数据、移动学习、智能化平台对英语写作教与学的作用日益彰显。信息化时代教学方式和学习方式的改变是一种必然趋势。

四、协作写作

近年来,以现代社会认知心理学、社会文化理论、现代教育技术学等理论为基础的协作学习(collaborative learning)进入了研究者的视野。基于社会交互的协作写作（collaborative writing）是协作学习的重要组成部分，但还未引起教师和研究者的充分重视。相关的研究文献较少，而且存在合作学习和协作学习概念混淆不清、理论探讨缺乏深度、实证研究匮乏零散等问题。协作写作不同于合作写作，其区别在于完成全部任务成员间劳动分工的程度（Dillenbourg, 1999）。协作写作是多人为了完成共同的写作目标通过合作的形式而进行共同的文本创作。"协作"是一种协调性的、同步的活动，成员共同工作以完成全部学习任务。在此过程中，他们之间没有稳定的分工，相互间的角色也经常转换。协作写作不仅涉及个体写作模式下的各种活动，而且还需要更多的活动来促进写作的顺利进行。协作写作具有许多独特的优势，协作写作过程的特殊性在于成员在写作全过程（从构思、产出观点、确定文本结构、进行文本编辑到修改等各个环节）都进行合作互动。这不仅仅是意见交换的过程，更涉及协商，即成员为了对写作的各方面达成共识而努力。这种写作模式可以最大限度地促进参与者的语言输出，充分发挥同伴互评的作用，在大数据、网络技术和自主学习平台辅助下的协作写作将会变得更有操作性，能更大地发挥其协作、互动的优势。

以Wiki、Blog、Blackboard等软件为支撑的网络协作学习由于不受时空限制被认为在语言教学方面具有巨大潜力。尤其是Wiki，作为多人协同写作工具，以其操作简易性、共享开放性、协作性等优势在国外二语教学中得到广泛应用，成为学生最喜欢的学习软件之一（Monje, 2014）。Wiki作为一种面向社群的协作式写作系统，将大数据、网络技术、个性化自主化的学习方式融为一体，为学习者提供协作式写作环境。学习者可以与同班同学两两一组、多人一组或者整班一起共同创作，甚至还可以同全球各地使用网络的人协同创作。倪清泉（2009）以计算机网络技术为支撑，尝试进行计算机网络环境下基于协作学习的英语能力培养。研究结果显示，计算机网络环境下基于协作学习的英语写作教学显著优于传统英语写作教学，不仅利于英语写作能力的培养，而且可以促进口语水平的提高，具有可操作性。俞婷（2010）在Wiki写作系统的基础上，开展了大学英语写作教学的实证研究，证明Wiki协作写作有助于提高大学生英语写作能力，激发积极性，促进协作学习能力的发展。李航、刘儒德（2011）利用校园网络学习平台Blackboard探索英语小组协作写作的可行性和优势。首先，针对英语互动写作交流需求开发了协作交流模块，供师生在此交互环境中通过英语写作交流、互动、反馈，发表自己的作品，评阅同伴的作品，并开展有序的小组写作活动。同时，利用班级通知模块提供教师写作指导与相应的支架式写作框架，规范小组交互写作活动的内容并调节各组间的参与程度。此外，充分利用Blackboard资源管理器中的后台监控管理功能，监控学生的写作进程，了解学生写作投入状态；并利用该平台提供的数据统计功能分析学生在网络写作中的参与情况，为教师调节教学活动、分析研究效果提供科学的参照指标。研究发现，基于网络平台的协作写作可以构建一个激发真实交流意愿的"写作学习共同体"，更大程度地优化写作教学效果，促进师生互动并增强学生对英语写作的兴趣以及写作效能感。

对如何利用 Wiki 等协作写作平台进行文本共建、合作写作的交互模式、协作写作的成效、学习者在协作写作中的角色等的研究表明，在线社群交互能够通过提供"集体支架"的方式拓展学习者的最近发展区，证实了数字化平台和信息技术在促进英语写作教学中的积极作用（罗凌，2017）。协作写作模式是大数据时代信息网络技术和语言教学深度融合的又一特点。

五、同题写作

在大数据时代下，人们可以依据数据分析，挖掘数据价值，积极参与数据信息的革命，改变自己的思维和行为方式。这不仅给自己的生活带来便利，也促进社会经济的稳步发展。同题写作是在大数据与英语写作智能平台基础上英语写作教学的创新方式。2016 年，第三届"百万同题英语写作"由北京大学提供写作题目——How Will AI Affect Our Life，聚焦人工智能将会带给人类的影响，引导中国学生对人工智能进行思考。从 4 月 6 日到 5 月 31 日，来自全国 32 个省市地区 9 384 所学校的 22 532 名教师参与活动，所提交的学生作文数目达到 1 739 660 篇，范围覆盖初、高、高职、本科等各个阶段的学生。与前两届相比，参与的学校、人数规模出现了较大增幅。2016 年"百万同题英语写作"构建了多元化、多维度、全学段的中国学生英语写作大数据，从不同角度解读，并对其展开研究，能有效探究各阶段学生的自主写作行为特点、语言表达能力的差异、写作教学教师角色的定位以及学生输出能力的人文素养等，从而促进英语写作教学的改革与创新（李书影，2017）。

同题写作活动使用前文提及的句酷批改网数字化写作评改平台，但是参与人数和数据维度都不同于任何一次写作体验活动，是大数据技术服务于英语写作教学最直观的反应和效果呈现。活动设计者从人机互动情况、数据维度变化、人工与机器反馈数据对比、AI 主题文艺作品等角度解读学习者的自主学习特点和语言产出能力，以促使写作教师尽快地完成从语言知识的"传授者"到"复合型角色"的转换，提升学习者的语言表达、思辨创新和终身学习能力。同题写作活动的组织和完善，是大数据时代学习者成为主体，个性化、多元化写作成功实践的有益尝试。证明大数据时代的写作活动和社会能实现无缝对接,具有时代性特点的写作话题能成为培养学习者语言表述、思辨创新、终身学习等能力的有效途径。

第四节　慕课、微课与翻转课堂

作为一种新型的教学理念和教育模式,慕课(Massive Open Online Courses, MOOC)时代的到来,对全球的高等教育都产生了巨大影响。2008 年,Dave Cormier 和 Bryan Alexander 首次提出了慕课理念。2012 年被称为慕课元年,此后慕课在全球如火如荼地展开。根据统计数据,目前主要的慕课平台有 10 种(Grainger, 2013;杨永林等,2014)。最知名的 MOOC 三大平台分别是 edX、Coursera、Udacity。2012 年,哈佛大学和麻省理工学院创立 edX (https://www.edx.org/),包括清华大学、北京大学、香港大学、香港科技大学在内,先后有 130 所大学和学术机构加盟。目前可选的在线课程 2 124 门,其中以英语为中介语的课程 1 913 门,1 400 万选修人数,5 200 万注册人次(数据截止到 2018 年 7 月)。Coursera(https://www.courera.org)由斯坦福大学创立,目前加盟大学和机构 150 多家,在线课程 2 700 多门,选课人数达到 3 300 多万(数据截止时间 2018 年 7 月)。Udacity (https://www.udacity.com/)始于斯坦福大学的一个实验:斯坦福大学教授 Sebastian Thrun 和 Peter Norvig,通过在线授课的方式,向全世界免费开放他们的课程人工智能概论,来自 190 个国家的 16 万多名学生报名参加了这门课,Udacity 随后正式创立。创始之初有 25 门在线课程、40 万用户。

国内影响比较大的慕课平台有"中国大学 MOOC"和"全国地方高校优课联盟"(University Open Online Course, UOOC)。"中国大学 MOOC"于 2014 年由网易与高等教育出版社联合创立,旨在向大众提供中国知名高校的 MOOC 课程。首批上线的大学有 16 所,包括北京大学、浙江大学、复旦大学等。目前加盟大学有 159 所,学术合作机构 17 家,拥有 7 920 门精品课程资源库。"地方高校优课联盟"由深圳大学发起创立,目前成员高校 125 所,上线 MOOC 课程 261 门,选课人数超过 30 万。中国慕课平台的开发和发展,对于我国精品课程的建设和教学改革具有重大意义。

微课平台出现于 2013 年,加州大学伯克利分校的 Armando Fox 教授提出了微课(Small Private Open Online Course, SPOC)平台的教学模式。微课平台主要是针对在校大学生开设的,它的出现为大学教育提供了更好的在线教学模式,具有鲜明的区域性和落地性特点,是现有课堂教学的有益补充。同时,相对于慕课的大规模而言,微课采用更精细化管理的教学模式,多开设学分课程,对选课人数也有限制。微课具有弹性化学习、多元化授课、海量资源选择的特色,被称为下一代的教科书。SPOC 是后慕课时代的产物,能够实现在线课程与课堂教学的结合,是使以 MOOCs 为代表的在线开放课程落地学校教育的一种"小型私有在线课程"形式。

来自美国的翻转课堂(Flipped Classroom)打破了传统的课堂教学模式,把线上线下学习有机结合起来,延伸了教学空间。翻转课堂把传统的课堂翻转过来,课前完成知识传授,课堂完成知识的内化。教师课前系统、合理地设计教学环节,整合在线学习资源,采用线上学生自主学习、线下教师引导学生内化知识的模式。随着慕课、微课、翻转课堂等理念与实践活动与现代信息技术的融合发展,海量教学数据的存储、提取、分析不但在技术上成为可能,而且也成了教学与研究的必然要求。SPOC 环境下的翻转课堂是"线上学习"与"课堂教学"的有机融合,是后慕课时期大学英语教学改革的必然产物,也是应用现代信息技术促进英语学科教与学的最好解读。大数据和 SPOC 平台技术结合,对学生学习行为和学习过程进行记录、监督、评价,"课堂教学"和"线上学习"互相作用,形成一个动态的学习社区,因而极大地丰富了传统英语写作教学的形式和内涵,缓解了英语写作课时不够的问题。大学英语 SPOC 翻转课堂目的在于解构与重构课堂教学,弥补传统课堂教学的不足,进而重构学生的英语学习过程,创新英语有效学习模式(王娜等,2016)。在翻转课堂模式下,教师课前利用大数据和数字化平台完成教学设计,给学生布置学习任务。学生课前借助信息技术手段完成线上自主学习,教师获取动态数据分析,了解学生学习状态和学习效果。课堂面授环节,教师根据课前学生知识学习和接受情况,引导学生深入探讨教学重点和难点,教师帮助学生解决线上自主学习时遇到的问题,布置课后写作任务。课后学生按要求进行进一步拓展与实践,提交习作。教师利用大数据和写作平台评估学生课后学习效果。最后是翻转课堂教学总结,在课程结束后,翻转课程并没有立刻结束。教师将各个环节数据进行整合分析,生成学生学习数据报告,构建新的资源库和数据库。

当然,目前的慕课、微课等产品也存在不足,比如,课程完成率低,缺乏教学过程管理,缺乏学生及教师激励,等等。但是大数据时代互联网的应用、MOOC 平台的构建和完善、微课的融入及 SPOC 翻转课堂在语言教学中的实现,使传统语言教学模式的重构和创新成为必然。在大数据的背景下,学生处于英语写作教学活动中的主体地位,学习的兴趣和积极性都得到极大的提高,学生的英语写作能力也能有效提升。当然,大数据给大学英语写作教学带来的变革远不止于此,如何利用大数据更好地体现个性化教学,以及如何将慕课、微课更好地与数字化学习平台融合起来,如何使 SPOC 翻转课堂更加深入,使教学环境更加灵活,学生学习的自主性和教师教学的创新性如何有机融合,这些都是大数据带给语言教学的思考。

第三章 大数据时代英语写作教学的改革与创新

大数据是当今世界发展的趋势,人们在存储、分析和利用巨量、高速、多变的数据的同时,自身的行为方式、思维方式也都在发生着改变。在大数据、人工智能、技术支持驱动下的外语教育改革不可避免。在今后的二三十年里,外语教育(主要是英语教育)会发生根本性的变化(刘润清,2014):教学模式、学习模式、教师认知和学生认知,包括科研方向和重点也会有根本性的改变。大学英语写作教学毫无疑问会因为大数据时代的到来面临新的变化、挑战与机遇。

第一节 大数据为英语写作教学带来的变化、挑战与机遇

一、变化

大数据的时代特点为大学英语写作教学,包括写作资源、写作目的、写作内容与组织、写作手段、写作评估以及写作能力的内涵带来从观念到行为等多方面的变化(王海啸,2014)。

1. 写作资源丰富化

传统的英语写作教学"一支笔""一本书""一张嘴"的模式不复存在。英语写作教材也不再是唯一的教学辅助工具。互联网上丰富的写作资源和数字化材料应有尽有,包括文本、音频、视频、课堂录像等,提供了大量的、多样化的指导。写作语料库及强大的数据检索引擎能在英语写作内容方面提供如词汇选择、词语搭配、单词使用频率、语境使用等个性化的帮助。跨学科、跨课程的信息资源又能帮助学习者极大地拓宽视野,丰富写作材料。

2. 写作目的明确化

英语写作的思维方式不同于中文写作，长期习惯于中文思维的中国学生在英文写作过程中往往容易受母语思维的干扰，写作过程不注重语言形式和思想性，更多关注内容和语言表达的正确性。写作总体缺乏目的性，写作的态度往往被动，为了写而写，为了完成任务而写。大数据时代自动写作软件和智能写作平台帮学生解决了语言形式和细节上的问题，使学生有更多的精力可以放在内容组织、逻辑架构、语篇思想等上面。同时，作为数据和信息的产出者和使用者，写作者成为写作行为的中心，写作者与读者的间隔被打破，写作者同时也是读者、他人习作的评估者和反馈者。写作不再是作者一个人的自言自语，任何作品都可以由写作者传到面向公众的数字化平台，通过双向的反馈和对话，实现写作者、读者、评价者与反馈者之间的有效互动。这种身份的互换无形中会增加写作者的写作兴趣，使写作者通过阅读、欣赏他人作品更明确写作的意义和目的，促使写作者更加注重提升自己的写作能力和思辨能力。

3. 写作内容可视化

这里的内容不仅包括写作者自己的习作内容，也包括通过计算机网络与他人共享的写作内容。网络使信息数据具有开放共享性，也搭建了相互交流、互动学习的桥梁，而这种交流互动是产生内容的重要途径。通过师生之间、生生之间、网友之间的讨论交互，更多的想法和创意得以产生。数字化写作平台又能提供各种语言内容信息，各种文字记录、绘制流程图和脑图的软件还能帮助写作者用图表形式把写作内容直观化和可视化。

4. 写作手段智能化

传统的写作手段无非是一张纸一支笔。计算机和笔记本电脑的普及使文字处理系统代替了纸和笔，从而减轻写作者的劳动量，提高人们的写作效率。大数据时代各种应用软件、智能写作平台、自动评估系统、移动写作系统、语料库系统、在线搜索引擎等从词汇、语法、句型结构、作文体裁、语篇欣赏等角度提供全方面的写作辅助。这些系统和技术支持极大地丰富了写作手段。写作者可以打破传统写作教学时间和空间上的局限，在任何时间、任何地点展开写作。

5. 评估和测试方式多样化

长期以来，英语写作教学都是学生写、老师改、老师反馈的单一评估过程。同伴反馈、生生互评的尝试丰富了评估主体和反馈方式，但是大数据时代才能把写作教师从评估和反馈的重担中解放出来。信息技术和数字化智能平台已经能在一定程度上将学生作文中的语言特征和系统语料库里的标准特征进行对照,实现自动评估,并即时给出同步反馈。互联网又进一步实现评估者和反馈者的身份互换。人机互动、生生互动、师生互动都改变了单一的评估反馈模式,丰富了评估反馈的内涵。测试方式不再只限于纸笔测试,机测、网测已经大规模出现并得以运用。

6. 写作结果数据化

在传统的英语写作教学中,学生完成习作后提交,老师批改反馈后返回给学生。少数学生根据修改建议进行修改,多数学生则从此就将写作作业束之高阁,写作无成果可谈。在大数据时代,写作已经是社会交际的一部分。写作活动从确定主题和内容,到如何写、怎么写好、互评反馈、修改完善、分享发表等,每一个步骤都可以是交际活动的一部分,都可以作为数据保存在网络或共享平台上。对写作结果进行的数据分析,又可以作为分析学生语言能力、评估写作能力发展情况的重要依据。

7. 写作教学社会化

大数据时代的写作教学已经不再局限于校园内的传统课堂内教学。大学校园的界限会变得模糊甚至被打破。数据共享、技术支持、智能互动等已经极大地延伸了课堂的时间和空间。移动写作、协作写作、同题写作等新的写作模式把教师的教学活动和社会有机连接起来。教师利用微信、微博等社交媒体,将其作为写作工具,发布写作任务、分享教学内容、鼓励生生互评、激励成果发表等行为都促成了写作教学与社会环境的无缝对接。此外,社会环境也可以成为写作教学课堂外的有益补充。比如,国内外主流媒体的门户网站都设有读者反馈与讨论的专门栏目,鼓励学生参与这些真实性和实时性的讨论,能满足学生的认知需求,提高学生的阅读和写作能力(王海啸,2014)。各个学校的国际交流交际活动——无论是交换生项目、国际学术交流,还是国际展会或体育赛事志愿者等都会涉及写作任务,能为英语写作教学提供丰富的参与计划,全面培养学生的英语写作能力和思辨能力。因为慕课平台课程的共享,学生只要拥有上网的机会,就能使用数据、生产数据,来自世界不同国家的学生都可以在网络上相遇、互动,成为学习伙伴,地域限制因此已被打破。当学习行为变得社会化,教育公平就有机会实现。

二、挑战

大数据和外语教育技术相结合具有的高速度、高效率、高性能、高体验的特点,把单调、固定、封闭的传统课堂转换成一个多媒体、多模态、多情境、多资源渠道的综合立体、开放式学习系统(胡加圣、靳琰,2015)。慕课平台对优质教学资源的开放共享,网络交互式、集体式、开放式、即时性的激发型互动学习体验让教师丧失了知识的权威地位。大数据时代为人们的学习方式带来新的理念与突破,也无疑为英语写作教学改革带来新的挑战。教师技能和素养必须与时俱进,才能应对大数据带来的挑战。

1. 课堂翻转,挑战英语写作教学课程内容

在大数据时代背景下,英语写作教学的教学资源呈现海量网络化的特点。慕课平台名师名课程的共享开放性给学生提供更多获取专业知识的途径。如果教师仅仅依靠传统的纸质教材,采取面授方式,课程计划因循守旧、单一扁平,授课内容照本宣科,毫无疑问,会受到学生的质疑。因此,面临这样的挑战,英语写作教师要构建多元化的教学方案来适应数据化网络环境下的写作教学。对教学目标、教学模式、教学内容都须加以提升、扩张和完善。写作教学的内容可以扩张到网络精品视频资源、语料库检索共组、写作辅助手段等多元化的教学资源。教学模式可以把课内讲授、课外自主学习、师生交流、生生互动等结合起来。教师通过给学生分享慕课优质写作课程,充分探索翻转课堂,采用个性化教学模式,鼓励学生的写作热情(李书影,2017)。比如,教师可以和自己的学生们一起登录Coursera,学习美国杜克大学的英语写作课程English Composition I: Achieving Expertise,作为自己课程内容的补充,然后与学生一起讨论自己的收获与学习感受。教师允许质疑、鼓励求证的平等互动态度是"教学相长"的最好例证。

2. 角色翻转,挑战教师写作评估方式

长期以来,写作教师都是采取单一的评估方式。学生完成作文上交,教师在一定时间内批改返回。如果教授的写作班级人数多,写作数量大,那么作业的批改实在是件费时低效的苦差事。有时教师花费心思在学生作文上留下的密密麻麻的批注和修改意见,学生却并不一定仔细阅读。有的学生看到布满红色批注的作文还会失去对写作的兴趣,根据教师建议主动做出修改的少之又少,除非老师要求提交二稿三稿。教师一直扮演着绝对权威的评估者和反馈者角色。在大数据时代,传统的教师角色受到挑战。自动在线写作评改系统、智能写作平台都能提供作文评估和反馈,并根据语料库对比数据提供修改建议。写作者提交作文后,可以及时通过数字化平台的自动评分与评语系统获得反馈信息,根据评改建议修改完善。想要看到自己分数不断提高的写作者还可以根

据即时的反馈和建议多次修改、多次提交。迅捷的在线反馈、人机互动、同伴互评使教师作为评价者和反馈者的权威身份在这一过程中被削弱。当然,自动评估系统由于自身的不足,如前文介绍批改网时提到过的缺点:不能评估文章内容切题与否,不能识别结构复杂的句子,对文章修辞没有反馈,尤其对文章的内部逻辑和关联性、文章的流畅性无法给出反馈等,这些都意味着教师的评估方式还是有着不可替代的优势。所以在应对这一挑战时,最好的做法是把教师评改和反馈与在线反馈、同伴互评、师生互改结合起来,打破师生之间身份的界限,使评估方式更多元化、立体化。

3. 挑战教师知识体系建构

英语写作教师目前所处的教育教学模式,是基于传统的课堂教学:固定的教材,灌输式授课,教案是经过不断的教学经验提炼而成的知识结晶,具有重复性。教师作为资源的占有者和知识的传播者,知识体系相对固定。大数据时代给这种有边界限制的知识传授方式带来冲击,固有的知识体系安全模式被打破,不变、不更新知识体系意味着被信息化社会的飞速发展所淘汰。当学生已经开始习惯用网络和现代技术搜索数据、观看视频课程、网上阅读、评论互动、获取最新资源时,教师如果还停留在照本宣科的年代,不能给学生提供教科书外的训练和知识,不能激发学生的创新思考和思辨能力,毫无疑问,是无法被新时代的大学生们所接受和认可的。程云艳(2014)在研究新教育范式下大学外语教师的机遇与挑战时指出,学校最受学生欢迎的十佳教师多数是35岁以下,善于把新的技术和理念融入教学中的人,而他们的学生的创造能力和批判性思维能力也远大于教师的预期。在大数据时代,如何利用现代科技获取知识和相关信息,如何更新教师的知识体系,实现教学方式重构,是教师们不得不面对的挑战。

4. 挑战教师信息技术应用能力

大数据时代教育技术与英语教育的深度融合变革了英语写作教学方式,英语写作教学的新生态环境也给英语写作教师信息技术应用能力带来了挑战。大数据技术让教师角色发生了颠覆性的变化,按刘润清(2014)一文中所描述的:教师从 God 变成 guide,从 sage on the side 变成 guide on the side,从 teacher 变成 helper,councilor 和 facilitator。写作教师要承担课堂的组织者和学习的引导者、学习资源的管理者和数据的整合者、知识的协商者和互动学习的指导者、写作过程的诊断者和写作成果的评估者等角色。比如,一个新时代的写作教师要进行一次完整的写作课程教学,课前要熟悉学生特征,选择适合学生学习用的课程视频,发布写前任务;课内根据学生学习反馈,组织课堂教学和讨论,布置写作任务;课后利用智能化平台或自动写作评估系统监督学生写作过程,结合在线反馈或生生互评等方式进行写作评估。提供公开课、在慕课平台分享课程资源的教师,还要录制授课视频,这又涉及相当多的技术细节:如何将视频模块化以便于学生利用零碎时间观看;如何在关键知识点嵌入交互式问题方便学生检查学习效果;如何嵌入超链接介绍背景资料;如何提取视频课选修者资料进行数据分析;等等。正如陈冰冰(2014)所指出的,要应对大数据时代英语教学变革的挑战,教师应该具有驾驭技术(信息技术与教育技术)、自主设计与实施课程的核心能力。

三、机遇

机遇总是与挑战并肩而行。基于大数据的英语写作教学面临挑战,也会带来新的发展机遇。

1. 基于大数据的英语写作教学使个性化的自主学习成为可能

大数据给教育领域带来的重要变化,正是对学习者复杂学习活动之海量数据进行个性化分类研究的重要机遇(陈坚林,2015)。基于大数据的英语教学的教育理念,使教学不再以教师授课为中心。教师作为教学活动的组织者和引导者,成为学生学习活动的辅助者和指导者。比如,学生可以主导慕课的讨论,发布讨论结果,与教师和同学交流信息;教师指导学生通过自主学习获得的数据挖掘和分析寻求最符合自身需求的写作方法和手段。各种智能化写作平台,优质在线资源,在线反馈和互动频繁的同伴反馈、生生互动和师生互动,打破区域界限的协作写作,随时随地学习的移动写作,等等,都是实现个性化自主学习的有效途径和保证。学习者与同伴有效的联结和互动构成规模庞大的学习群体,而这种以学习者为中心的教学和学习模式,也使得教师可以利用大数据分析,了解学生对数字化平台和网络的使用情况,进而明确学生多样化的学习需求,并以此为根据设计更适合学习者特征、满足学习者需要的教学活动,为个性化的自主学习提供多样性的资源、选择和学习指导服务,从而提升学习者的写作能力,最终达成自主学习能力的最优化。

2. 基于大数据的英语写作教学使新型写作课程体系得以优化

基于大数据的在线教育、网络课程的核心竞争力就是课程内容。Coursera和edX这些慕课平台的数字化课程资源涉及各门各类学科,授课语言选择丰富。edX所使用的课程语言多达15种,总课程数量2 124门,其中英语为中介语的课程为 1 913 门,占 90%。Coursera 的课程总数达到 2 700 多门,它的创始人 Andrew Ng 在访谈中更曾指出,Coursera 一年内收集的教育数据,超过了过去 5 000 年所有的教育数据总和。

表 3.1　edX 平台 MOOCs 课程前 10(按数量)

课程名	数量/个	占比/%	课程名	数量/个	占比/%
Computer Science	584	27.5	Data Analysis & Statistics	223	10.5
Business Management	436	20.5	Science	202	9.5
Engineering	313	14.7	Economics & Finance	197	9.3
Social Science	287	13.5	Biology & Life Science	158	7.4
Humanities	240	11.3	Physics	145	6.8

表 3.2　edX 平台 MOOCs 课程(按语言分类)

语言	课程数量/个	占比/%	语言	课程数量/个	占比/%
English	1913	90	Portuguese	5	0.2
Spanish	188	8.8	Dutch	3	0.1
Chinese-Mandarin	57	2.7	Turkish	3	0.1
French	47	2.2	German	2	0.1
Italian	26	1.2	Korean	2	0.1
Russian	5	0.2	Arabic,Chinese-simplified,Hindi	1+1+1	0.1

各种慕课平台和网络精品课程,就像一个巨大的开放性课程自选超市,质优价廉,选购方便。想象一下,坐在家中或者走在路上就可以收看哈佛名教授的授课,这对于学习者来说,是不出国门就能获取最优教育资源的机会,而且这些资源还在持续更新和增加中。面对国际国内海量的优质教学课程,教师们必须重构课程体系,合理整合线上线下的教学内容,与翻转课堂理念相结合,用技术手段作支撑,实现写作课程的最大优化。优化的可能之所以存在,是因为在线课程的课程设计内容面对的是全球的学习者,没有针对性。而由于教学对象的特点、需求不一样,即使是来自世界名校的著名教授的课程,也无法完全满足所有学习者的需求。此外,在线课程的互动性和完成率(完成率只有个位数)也是无法和课堂教学相比的。基于此,教师可以结合技术手段和大数据分析,结合在线课程的优势,依据教学对象的特点和个性化需求,设计更合理的课程内容,构建更完善的课程体系。

3. 基于大数据的英语写作教学促进教师向专业性、复合型发展

大数据时代带给英语教学的挑战和冲击是毋庸置疑的。英语写作教师除了要更好地提升自己的专业知识，优化写作课程设计外，还要提升信息技术能力和综合素养。在人机一体化的数字化教学环境下，除了传统的课堂组织和管理、学习引导和激励外，教师还应对教学技术和手段、网络媒体和平台、资源建设和开发、数据收集和分析等熟练掌握和运用。这也就意味着教师以前不太要求的专业能力和综合素养都可以因为大数据环境而得到孕育、发展。以数据的产生、收集和分析为例：学生对写作任务或授课视频的每次点击；在观看授课视频中途有没有暂停；写作；写作任务是否按要求完成、是否修正、修正次数、花费时间；在互动评论里写了些什么，获得了怎样的反馈；等等。通过解读数据，写作教师可以更科学地把握英语学习者自主写作的行为特点，更准确地判断其语言表述能力的发展倾向，分析出学习者的写作风格、认知倾向、写作策略、动机类型、人文素养等。教师在对学生的数据分析和解读过程中更了解自己面对的学生，更能因材施教，制定有效的教学策略，合理设计教学活动。这一过程的实施和完善也促使教师不断根据数据反馈反思自己的教学理念、认知方式、角色定位，从而全方位地提升教学能力。

基于大数据的新生态教学环境也使单打独斗、孤军奋战的教学模式格格不入。教学可以依靠智能化的写作系统和数字化教学手段，把个体劳动转化为团队合作，最大限度地减轻教师的重复性劳动，促进专业团队建设发展。大数据环境也使跨空间、国际化的合作形式成为可能。

四、小结

随着信息技术的进一步发展，大数据会给英语教育带来更多的变化、挑战和机遇。大数据创新了英语写作教与学的方式，促使教师改变思维，与时俱进。大数据支持的数字化写作环境，为英语写作教学与研究提供了更广阔的发展空间。

第二节　大数据时代英语写作教学模式重构

长期以来,我国的大学英语写作教学存在教学目标不够明确、教学内容单一扁平、写作课堂缺乏互动、评价反馈费时低效等问题,写作效果不尽如人意,学生写作能力提升不明显。大数据时代的海量资源和智能写作系统、在线反馈和移动学习模式对教师的教学行为和学生的写作行为都产生了重大影响。教师的教学方式、课程内容、教学手段、评估方式和学生的写作目的、写作内涵、写作环境和写作结果等都发生了巨大的变化。在大数据环境下,英语写作教学模式重构成为不可回避的趋势。

中国教育网2010年刊发的《国家中长期教育改革和发展规划纲要(2010—2020年)》专门阐述了教育信息化的发展目标,指出"信息技术对教育发展具有革命性影响,必须予以高度重视",要"充分利用优质资源和先进技术,创新运行机制和管理模式,整合现有资源,构建先进、高效、实用的数字化教育基础设施";同时,要"加强优质教育资源开发与应用","提高教师应用信息技术水平,更新教学观念,改进教学方法,提高教学效果,鼓励学生利用信息手段主动学习、自主学习,增强运用信息技术分析解决问题的能力"。现代化的信息技术与课程的整合优化是提升学科质量,进而提升学生能力的有效途径和方法。整合不是"技术+教学"的简单叠加(王娜,2014:68)。当前很多英语教师把PPT课件设计得很"炫",课堂活动热热闹闹,音频视频轮番登场。表面上学生上课上得高高兴兴,但检测教学质量和学生学习能力时,却发现并没有得到有效提高。这样的课堂教学并不是对技术的成功整合和应用,也不是在数字化环境下应该倡导的教学模式。基于大数据语境的英语写作模式重构,是信息技术和英语写作教与学深度融合的产物,有利于扩大英语写作课堂教学的深度和广度,是充分能动地培养学生自主学习能力、提升写作能力的有效途径。

各学校、各写作教学与研究团队立足大数据背景,从内容和形式上对英语写作教学模式重构做出了设想和尝试。吴晓蓉(2004)建议从写作主体、写作客体、写作文本、写作受体四个维度重建,来应对数字化的冲击。陈庆斌(2016)则从教学目标、教学资源、教学形式、师生和生生互动关系及考评体系等角度提出了构想,指出从五个方面进行写作教学的重构:培养新型读写能力,整合教学内容及资源,更新传统教学方式,建立新型师生、生生关系,健全新型考评体系,等等。胡加圣、靳琰(2015)从跨学科的角度出发，以外语教学和语言学理论、教育学及心理学等教学法为基础，以教育信息技术等为基本构成要素，构建跨学科的教学体系。针对英语写作技能，设计"英语读写"课程模式，将读与写紧密结合起来，以读促写，以写促读。这样的教学设计，既不排斥课堂内读写的功能，又能融合网络读写的优势，扩大阅读面，增加写作量。学生通过阅读解码输入，然后整合分析语言现象并输出。学生之间的语言输入和输出又可以进行交互反馈。在强大的语料库支撑下，采用多元化写作机制，提供给学生大量写作素材，建立有效评估机制以促成写作能力的提升。

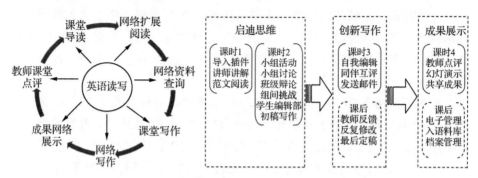

图 3.1　读写课程动态图(胡加圣、靳琰,2015:117)

另有研究者提出英语写作教学新模式并进行了实证研究。邵春燕(2016)基于社会文化理论和英语专业写作教学的特色出发，提出了多角色参与的英语写作教学模式，并对英语专业二年级两个平行的写作班级进行了为期16周(一个完整的教学学期)的实验研究。通过创设不同的活动情境，促进学生的社会互动与合作，创建最近发展区，尽可能发挥学生在写作中的主体性作用。她的研究发现，该模式有效提高了学生的习作质量，对学生写作能力的后期发展与自主性学习能产生持续性影响。王保健等(2017)尝试在数字信息化背景下构建大学英语过程写作教学模式。结果表明，过程写作教学模式有助于学生写作能力的提升，写作效果优于传统的结果写作教学法；学生写作成绩跟实验前比有明显提高。学生整体对该教学模式持肯定态度。

2011—2012年第二学期，北京科技大学英语系"数字化英语写作教学团队"，在全国高校中首次尝试开设了数字化英语写作实验课程。该课程体系基于清华大学杨永林教授所带领的体验英语教学团队主导开发的"体验英语——写作教学资源平台"(Teaching Resources Platform, TRP)，构建数字化英语写作教学模式。这种教学模式充分利用了TRP的特点，把信息技术和英语写作课程进行深层次融合，探索数字化写作教学对学生写作能力及写作动机的影响及对传统写作教学模式的创新重构(陈娟文、王娜,2016)。

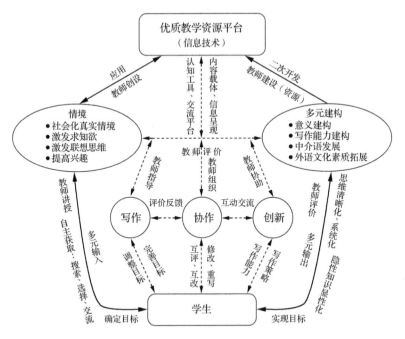

图 3.2　数字化英语写作教学模式图(王娜,2014)

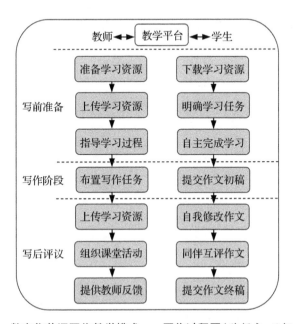

图 3.3　数字化英语写作教学模式——写作过程图(陈娟文、王娜,2016)

数字化英语写作教学模式以建构主义的学习理念为基础,采用过程体裁教学法,将数字化学习资源与英语写作紧密结合,创建真实、自主、交互的学习环境。授课教师上传信息、资源至平台供学生使用;学生在学习过程中不断通过搜索、浏览、分享、写作、测验、互评等方式完成学习任务。以数字化学习资源建设为起点,师生互动、协作开发生成开放性资源。教师评改的课堂范文、学生提交的多稿作文、同伴互评的赏析妙语、平台自动评改系统的三级评议等都是语料库来源。借助于TRP,数字化英语写作教学团队建构了300余万字的中国学生英语写作语料库。通过对这些原汁原味的真实文本的分析,形成了基于海量数据的错误类型语料库(杨永林等,2014)。

大数据时代的数字化英语写作教学的新模式,通过创设真实情境的意义建构,来促进学生主动认知知识结构的建立,从而革新以教师为中心的传统英语写作教学模式。新教学模式以学生为中心,师生协作,共建数字资源平台,一方面极大地丰富了写作语料库,另一方面也使学生置身于真实互动的学习环境中,多元化学习资源与写作过程环环相扣,满足了个性化的学习特点和多样化的学习需求,真正激发学生的写作兴趣和热情。学习资源的多元化和微型化不仅有效地支持了课堂教学,也有助于培养学生自主学习的能力。数字化英语写作教学模式是在线学习与课堂教学、自主学习与互助学习的有机结合,既可降低写作教师的工作强度,提高作文评改的质量,又能促进学生自主学习能力的养成,提高写作能力。它的构建和成功实践,为大数据时代英语写作教学改革与研究提供了更广阔的发展空间。

第四章 大数据时代英语写作中的身份建构

随着社会学、心理学、语言学等学科的发展,身份(identity)研究已经成为国外语言学等学科的研究热点。Norton(2000:5)认为,"身份"是指一个人如何理解自我和世界的关系,如何在时空中建构这种关系,以及自我如何理解未来的各种可能性。在 Norton 看来,二语习得的过程不仅是通过刻苦和专注学习获得语言技能的过程,也是复杂的社会实践,在各个方面都涉及语言习得者的身份(Norton,2000:132)。Ivanic(1998)也提出,写作者身份不属于作者个人,是身份与社会、文化等各种变量同时作用,并最终在作者个体上体现出来。

国外有关写作者身份的研究出现较早,研究方法多是用语料库方法,探索隐含于语篇中的写作者身份特征。近年来,国内也开始有学者关注身份研究(李战子,2005;欧阳护华、唐适宜,2006;徐昉,2011,2012,2017;吴格奇,2013;唐芳、许明武,2015;杨欣然,2015)。身份研究的视角从社会文化维度转向二语写作者。以往的研究主要集中于写作者身份特征、身份意识、身份构建、身份的影响因素等方面,研究方法既有定量方法与定性方法,也有定量方法和定性方法的结合,但跟国外研究相比关注度明显不够。在中国知网(CNKI)搜索到的相关文献寥寥无几。英语写作中的身份研究可以帮助提升语言学习者的语言敏感度,提高语言使用能力。写作者身份的建构过程因而成为学者们身份研究中关注的重点。探讨英语学习者的写作者身份、如何实现自我身份构建的研究能够揭示学习者在学习、写作过程中的发展变化,促使其成为有自我的学习者和写作者(唐芳、许明武,2015)。

大数据时代无疑给写作者身份研究带来强大的助力和推动力。写作者身份研究多采取语料库的研究方法,需要大量使用数据对文本进行分析对比。网络信息化时代使数据检索和收集、语料库创建和统计分析变得更为方便,更为快捷,研究结果也更具有说服力和应用价值。无论是学术写作语料库还是体裁写作语料库,本科生还是硕士生、博士生论文写作语料库,中文写作还是英语写作,国内、国际还是跨国间的研究,大数据时代都使得这些领域内的身份研究和建构成为可能。

第一节 基于语料库的英语写作者身份研究

关于二语学习者身份的理论研究对写作者身份的定义因为视角的不同而未能达成一个统一的定论。Ivanic 是研究写作者身份的标志性人物,她对学术语篇与作者本人之间关系的研究厘清了学者们对写作者身份概念的理论解读。

Ivanic(1998)提出写作者身份由"自传式自我(autobiographical self)""语篇自我(discoursal self)""作者自我(self as author)"三部分构成。自传式自我,她认为写作是作者身份建构的动态过程,写作者身份具有多重性。语篇自我指人们在写作中凸显的自我形象。作者自我指作者在写作中表达立场和观点的自我。2010 年 Ivanic 和 Burgess 就写作者身份的语篇架构设计了一个框架图(图4.1),解释各部分的互相作用。

Hyland 是二语写作身份研究的另一个代表性人物。他长期关注写作与写作者身份之间的关系。他提出,写作中的身份概念是由社会界定的,身份之间的沟通通过写作者在语篇中做出的选择进行(Hyland, 2005)。在 2015 年的研究里,Hyland 进一步强调社区和写作者身份的关系(the relationship between community expectation and individual writer)。他认为社区的合作实践使写作者趋于一致,促使写作者融入社区,并提供写作者承担某种身份的机会。对学术写作而言,身份是他们作为个体赢得的信誉和获得的声望(Hyland, 2015)。

图 4.1 写作者身份的语篇架构框架图
(Burgess & Ivanic, 2010)

学术语篇是作者高度参与的社会性言语行为。写作者身份通过学术语篇实践得以构建,并且具有多样性。学术语篇中写作者身份的不同侧面也比较多地引起了研究者们的关注。在国内,研究者们用语料库研究方法,探讨学术论文中作者自称与身份构建的方式(柳淑芬,2011;吴格奇,2013;杨欣然,2015)。吴格奇建立了一个包括 90 篇期刊论文的语料库,总计 705 364 字。前期的语料收集,用电子邮件求证写作者背景;中期用软件转换文档,用 Wordsmith 进行数据检索;后期数据统计和软件等技术手段都使研究的效度和信度得到保障。吴格奇认为学术论文作者身份由四个侧面构成:研究者身份、话语构建者身份、观点持有者身份及评价者身份,其中研究者身份和话语构建者身份是写作者身份的主要方面。这四个方面的写作者身份并非独立存在,而是相互交错、互动作用,最后构成了写作者身份。柳淑芬(2011)把国内五种核心期刊的 80 篇语言学论文摘要和国外四种最权威的语言学期刊 80 篇论文摘要中的作者自称语使用作对比分析,发现国内作者的参与度明显偏低。杨欣然(2015)借助数据检索工具 AntConc 2.1,创建了中国学生学术写作语料库(Chinese academic writing,CAW)和北美学生学术写作语料库(North America academic writing,NAW),考察了国内和北美(美国和加拿大)英语语言学和应用语言学专业硕士学位论文中的作者自我指称使用特征。通过使用语料库检索工具 AntConc 3.2.1 进行统计分析,采用对数似然比检验,检验上按频次和标准频率报告分析结果后发现,中国和北美学生在用于自称的第一人称代词使用频次和语篇角色选择方面都存在显著差异。中国学术写作中的写作者身份相对"隐性",缺乏权威性。这一研究结果与 Hyland(2002)、欧阳护华和唐适宜(2006)、徐昉(2011)等的研究结论一致。杨欣然在研究中指出,因为传统角色定位的影响,中国学术论文写作者的身份重构面临困难。一方面,他们把自己定位为谦逊的学习者而不是拥有较多话语权的专家,以降低对自己观点或结论所承担的风险;另一方面,他们也要表现出与权威的协同,以融入学科专业领域获得认可。这种矛盾导致了英语写作者身份建构处于英语学术语篇共同体边缘地带(杨欣然,2015)。徐昉 2017 年的论文把目光投向了中国外语教学研究者们在国际发表中的写作者身份建构。从研究者、写作者和审稿人三个角度出发探究如何实现研究者们写作者身份的合理建构和转型。

基于语料库的研究方法除了被用于学术英语写作者身份研究外,也有学者用来做体裁写作者身份研究。欧阳护华和唐适宜(2006)对中国大学生英语议论文写作中的作者身份进行了实证调查。他们选取中国学习者英语语料库中 117 篇学生的英语议论文作为研究对象,用 Wordsmith 检索软件对目标代词进行词项和词频统计,进行数据分析。结果表明,中国大学生议论文中写作者身份的建构是隐性的,写作者的个人观点被常识化、常规化。写作者习惯于自我模糊,用"包含性的你"的指称来寻求与读者观点的一致。

　　虽然中国论文写作者在国际发表中的投稿数和发表率在逐渐增加,中国外语研究者在国际发表圈能发出声音并拥有一定的话语权,但分量跟国际发表大国相比还远远不够。在国际学术圈中,中国研究者们的写作者身份建构还任重道远。此外,对于中国高校的英语学习者来说,众多研究者的研究结果都表明英语学习者的写作者身份意识普遍较弱,身份建构的理论和实践欠缺。中国写作者强烈的"集体化声音"与西方写作者强调的"个性化声音"呈现出截然不同的特征(欧阳护华、唐适宜,2006)。究其原因,中文作为母语,对英语为外语的英语写作有负迁移,但也说明在国际化速度加快、文化融合加速的大数据、信息化时代,中国学生作为写作者的身份建构应当引起更多写作教师和应用语言学研究者们的关注。尤其是中国语境下的英语写作者身份研究还是一个全新的跨学科领域,存在不少值得探讨的课题。

第二节　英语写作教师身份研究

　　对于身处汉语社会文化背景下的中国英语写作者而言,需要突破母语文化中的束缚因素实现身份重构;而对于英语教育者,特别是英语写作教师而言,则是尝试建构新型的教师和写作者双重身份。

一、写作教师的双重身份:写作教师身份和写作者身份

　　总体而言,关于国内英语写作教师的身份研究屈指可数。正如英语写作领域其他研究一样,大部分的研究关注主体还是以写作者为中心进行的。事实上,不止在国内,国外以写作教师为主体的研究也相对较少,虽然关于写作教师的职业身份(professional identity)的文章在逐渐增加,但写作教师作为写作者身份的研究仍然十分匮乏(Cremin & Baker, 2010, 2014; Gardner, 2018)。Gardner认为这是由文化和社会经济方面的原因导致的,他指出写作教师通常会认同自己同时也是读者的身份,但很少会认为自己也是写作者。与国内相比,有越来越多的国外研究者开始关注写作教师的身份建构,以及他们跟写作者身份互相作用会产生的结果。一般认为,写作者身份不是静止不变的,它的建构是一个持续的、动态的过程,会随着时间、环境等各方面因素影响发生变化(du Gay et al., 2000; Ivanic, 2006; Lemke, 2000, 2002; Sfard & Prusak,

2005）。而对于写作者身份建构影响最大最直接的,是写作者的教师,即教师身份建构对学生的影响。

Cremin 和 Baker（2010）采取个案调查和定性分析的研究方法,采用课堂观察、访谈、视频回顾、写作文本检测等形式对两名英国写作教师的身份构建进行调查,研究英国教师如何对自己的教师身份进行构建,以及如何主动构建写作教师——写作者的双重身份,以求为学生提供有力的写作支持和指导。长期以来,学者们对写作教师在课堂内外构建自己的写作者身份给学生带来的意义和价值一直有争论。支持者们认为,写作教师作为写作者参与学生互动,做写作示范,展示他们的写作能力,与学生分享写作过程中的困难和挑战,会使学生受益匪浅（Atwell,1987；Draper et al.,2000；Grainger et al.,2005）。关于"国家写作项目"（National Writing Project,NWP）的一些研究也肯定了写作教师采用写作者身份的积极意义。但是这些研究基本都是分为两类：一类是小范围、小规模的自我检测报告；另一类是以学生学习结果为导向的,基于 NWP 项目的大规模的定量研究数据。前者的研究结果取决于"exemplary writing instructors"的个人行为（Cremin & Baker,2010：9）,对研究者来说有不可控性；后者的数据来源是基于不停变换身份角色的教师,因而结果也不一定可靠。

二、写作教师双重身份构建——基于个案研究案例的报告

Cremin 和 Baker(2010)的个案调查在数据收集阶段给每名研究对象配置了一名研究人员,研究对象是来自英国两所学校的写作老师。研究人员在一个月的时间内分四次去学校进行数据收集：第一次是深度访谈,了解两名研究对象的写作背景和历史及对自己作为写作者的看法。后面三次（每周一次）对每次课堂教学活动进行课堂观察并录像,记录教师的写作示范和师生合作写作行为,如教师转换为写作者身份时会离开讲台,坐在学生当中一起写作。每次课堂教学过后,教师们接受访谈,思考同时作为写作教师和写作者的感受。

数据收集过程如下：
- 初始深度访谈(1.5 小时 ×1)
- 课堂观察、录像(1.5 小时 ×3)
- 课后反思性一对一访谈(1 小时 ×3)
- 教师个人日志
- 与两位教师一起的小组访谈：最后一次课后,用课堂录像视频作为回顾(3 小时 ×1)

- 与6名随机抽取的学生的小组访谈:最后一次课后(0.5小时×1)
- 与两位教师的最后一次小组访谈:3个月后(3小时×1)

两名研究对象,Jeff 和 Elaine(均为化名),都有12年以上的教学经验,都有教育学的理论知识。Jeff 5年前获得硕士学位,目前所教学生为9~10岁;Elaine 正在攻读硕士学位,目前所教学生为7~8岁。有趣的是,对两位教师的深度访谈揭示了截然不同的写作背景。工作之余,Elaine 私下也喜欢写作,但在上学期间对写作方面并没有信心,直到遇到她中学的写作老师。Elaine 的写作老师非常重视学生的写作:"He made us feel like writers, like we had a voice, we had a say. It just made such a huge difference"(Cremin & Baker,2010:14)。这位写作老师不仅让 Elaine 对自己写作更为自信、更喜欢写作,而且也给 Elaine 后来的写作教师职业带来了非常正面的、积极的影响。另一位教师 Jeff 则有完全不同的写作经历。他把小学阶段的写作体验描述成 horror,中学的写作也没有多好。到了大学阶段,当他可以更自由地表达自己想法的时候,Jeff 开始找到了写作的乐趣,并逐渐找到了写作的自信和意义。Jeff 作为写作教师的写作体验主要是工作中需要的应用文写作,如学校计划、报告等。

从两位研究对象的写作背景可以看出,两人的共同点在于一开始对写作都缺乏自信,但后来都有改变。Elaine 在学生时代还只是一个写作者时,跟写作教师有积极的互动和互相作用,从不自信到自信,从不喜欢到喜欢的写作者身份直接来自写作教师的正面影响和反馈。Jeff 没有这方面的身份建构体验,他作为写作教师身份的经验来自自己的理解和领会。

数据分析过程分为好几个阶段。所有的访谈被录音并由研究人员转写,生成类别数据。然后用聚类分析法(categorical analysis)进行归纳,并由研究人员进行交叉审核,对教师身份构建形成影响的三个类别数据被确认:interpersonal, institutional 和 intrapersonal influences。最后,为了保证研究的信度和效度,研究人员也采用了参与者数据核实(member check)方法,邀请研究对象对数据进行评判、核实、补充,以确保研究者们的数据解读准确。并分别在个案调查结束的3个月和1年后,再次邀请研究对象进行数据核实(Cremin & Baker, 2014)。

Elaine 的教师—写作者及写作者—教师身份互换的建构过程如表4.1。

表4.1 Elaine 的写作示范节选——口头稿（Cremin & Baker,2010:15）

Elaine	Right, I'm going to read this back, just to make sure that it makes sense to me, then it'll make sense to my readers. (*reads*) "I looked at Mary's face, for some reason I was drawn to her eyes. Suddenly she blinked"… I'm probably going to be sort of … unbelieving, disbelieving. (*pause*) So I need to convey that, I might say … (*pause*) "I couldn't believe it".
Paul	I couldn't believe my eyes?
Elaine	I appreciate your idea, Paul, but I'm going to have a think myself first, though I may need help in a little bit, but I'm trying to sort of get my own ideas down first … (*writes and reads aloud*) "Was I imagining it? I looked at her eyes again—they were"… (*long pause, Elaine looks at her own writing apparently thinking about options*)
Nathan	Glowing?
Paul	Beautiful eyes?
Elaine	(*acknowledges the suggestions, then turns back to the flipchart*) I'll say "they looked … they were full of kindness" (*writes*) "full of kindness." (*re-reads*) "I looked at her eyes again—they were full of kindness" (*pause*) I don't know what to say now (*long pause*). I want to say something else happened, not blinking, like … maybe … I kind of want her to come to life, but I'm not sure … (*looks uncertain and uncomfortable*)
Several Children	(*multiple suggestions from children calling out simultaneously*)
Elaine	Oh, thank you very much but I won't be able to concentrate if you're giving me ideas. I might get confused if people are shouting things out. (*long pause, Elaine still looks unsure*) (*Writes and reads aloud*) "And then her lips began to twitch" (*long pause*)
Elaine	Could you finish it off for me, guys? Because I don't know what to … I want to say "eventually she smiled"—you know—that kind of thing?
Paul	How about "until she smiled"?
Elaine	Okay how about (*writes and reads aloud*) "until she smiled so brightly at me! It was a miracle".

从节选的数据一开始可以发现，Elaine 在写作示范之初是想要按自己的想法来进行写作的。自然而然地，她的写作者身份促使她采用了以写作者为主、

教师为辅的身份定位。然后她无意中留出一个可供学生们参与进来的切入口，在面临写作困难时，她向学生寻求帮助。然后她停止写作示范，要求学生自己进行写作练习，Elaine这时不是坐在讲台前继续完成写作，而是以一个写作同伴（fellow writer）的身份坐在学生中间一起写。

文字稿：I looked at Mary's face, for some reason I was drawn to her eyes. Suddenly she blinked. I couldn't believe it! Was I imagining it? I looked at her eyes again—they were full of kindness. Then her lips began to twitch, until she smiled so brightly at me. It was a miracle.

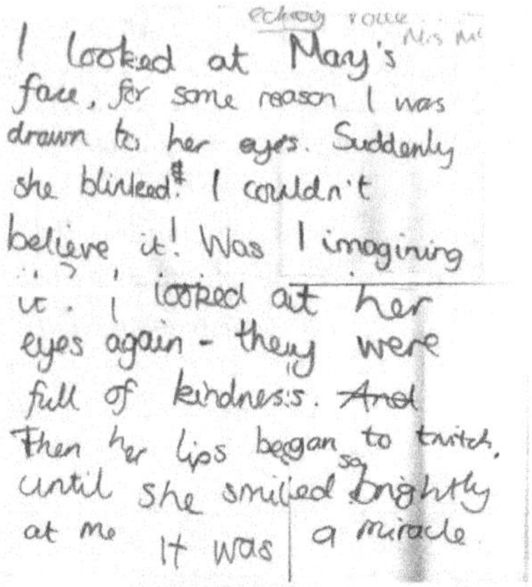

Elaine的口头稿和电子稿都表明，她在进行写作示范之初以写作者身份为主，教师身份为辅，真实地表达自己的想法。写作者身份在她

图4.2　Elaine的写作示范课节选——文字稿
（Cremin & Baker, 2010:16）

坐在学生当中（如图4.3），以同伴写作者身份一起进行写作时建构完成。随后，Elaine停止写作，站起来在教室里四处走动，查看学生写作情况，回答学生写作时碰到的问题。至此，Elaine从写作者身份转换回教师身份。

图4.3　Elaine（中）与学生一起写作
（Cremin & Baker, 2014:47）

Jeff的教师—写作者及写作者—教师身份互换的建构过程如表4.2。

表 4.2　Jeff 的写作示范节选——口头稿（Cremin & Baker，2010：18）

Jeff	I'm going to do now what you're going to be invited to do in a minute, write about someone in my family. Whilst I write I'm going to talk about what I'm thinking, just to see if that helps you when you come to write, 'cos I'm a writer too and it's not easy—writing. Who do you think I've chosen?
Chris	Your nan?
Jeff	Yeah, well done, Chris, my gran. I'm talking a lot at the moment 'cos in my head I'm thinking what I'm going to write. What do I want tell you about her? (*pause*) I'm not sure and I'm putting it off. But I'm gonna do my title (*writes*), "MY GRAN", though it may change later. I've done it in capitals because she's important—she's special to me. The hardest part for me, I think, is starting, I'm not sure (*pause*) um … (*long pause, then writes and reads aloud*) … "The gentle rhythm of the car." For some reason I've started in story mode, instead of saying my gran was this, my gran was that, which would be boring. I'm in the car on the way to her house (*rereads*) … "the gentle rhythm of the car" (*writes and reads*) "and the sound of …"
Callum	The engine
Jo	A train
Elaine	(*writes*) "The engine slowly rocked me to sleep." I'm trying to remember her and cos she's dead, I find it hard, so I think perhaps if I dream about her she'll be more vivid. (*writes*) "Now in my memories I can remember and hold on to those precius [sic] memories." I've used that word twice (*underlines memories in both places*) and it doesn't sound right to me (*crosses out "remember and" and the repeated use of "memories" and changes it to "moments"*). Does that sound better? (*rereads*) "Now in my memories I can hold on to those precius [sic] moments."
Several children	(*simultaneously*) Yeah, much. It's fine. (*Murmurs of agreement*)
Jeff	I'm not sure "precius" is right?
Class teacher	Mr. Mac, don't worry about the spelling now, it's not important, just underline it and come back to it later.
Jeff	Oh, okay. (*looks unsure but underlines it*)
Callum	Mr. Mac, it's got an "o".
Jeff	Thanks, Callum, I'll come back to it.

Jeff 在写作示范的一开始,也是采用写作者为主、教师为辅的身份建构。他解释了他的写作构思,表明自己在这个写作话题上的情感表达倾向,分享他写作中可能会碰到的困难。随后他也选择坐在学生中间一起写作,而不是以一种更权威的教师角色站在学生面前。与 Elaine 不同的是,在课堂纪律有点失去控制时,Jeff 没有把写作者身份立刻转换回教师身份,而是继续坐在学生中间写作。直到最后噪音太大,才进行一定程度的教师身份切换来管理课堂秩序。但他最后说的一句话是:"… then we can keep our thinking going, okay? I can't do justice to my gran with all this noise."(Cremin & Baker,2010:19)这说明 Jeff 到最后还是停留在写作者身份建构中。Jeff 在后面的访谈中解释说,他这样做的目的是让学生建立起"老师也可以是同身份的写作者"的认知,帮他们树立如何解决问题的观念,以及在处理这种写作话题时应该具有的情感和如何写出让自己满意的作文。

经过数据分析发现,两位写作教师在进行教师身份—写作身份/写作者身份—教师身份的互换和建构的过程中都伴随有相当程度的紧张和困难,也就意味着在学生面前进行即兴写作示范是有挑战性的。但总体来说,两位写作教师都肯定了这种身份互换和建构的尝试。Elaine 喜欢这个过程,不管是为了应付学校课程要求而写作,还是为了自己而写作(图 4.4),因为感觉可以时不时地受到鼓舞和推动("constantly feeling pushed and pulled indifferent directions")。

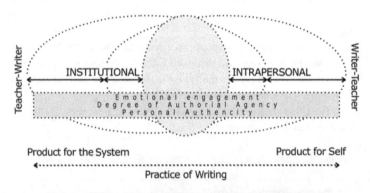

图 4.4 教师—写作者/写作者—教师的身份建构连续体
(Cremin & Baker, 2010:20)

上图连续体模型中教师与写作者身份的互换和建构是流动的、持续的。在为了完成学校教学要求而写作时,写作中的身份建构偏向以教师身份为主、写作者身份为辅(teacher-writer identity);而当写作是为了抒发自己的情感,为自己而写时,写作中的身份建构偏向以写作者身份为主、教师身份为辅(writer-teacher identity）。

Cremin 和 Baker 的个案调查研究发现，当两位写作教师以"写作同伴"（fellow writer）的身份坐在学生中一起写作时，通过强调写作者身份和选择的重要性，他们寻求给学生提供更多作为写作者的权利：比如，选择写作主题、写作形式和读者。Elaine 和 Jeff 也努力为学生提供机会分享他们在写作过程中的参与感，讨论学生写作者们对自己习作的感受。通过感知学习者写作过程中的问题和困境，两位教师也站在学生们的角度思考学生们完成学校课程要求的"为了写而写"是否太频繁及教师的课堂话语和行为对学生有怎样的影响。通过对身份互换和建构尝试的反思，两位教师更加能感知把教师身份转换为写作者身份，参与写作过程对学生写作者的影响，更关注学生的写作者身份建构，也能更好地帮助学生提升写作能力。反过来，对写作者身份的理解和专业化知识也能进一步帮助写作教师认同自己的教师身份，发现学生的多样性，探索怎样使用课堂语言和行为帮助学生建构写作者身份。

三、小结

当前国内关于写作教师身份的研究匮乏，笔者通过对 Cremin 和 Baker 的个案调查研究进行报告、提炼与总结，意在为中国研究者们提供相关领域定性研究的借鉴和思考。对写作教师进行课堂观察和个案研究，可以帮助研究者们熟悉在写作过程中教师身份与写作者身份互相作用的过程，以及这种身份互换和建构对学生写作者产生的积极影响。不可否认，在课堂内即兴进行写作示范有很大的挑战性，会受到多方因素的干扰，这种身份互换的即兴写作示范模式更适合小范围（比如小组）的写作教学活动。在 Cremin 和 Baker（2014）的后续研究中，他们对课堂录像资料做了进一步的数据分析，邀请研究对象一起对教师课堂话语、教师肢体语言、面部表情等进行深度回顾和剖析，给写作示范和同伴写作的多模态互动语篇分析提供了更多的数据细节。在这次后续研究中也证实写作教师转换为写作者身份，作为写作同伴与学生一起参与写作过程和讨论受到了学生的认可和肯定。此外，Kajee（2015）也对南非一所大学的教育专业 35 名大学生的叙事性写作进行了个案调查，来探究学生在写作者身份和准教师身份之间的协商和身份建构。这些研究都给英语写作教师身份研究领域提供了有益的参考。

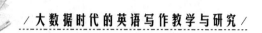

第三节 写作中身份研究的意义

国内外研究表明,二语/外语甚至母语写作者身份的构建都面临不少困难,写作者身份研究可以让写作教师认识到写作教学不仅仅是语言层面知识的传授,更是帮助学生了解自己在学习、写作过程中的发展变化,建构二语写作者身份并有效与社区、社会环境互相作用获得认可的过程。Bhatia(2008:144)认为写作教学应该包含语言、语类以及社会三个层面的语篇能力。在语言层面,除了培养学生遣词造句以及如何保持语篇的衔接和连贯的能力之外,教师还应培养学生选用得体的措辞来传达自己的态度、立场和观点的能力。在语类层面,应该传授给学生如何根据学术论文的语类特点来呈现研究过程和结果的方法,以及在相应的语类规范下如何更好地表述自己在研究中得出的观点和看法。就社会层面而言,写作教师应培养学生在写作时考虑与潜在读者的社会距离、权利差距以及自己的表述对读者可能产生的影响,从而使用更合适的语言策略来与读者进行有效交流,使自己的论点更容易被接受(吴格奇,2013)。身份研究对学术写作者尤其意义重大,可以帮助他们熟悉国际发表中常规的语言与形式,增加相应的学术圈话语权。

同时,写作教师的身份研究,尤其是对教师—写作者身份互换和建构的实践和理论研究,给英语写作教学提供了新的发展空间和创新方式。研究证明学生觉得这一改变传统写作课堂的教学实践非常有趣,对写作更有兴趣,更愿意与教师分享写作想法和写作过程中遇到的问题(Cremin & Baker, 2014)。教师身份建构在学生写作者的身份建构中起到举足轻重的作用(Shand & Konza, 2016),反过来,学生的写作者身份建构也反映了教师身份建构的成功与否。学生与包括教师在内的学习环境的相互作用是一种独具匠心的教学设计,能反映出教师打破认知障碍的能力,以及学生应对高期待值的能力("… reflect the power of teachers to break down perceived barriers, and the capacity of students to respond to high expectations, and well-crafted teaching")(Shand & Konza, 2016:159)。

写作者身份研究正在成为外语界应用语言学领域的研究热点,也是难点。大数据时代信息获取的快捷、研究手段的丰富、技术支持的保障都给写作者身份研究带来新的发展契机。技术融合型的写作教学与研究为新时代的英语写作者们提供更多机会去深化多文化、多层面学习环境中写作者身份的了解和建构,也为跨学科、跨国际的研究合作提供了无限的可能性。

第五章　大数据时代英语写作的资源运用与评估

英语写作从传统的使用纸、笔写作,到现今使用电脑和在线系统写作,到使用手机或 iPad 等平板电脑的移动写作,写作方式和评估方式都发生了重大的变革。而网络资源的极大丰富、写作素材库和语料库的技术支持,使英语写作变得数据化和社会化。在大数据时代,学生可以利用网络输入作文话题关键字,轻松获取海量的话题资源和数据。强大的搜索引擎和数字化平台还能提供多样化的写作指导、测试与反馈。传统的写作教师角色和学生角色发生改变,对写作资源的运用和评估,也成为写作教学改革的一项重要内容。

第一节　网络资源与数据库

信息化时代,网络作为传输信息的载体,从某种程度上来说就是一个巨大的资源库。网络资源的交互功能使学习资源的形式变得越来越生动。英语写作课程网站及各种写作素材库和数据库的建立,使英语写作过程更数字化,写作手段更丰富。海量的英语写作教学资源也削弱了传统教材和传统教学方法的地位。单一的教学方式和评估手法必须适应时代的变化。教师需要更多地发挥自主权,合理运用现代技术手段,自由整合各类写作教学资源,借助大数据将具体教学内容向外辐射,筛选适合自己学生学习的最新的音频、视频语料,服务于教学。在大数据的支持下,学生的自主学习和社会化学习成为可能甚至常态。通过网络资源,学生可以接触到原汁原味的英语材料,方便、快捷地查询需要的资源。比如,如果需要写作素材,可以搜索 Resources for Writers and Writing Instructors。Web Quest 为英语学习者提供不同层次和难度的任务模式,让学习者在完成任务的过程中相互合作。普度大学的在线英语写作实验室(Purdue Online Writing Lab,OWL)是美国比较完善的写作实验室之一,提供超过 200 个写作课程的讲义，如语法、各种领域写作方法等。

网络数据库也是极其方便的语言学习和研究资源。教师可以利用网络语料库引导学生的学习，推荐适合的写作语料库来完善学生的英语学习环境。号称目前最大免费英语语料库的美国当代英语语料库（COCA，Corpus of Contemporary American English，https：//corpus.byu.edu/coca/），是一个动态的历时语料库，具有很强的文本实时性。COCA 收集了从 1990 年至今的现当代美国英语用法，每年更新约 2 000 万字的词汇数量，目前包含有 5.2 亿词的文本，这些文本分别由小说、流行杂志、报纸、学术文章等语料构成。即使拥有这么庞大的语料库，COCA 的搜索速度依然非常之快。注册账号后可以无限制使用搜寻功能，不注册登录的用户也可以每天搜索 10～15 次。COCA 的英语语料来自专业正式文本，如美国英语使用情境下的口语演讲、小说、杂志、报纸、学术期刊等。和其他网络用语素材相比，COCA 的语料来自有更多严谨检查与使用的专业或正式文件，相对而言更能避开有争议的用法，更接近正式的语法。这为英语实用文体写作提供了更专业、正确的查询和语料参考。COCA 语料库也提供单词的词频信息，有助于学习者了解该单词在实际应用中的出现频率及单词的使用语境，从而帮助学习者在英语写作中更准确地用词。语料库还能提供模糊搜索、同义词、单词搭配、搜寻一个词汇的所有变化形态等功能。使用时只要在网页搜寻栏内输入要查询的英文单词、词组或句子，就可以找到相关的语料，比较同义词近义词，确认语言表达是否地道、语境是否合适，等等。对于中国的英语学习者，尤其是英语写作者，COCA 是功能非常强大的语料库。图 5.1 是 COCA 使用页面截图，笔者在搜索框输入"I guess"，点击"See frequency by section"，就会看到这个词组的使用频率：在口语中出现超过 2 万次，在小说中是 1.3 万次，但在学术文章中只出现了 566 次，这说明它在学术文章中的使用频率偏低。对比一下"I think"这个词组的使用频率和语境（图 5.2），会看到后者在所有语境中都高出很多。

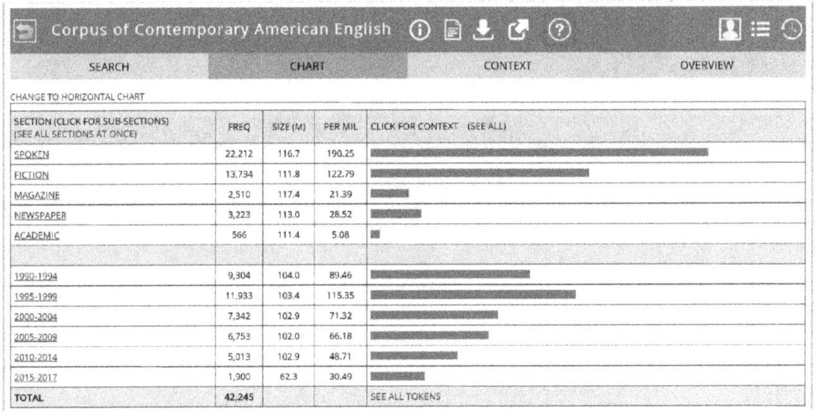
Corpus of Contemporary American English

SEARCH | CHART | CONTEXT | OVERVIEW

CHANGE TO HORIZONTAL CHART

SECTION (CLICK FOR SUB-SECTIONS) (SEE ALL SECTIONS AT ONCE)	FREQ	SIZE (M)	PER MIL	CLICK FOR CONTEXT (SEE ALL)
SPOKEN	22,212	116.7	190.25	
FICTION	13,734	111.8	122.79	
MAGAZINE	2,510	117.4	21.39	
NEWSPAPER	3,223	113.0	28.52	
ACADEMIC	566	111.4	5.08	
1990-1994	9,304	104.0	89.46	
1995-1999	11,933	103.4	115.35	
2000-2004	7,342	102.9	71.32	
2005-2009	6,753	102.0	66.18	
2010-2014	5,013	102.9	48.71	
2015-2017	1,900	62.3	30.49	
TOTAL	42,245			SEE ALL TOKENS

图 5.1　COCA 语料库“I guess”词频与语境使用图

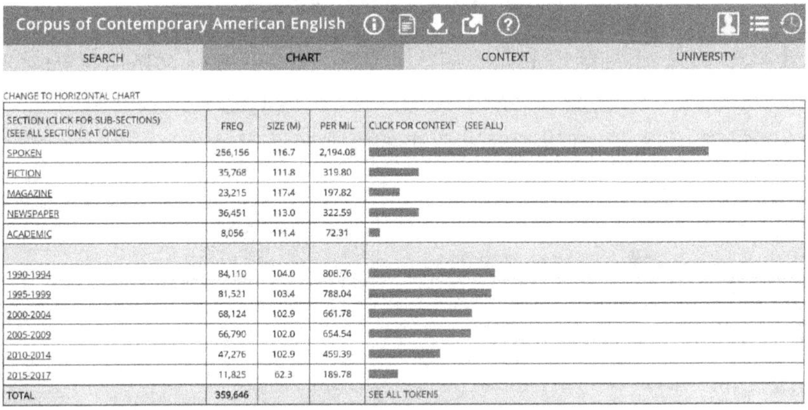
Corpus of Contemporary American English

SEARCH | CHART | CONTEXT | UNIVERSITY

CHANGE TO HORIZONTAL CHART

SECTION (CLICK FOR SUB-SECTIONS) (SEE ALL SECTIONS AT ONCE)	FREQ	SIZE (M)	PER MIL	CLICK FOR CONTEXT (SEE ALL)
SPOKEN	256,156	116.7	2,194.08	
FICTION	35,768	111.8	319.80	
MAGAZINE	23,215	117.4	197.82	
NEWSPAPER	36,451	113.0	322.59	
ACADEMIC	8,056	111.4	72.31	
1990-1994	84,110	104.0	808.76	
1995-1999	81,521	103.4	788.04	
2000-2004	68,124	102.9	661.78	
2005-2009	66,790	102.0	654.54	
2010-2014	47,276	102.9	459.39	
2015-2017	11,825	62.3	189.78	
TOTAL	359,646			SEE ALL TOKENS

图 5.2　COCA 语料库“I think”词频与语境使用图

此外，还有如图 5.3 的 WebCorp（http://www.webcorp.org.uk/）。WebCorp 是基于网络语词的功能强大的语料库，提供高级搜索选项，用户可以根据自己的需求设置搜索条件，选定特定的主题领域，设置时间范围，等等。WebCorp 不仅提供共时的网络语料库，也提供历时的网络语料库。

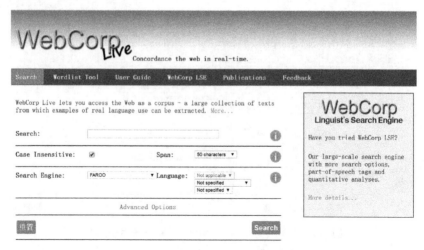

图 5.3　WebCorp 语料库界面图

图 5.4 是英语国家语料库(BNC，British National Corpus，http://www.natcorp.ox.ac.uk/)，也是一个来源渠道广泛、多达 1 亿字英语书面语和口头语样本的语料库，代表了 20 世纪晚期以来的英式英语用法。

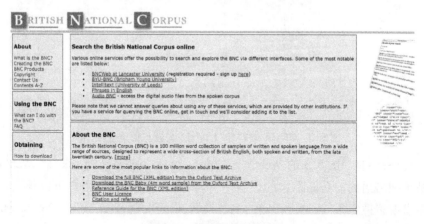

图 5.4　英语国家语料库

除了这些语料库，还有语料库检索工具软件，如 Wordsmith，Antconc，PowerConc 等，在检索语块、词语索引、单词使用频率、词语搭配、语境使用情况等方面都能给教师和学习者提供便捷。基于语料库的写作能够为学生提供丰富的、真实的语料，帮助他们克服母语负迁移的影响和对英语语言的错误认知，让英语写作更地道，更接近英语国家本族语使用者。

第二节 自动写作评估系统

随着计算机和网络技术的飞速发展及自然语言处理技术的发展,基于自然语言处理的各类算法、模型、机器学习法等纷纷涌现。20世纪60年代至今,英语自动写作系统的研究领域不断交叉,逐步涵盖了认知心理学、计算机科学、教育测量、语言学、写作研究等学科。自动写作评估系统被认为比人工评改更加稳定,可消除人类评分员因其特质行为(如光环效应、疲劳、趋中性、松紧度等)造成的信度损耗。由机器计算出的分数在统计学意义上具有可靠性,作为质量评估的有效指标对学生的写作水平加以区分,具有解释力和使用意义(Attali & Burstein,2006)。

自动写作评估系统(Automated Writing Evaluation,AWE;或 Automated Essay Scoring,AES;或 Automated Essay Evaluation,AEE)开发的初衷是帮助写作教师提供更高水平的写作反馈,加速写作反馈的过程及更好地激发学生的写作动力,提升写作质量(Wilson & Czik,2016)。经过多年的发展,各种自动写作评估系统已经初具规模,并且有了一批忠实的用户群。国外的自动评估系统比国内开发得早,类型更多,相关的研究文献也更丰富。对于自动评估系统的开发研究最早可见于20世纪60年代由Ellis Page教授团队开发的写作自动评分系统(Page Essay Grade,PEG)。随后,更多的自动写作评估系统如IEA(Intelligent Essay Assessor)、E-rater(Electronic Essay Rater)、BETSS(Bayesian Essay Test Scoring System)、IntelliMetri、Criterion、MyAcess 等陆续成功开发,数量已达10余种。国外关于自动写作评估系统评介研究也随之引起众多学者的关注。国内的自动写作评估系统开发相对较晚,数量也更少,使用最为广泛的有句酷批改网(http://www.pigai.org)和极智批改网(http://www.smartpigai.com)。前者简称批改网,拥有国内高校规模较大的用户群。此外,引起广泛关注的在线智能写作平台还有由清华大学和高等教育出版社合作开发的"体验英语——写作教学资源平台"(Teaching Resources Platform,TRP)。

第三节 自动写作评估研究与实践

国外研究者们对基于大数据技术的在线自动写作评改系统评价褒贬不一。一方面,AWE 系统写作测试场景的可靠性得到了很多研究者的认可(Attali et al., 2013; Attali & Burstein, 2006; Elliot, 2003; Shermis & Hamner, 2013; Ware & Warschauer, 2006)。这种正面评价促使更多的研究者把研究视角进一步扩大到教育领域,通过基于写作课堂的实证研究来求证 AWE 系统对于教学的积极影响。他们的研究结果肯定了自动评估系统的优势:能够给学生提供适合的语言质量反馈,让学生有更多修改文稿、练习写作的机会(Attali, 2004; Kellogg et al., 2010; Li et al., 2015; Moon & Pae, 2011)。这种功能也在一定程度上解放了写作教师,使他们能够把花在修改语法错误上的时间省下来,集中精力给学生提供文章内容和结构方面的个性化建议(Ferris, 1999)。另一方面,学者们也发现 AWE 系统存在诸多不足。Weigle (2013)指出,由于系统的技术发展还有欠缺,系统给出的关于语言质量的反馈比较表面化,不能提供更高质量和更深层次的建议。Fang (2010)在肯定 MyAccess 系统正面作用的同时,也指出依赖这个系统的评分会使学生更关注写作表层的东西而忽略写作内容。综合来说,研究者们发现 AWE 系统在写作内容、结构、写作风格方面给出的建议反馈都非常有限。此外,学者们在评估学生和自动写作评改系统的相互作用时也发现学生的参与度非常欠缺(Warden, 2000; Attali, 2004; Grimes, 2005; EI Ebyary & Windeatt, 2010; Zhang & Hyland, 2018)。Warden (2000)对 42 名二语写作学生在获得自动评估系统给出的反馈后的反应做调查后发现,每名学生平均只花了 6 分钟查看系统评估后的文稿。Grimes (2005)也指出,学生对于 AWE 系统的反馈和互动仅停留于表面,学生呈现出一种很明显的修改趋势——在提交第一稿后,根据自动写作系统的评估稍微修改几处错误后会尽可能快地提交第二稿。Attali (2004)的研究报告显示,有超过 2/3 的学生在收到 AWE 系统反馈后从不提交第二稿。类似的学生写作者行为也在 El Ebyary 和 Windeatt (2010)的研究中得到证实:有一半学生在得到自动写作系统评估反馈后从不提交修改稿。Vojak 等(2011)更是在写作研讨会上明确表示反对使用自动系统进行写作评分。

国内关于自动写作评估系统的研究起步稍晚,但近年来随着大数据技术的发展及信息化和自然语言处理系统的融合,相关研究也在快速增长。从最初对国外 AWE 系统的引介研究,到基于批改网、智能写作平台等国内写作系统的本土化的实证研究,国内写作教学领域的学者们开始涉及在线写作的方方面面,为基于数据技术的新型写作教学提供了强有力的理论支持。在对国外 AWE 系统的评介研究里,梁茂成和文秋芳(2007)对国外三种最知名的自动写作评估系统(PEG,IEA,E-rater)的分析最具代表性。他们详细评估了每一种自动写作评估系统的优势和不足。简而言之,这些系统跟人工评估和反馈相比,在语言评估质量、机器评分效度等方面存在问题。IEA 重内容,轻形式;PEG 重形式,轻内容;E-rater 相较前两种而言结合了对内容和形式的分析,但对作文质量和语言质量的分析还不够全面。

关于本土自主开发建立的自动写作评估系统的研究里(以关于句酷批改网的信度和效度研究为主),研究者们大多对其应用价值和对英语写作教学的正面作用做出了充分肯定(何旭良,2013;蒋艳、马武林,2013;杨晓琼、戴运财,2015;Lv,2018)。一方面,批改网写作评估系统的积极意义在于,它能就学生语法、词汇、表达规范性等给予修改建议,能够如实记录学生提交、修改作文的历史轨迹,并保留所有的修改数据,形成个性化的学习者写作数据库。写作教师也可以随时调阅学生作文,布置学生进行同伴互评和群批,对系统已批改作文做人工评改,能读取数据,对数据进行整理分析,等等。笔者在实践中也发现,由于系统在线批改与反馈的即时性,学生在提交作文后会立刻得到评分与反馈。笔者的学生为了提高作文评分,会按照系统语料库的建议,修改自己习作里的用词,调整句子结构,等等。高达几十次,甚至上百次的作文修改和语言提炼对学生语言能力的提高无疑是有帮助的。另一方面,批改网也存在弊端(何旭良,2013;蒋艳、马武林,2013;杨晓琼、戴运财,2015),尤其是与人工评改相比,不能评估文章内容切题与否,不能识别结构复杂的句子,对文章修辞没有反馈,尤其对文章的内部逻辑和关联性、文章的流畅性无法给出反馈,等等。与人工评改相比,批改网给出的分数显著偏高,这也意味着自动评改系统的信度还有待提高。

国内外研究者们对基于技术支持的在线自动写作评估系统的调查分析有一个共同点:AWE 写作评估系统确实给写作教师和学生带来便利,于教师而言,节省了批改作文的时间,可以把更多精力用来培养学生其他方面的写作能力;于学生而言,AWE 系统能减轻写作焦虑,增加自信心,促进自主学习能力养成。但不可否认的是,自动写作评估系统在很多方面还存在不足,它们可以用来辅助英语教师的评改和反馈工作,却不能用来替代教师的人工评价和反馈。最有益于学生写作能力发展的评价与反馈是自动在线评改反馈与写作教师的人工评改相结合的模式(蒋艳、马武林,2013;Wilson & Czik,2016;李奕华,2016;黄礼珍,2017;Zhang & Hyland, 2018)。

纵观自动写作评价研究50年的发展,从单一分数评定阶段,到合作分数评定阶段,再到人机交互评改阶段,从重形式到重内容,再到二者兼重,呈现出非线性和多维的特征,为写作教学和写作评估提供了一条有效、高质的途径。自动写作评价研究从关注可行性和信度(机器评分快/准),到关注效度(机器要包括越来越多的语义和修辞特征),再到关注后效(机器要激发学生的有效写作学习),似乎契合了三个科技革命(工业革命、电力革命、生命科学和移动互联网革命)的重心,即从标准、规范到科技、创新再到个性、快乐。科技的发展最终以人的个性化发展为本,而写作评估的本质也该如此(王勃然等,2015)。

第四节 小 结

本章介绍了在大数据背景下用于辅助英语写作教与学的网络资源、数据库与自动写作系统的评价与实践。资源整理和对国内外相关研究的梳理,为科学、合理地利用语料库技术和信息资源,更好地使用技术支持的自动写作评估系统提供理论支持与依据,并为接下来对每一种写作反馈方式的具体讨论与案例分析做铺垫。

第六章 大数据时代英语写作的评价与反馈

第一节 英语写作反馈的理论基础

长期以来,写作的评价与反馈一直都是研究者们关注的焦点。在过去的20年里,关于二语写作的评价与反馈研究有了很大的增长,从最早的书面修正性反馈,到同伴互评反馈/同伴互评,再到如今大数据时代的在线反馈与自动评估,研究内容更深入,也更多样化。计算机和网络技术飞速发展使自然语言处理技术获得了长足的进步,从而带给英语写作评价和反馈新的内涵,研究手段更丰富和科学化。

写作反馈一直被认为是英语教学研究领域提高学习者能力和巩固学习成果的重要手段。写作反馈质量的高低,直接影响学习者写作水平的提高程度和教师的写作教学成效。写作反馈的两个基本要素是评分(Evaluation)和修正(Correction)。评分就是教师(评估者)基于语言质量、写作内容、行文规范等给出的分数;修正是教师(评估者)关于作文错误的细节性解释和修改指导。最早的英语写作教师反馈,从形式上来说,分为口头反馈和书面反馈。随着写作评价与反馈方面的研究与实践,更多的反馈方式随之出现,如同伴反馈、基于自动写作系统的在线反馈、线上线下的多稿评改与反馈等,但是教师反馈依然对学生写作能力的培养起着不可替代的作用。

英语写作教学法经过多年的理论研究与实践,也经历了多次变革与创新。曾经占主导地位的"结果教学法",注重帮学生掌握正确的语言形式,教师的反馈也多是以终结性的单向反馈为主。20世纪70年代,以学生为主体,强调写作过程和师生互动、生生互动的"过程教学法"出现并逐渐流行,反馈理论作为过程写作理论的一个有机组成部分,正式与写作教学法结合起来。Swain(1993)

提出了"输出假说",强调语言输出在二语习得过程中的重要作用。英语写作作为一项重要的语言输出技能,学生在用语言表达自己想法时,通过内部、外部反馈的共同作用,会意识到自身在语言方面的不足,而去寻求更精准有效的表达方式,从而提高学习者的自我反思能力和语言学习主动性(Schwind & Siegel,1994)。Long 在 20 世纪 80 年代初提出的互动假说理论,在 90 年代中后期进行了更新。Long 认为以意义协商为形式的言语互动能够修正并调整互动结构,使语言输入可理解,从而促进语言发展。在语言学习进行"输入—反馈—修正—重新输入"的过程中,反馈对英语写作就显得非常重要。通过写作反馈,学习者了解自己的语言错误和不足并及时进行修正,最终可以用正确的语言知识代替原有的对目标语言的错误假设(Long,1996;Bitchener & Knoch,2009;Freeman & Ambady,2011)。

第二节 教师反馈与案例分析

一、教师反馈

在二语习得领域,教师对学习者的语言错误做出的回应被称为修正性/纠错性反馈(error correction, error treatment, corrective feedback)。写作教师对学生作文中出现的错误给出的反馈,则称为书面修正性/纠错性反馈(written corrective feedback, WCF)。国内外关于二语写作的修正性反馈的研究由来已久,对它在英语写作教学中所起的作用也不乏争论。"错误",按 Lennon 的定义,"is a linguistic form or combination of forms which in the same context and under similar conditions of production would, in all likelihood, not be produced by the speakers' native speakers counterparts"(Lennon,1991:182)。有学者认为纠错过程是学生学习新知识的一种重要渠道,它能让学生更熟知自己语言输出成功与否,给学生提供更多对语言的理解和产出(Yılmaz, 2013)。

在纠错性反馈的有效性上,研究者们有两种截然不同的观点:认为它无用甚至有害因而反对使用的(Polio et al., 1998;Truscott, 1996, 1999, 2004, 2007);肯定其积极作用并推崇的(Ferris, 1995;Chandler, 2003;Ashwell, 2000;Muncie, 2000;Ferris & Roberts, 2001;Russell & Spada, 2006;Sheen, 2007;Bitchener, 2008;Bitchener & Knoch, 2008, 2009;陈晓湘、李会娜,

2009）。持反对意见的代表性人物 Truscott 多次撰文，坚持认为纠错性反馈是"ineffective""harmful"。他认为写作纠错不能减少语法错误，因为语法结构的习得是一个渐进的、缓慢的过程，不是一次纠错就能获得的（Truscott，1996）。相反，为了尽可能避免错误，学生会选择使用英语短句，或者尽可能缩短文章长度。长此以往，这样的做法会影响到学习者的思维方式和写作水准。他对研究书面反馈有效性的文献做了回顾后，指出这些研究存在严重的方法论错误，因此其研究结论缺乏说服力。语言纠错只会带给接受方沮丧和挫败感；教师不做纠错反馈节省下来的时间可以花在其他更有益的事情上。他的观点遭到了很多学者的反队，并且越来越多的人采用实证性研究来证明纠错反馈的益处，其中最具代表性的学者为 Ferris。Ferris 认为，纠错性反馈可以帮助学生提高语言的准确性。对于教师而言，学生习作中的错误能够揭示学生在语言使用过程中出现的问题，从而让教师在布置写作任务时更有针对性，给学生的写作过程提供更好的帮助（Ellis，2009）。更多的学者们证明学生会在完成一篇新的作文时参考写作教师在上一篇作文中给出的纠错性反馈（Bitchener et al.，2005；Sheen，2007；Bitchener，2008；Bitchener & Knoch，2008，2009）。Bitchener 和 Knoch（2009）更是指出，反对者在数据分析、研究工具等方面存在缺陷将导致研究结果不准确。

在肯定纠错性反馈积极意义的研究中，还涉及了纠错反馈的策略选择：直接反馈（direct feedback，explicit feedback）和间接反馈（非纠错性反馈）（indirect feedback，implicit feedback）。直接反馈是对学生的错误直接给出书面修正；间接反馈是用红笔圈出或画出错误或做记号，但不改正错误。学者们对教师纠错策略的选择也有不同的看法。在肯定两者各有优劣的基础上，一部分学者认为直接纠错更富有成效（Chandler，2003；Sheen，2007；Bitchener，2008；Bitchener & Knoch，2008；陈晓湘、李会娜，2009），如 Chandler（2003）就提出，直接反馈是一种能帮助学生写出语言规范、用词正确的作文的最快最容易的方法。与他们相反，另一部分学者们则认为间接纠错整体上更有利于学习者写作水平的提高，因为反馈的间接性可以促使学生更关注语言形式，引导和激励学习者参与问题的解决（Ashwell，2000；Ferris，2002，2003，2006）。

在进行纠错策略选择时，写作教师们应该把写作教学的理论背景考虑进去，因为有理论依据的反馈能更有效地使学生获益。影响到教师们选择直接反馈还是间接反馈的因素有很多，比如，纠错的内容和时机：到底对什么进行纠错？什么时候该纠错？换句话说：怎么纠错，改多少错，如何给反馈等是会随着语言学习的环境变化而变化的（Ellis，2010）。不同的纠错方式对不同的错误类型会有不同的效果。但公认的一点是，系统性的、有选择性的和针对性的纠错反馈更有效果。学者们对反馈方式做对比性研究的结果表明，直接反馈更适用于语言规则性的学习（rules learning），间接反馈则多用于类别（items learning）。辅以示例地直接讲规则的反馈，比间接地给出词汇比较、相似语音对比类的反馈有效。此外，直接反馈似乎对长期的学习效果更为重要，比如对过去式和定冠词用法会有正面影响（Bitchener et al., 2005）。国内学者也对两种反馈方式进行了对比分析，李竞（2011）的研究发现间接反馈（非纠错性反馈）主要针对学生作文的思想内容，同时兼顾作文的其他方面。李竞在2013年的个案研究中进一步证实间接纠错能引导学生更关注文章内容、结构等深层特征。吴雪峰（2017）在探讨直接反馈、间接反馈对英语写作词汇、句法层面复杂度影响的研究中发现，直接反馈对从句长度的促进作用较明显，而间接反馈更能帮助学生提高从句的使用率。

学生犯错误的频率也是纠错反馈时要考虑的因素之一，写作教师应该在学生学习的每个阶段都能做错误分析，以帮助学生创建自己的错误层级表（error hierarchy）。学者们（Ferris & Roberts, 2001; Ferris & Hedgcock, 2005）针对写作中频繁出现的错误做了分类，它们是：动词错误、拼写错误和其他类型错误。错误层级表也可以用来发现纠正性错误和不可纠正性错误（treatable errors and untreatable errors）。一般来说，写作教师对 treatable errors 选择直接反馈方式，对 untreatable errors 选择间接反馈方式。

学生对不同反馈方式的喜好和接受度也是写作教师们选择反馈策略时的一个重要影响因素。有研究表明，学生在不同的语境下会选择不同的反馈方式。如在 Ferris 和 Roberts（2010）、Rennie（2010）的研究中，学习者更偏好直接反馈，而不是间接反馈。Lee（2004）的研究对象则更喜欢间接反馈，认为这种反馈方式更有助于帮助学习者提高语言正确率。金晓宏（2016）关于学生对不同反馈方式的接受度的研究证明，学生尤其欢迎标注错误类型的间接反馈，而不是直接改正错误的直接反馈。

从学习者的角度出发，除了学习者对反馈方式的接受度和偏好，学生学习二语的目的也是教师在选择反馈策略时需要考虑的。短期课程项目里，直接反馈更有效；相对的，长线写作课程，特别是以学术写作为目的课程，间接反馈更有效（Ferris, 2002）。

学习者的语言水平也会对写作教师选择反馈方式产生影响。处于英语学习初级阶段的学习者还没有全面的、系统的语言学理论知识，自己也不具备改错的能力，因此直接反馈对他们更有帮助。当学习者英语能力发展趋于成熟，达到更高级的阶段时,教师可以使用间接反馈,只标示错误位置,而不直接修正错误。其他方面,如学习者的性格特点、学习动机等个体性差异,也或多或少会对教师的纠错反馈方式产生影响。

从社会文化角度来看,处于 ESL(English as a second language)和 EFL(English as a foreign language)语言环境的学习者也会对教师反馈有不同的需求和要求。EFL 语境的学习者在课堂外通常没有太多接触和使用语言的机会,语言浸入环境与 ESL 学者全然不同。关于反馈方式的研究,也更多是与在 ESL 环境下的教学和学习相关。在国外为数不多的以 EFL 为背景进行的研究里(Ellis et al.,2008;Shintani et al.,2014;Stefanou & Revesz,2015),相比较 ESL 学习者而言,直接性反馈的效果似乎显得不那么有效。Ellis 等(2008)从关于日本一所大学的英语学习者直接纠错反馈效果的调查中发现,在三次试验后,焦点组(使用直接反馈的组,只收到文章的错误修正)并没有比非焦点组(使用间接反馈,收到文章错误位置以及其他如过去时、介词和词汇方面的错误标识)的表现更好。更有趣的是,即时后测结果表明,焦点组和非焦点组与对照组相比没有优势,但是在延时后测中,两组均比对照组表现要好。Stefanou 和 Revesz(2015)选择文章中"特指"和"泛指"两个语言特征来进行反馈效果研究。他们发现,尽管使用直接反馈和混合反馈(直接反馈+元语言分析)的焦点组在使用"特指"时表现都优于对照组,但是对于"泛指"的运用都没有优于对照组。Shintani 等(2014)的研究增加了写作中目标语言特征的数量,对英语中不定冠词和虚拟条件句的习得进行一次性反馈实验:一组学生接受反馈后将原来作文修改重写,一组不做修改重写,所有实验组学生在接收语言特征反馈后都要写一篇新的作文。研究结果表明,关于特指的用法不存在组内差异或组间差异。而对虚拟条件句的用法,所有四个实验组在即时后测中都比对照组表现出色,但是在延时后测中,仅有接受了直接反馈并修改重写作文的实验组表现超过对照组。国内的英语学习者处于 EFL 语境下,所以直接纠错性反馈方式还是占主导地位(李竞,2011)。学生非常重视教师的书面反馈并且大部分能认真对待,有效的反馈能激发学生学习的兴趣,促进学生习作技能的提高。陈晓湘和李会娜(2009)的实验研究表明,学生接受直接反馈的提高程度比接受间接反馈的提高程度更显著。涉及书面纠错性反馈对英语写作复杂度(如词汇复杂度和句法复杂度)的作用时,直接反馈和间接反馈对于 EFL 学习者的效果就没那么明显了。吴雪峰(2017)指出,直接反馈和间接反馈都未能显著提高词汇复杂度和学生使用从句的种类数量,但对句法复杂度有一定的促进作用。

综上所述,教师的书面纠错性反馈(修正性反馈)对英语写作者的有效与否取决于多种因素，如教师对纠错内容、纠错时机、纠错策略的选择；学生的学习目的、语言水平、语言错误频率、对纠错方式的偏好、语言环境等。大数据时代的信息化技术和发达的网络媒体给写作反馈方式提供了新的方法和途径，同伴反馈、在线反馈等多元化反馈方式的出现，极大地补充、丰富了传统的、单一的教师反馈模式。在各类反馈方式中，虽然教师反馈的作用和效果最受学生欢迎，也被国内外研究证明了其不可替代性，但是如何在英语写作教学中更有效地、更有针对性地优化运用各种反馈方式，提高学生写作能力和培养学生自主学习能力，将仍然是写作教师们要思考和研究的议题。

二、案例分析

1. 案例分析对象

笔者选取近两年来的学生习作的反馈数据，对学生的反馈接受度和效果进行分析、总结、归纳。学生均为国内高校英语专业大二学生，涉及四个写作班级。写作内容包括段落写作和篇章写作。写作体裁包括记叙文、说明文、议论文等。学生大部分时候提交纸质版作文，或者按要求提交电子版作文。学生写作的频率基本为两周一次，整个流程包括写前准备（确定主题、头脑风暴、列提纲等）；学生起草第一稿，学生自己修改；同伴互评和反馈（不定时）；提交自己的最终稿。必须说明的是，习作反馈以教师反馈为主，以同伴反馈和在线反馈为辅（这一部分会有专门章节进行分析探讨）。有一部分学生因为本身语言水平基础薄弱，不对同伴进行互评和反馈，但是接受其他同学的评价与反馈。

本节提供的反馈实例主要是笔者针对第一次写作课作文提供的反馈（最后一次课的部分学生习作在最后一章提供）。此外，笔者还对第一次写作课作业和最后一次写作课作业的教师反馈数量、反馈类型做了对比。第一次课和最后一次课写作作业都是记叙文写作。第一次作业在学期初、写作课课程伊始，四个写作班一共提交了96篇作文。最后一次写作课作业在一个教学年之后（包括两个教学学期，每学期16个教学周，写作课课时为一周一次），共收到95篇作文。

2. 教师反馈类型和数量

教师对15级、16级第一次作业的反馈处理略有不同：15级以间接纠错性反馈为主，很少涉及直接纠错性反馈；16级则是直接纠错性反馈和间接纠错性反馈结合。笔者参考了Ellis(2009)对教师书面反馈的分类，将本研究中出现的所有反馈分为9类，如表6.1所示。

表 6.1 教师反馈类型

教师写作反馈类型		
A. 纠错性反馈	1. 直接纠错性反馈	
	2. 间接纠错性反馈	
		1）指出错误并标注位置
		2）仅指出错误的存在,不标位置
		3）指出错误,并使用错误代码
		4）指出错误并简要说明、解释
	3. 重新表述	
B. 非纠错性反馈	1. 关于思想内容的评语	
	2. 关于逻辑、组织结构的评语	
	3. 关于词汇、语法、句法等语言质量的评语	
	4. 总体评价(局部、整体);改进建议	
	5. 鼓励(好词句、用法)	
	6. 分享范文	

表 6.2 15 级和 16 级两次写作作业教师反馈数量和类型对比 *

教师写作反馈类型	15 级反馈数量/个		16 级反馈数量/个	
A. 纠错性反馈	第一次	最后一次	第一次	最后一次
直接纠错性反馈	34	272	138	295
间接纠错性反馈	170	64	103	97
B. 非纠错性反馈	31	11	28	5
C. 总体性评价	47	45	49	50

注 1：统计教师反馈数量的时候,这里的非纠错性反馈没有把总体性评价计算在内,因此把总体性评价与非纠错性反馈单独分开来计算。

注 2：15 级、16 级最后一次写作作业体裁虽然还是记叙文,但是写前教师着重强调不限字数、不限主题,所以所有学生的作文字数都比第一次作业多出一倍以上。写虚构类小说的文章字数长达数千字,所以两次的反馈数量有比较明显的差别。

注 3：16 级第一次和最后一次的写作作业都没有使用其他反馈模式,学生写完后直接交给教师。15 级学生第一次作业没有其他反馈,但是最后一次作业 45 人中有 12 人的作业是经过同伴互评和反馈后交给教师的。

表 6.3　15 级和 16 级两次写作作业教师不同反馈类型占比

教师写作反馈类型	15 级两次反馈数量				16 级两次反馈数量			
	第一次		最后一次		第一次		最后一次	
A. 纠错性反馈	占比/%	人均/%	占比/%	人均/%	占比/%	人均/%	占比/%	人均/%
直接纠错性反馈	12	0.72	69.4	6.04	43.4	2.80	66	5.67
间接纠错性反馈	60.7	3.61	16.3	1.42	32.7	2.10	21.7	1.94
B. 非纠错性反馈	10.9	0.66	3	0.24	8.8	0.57	1	0.1
C. 总体性评价	16.7	1	11.4	1	15.4	1	11.1	1

3. 两次写作作业反馈类型和数量的讨论

从上表中可以看出,虽然 15 级和 16 级第一次写作作业的反馈方式有所区别:15 级更多采用间接纠错性反馈,比较少使用直接纠错性反馈;16 级则是结合直接纠错性反馈和间接纠错性反馈一起进行。但是两个年级最后一次写作作业的直接纠错反馈数量的人均个数非常接近(6.04 个 *vs.* 5.67 个);直接纠错性的反馈数量占反馈总数的比例也相差无几(69.4% *vs.* 66%)。而间接纠错性反馈数量和占比就有比较大的区别:15 级第一次使用间接纠错性反馈的占比数量很大,达到 60.7%(16 级为 32.7%),最后一次写作作业的间接纠错反馈占比两个年级都有明显减少,尤其是 15 级,从 60.7% 减少到了 16.3%;16 级从 32.7% 减少到了 21.7%。导致间接纠错数量明显下降的原因之一,可能是因为在 15 级最后一次作业的 45 篇作文中,有 12 篇在教师最终评改和反馈前,采用了同伴互评和反馈,作文经过修改后再提交。这 12 篇经过同伴反馈的文章,教师的间接反馈数量仅为 17 个,人均 1.41 个,有 7 人的文章教师没有给出间接纠错性反馈。

因为最后一次写作不限主题、不限字数,只要求是叙事文,所以最后上交作文的长度、词数,跟第一次作文比,都有成倍地增加。第一次作业几乎所有同学的作文词数都在 200～300 词。最后一次作业普遍在 400～500 词,为数不少的同学作文字数超过 1 000 字,甚至 2 000 词。虽然有理由相信文章词数的明显增加会导致直接纠错性反馈数量的相应增加,但无法得到证实。但是在间接纠错性反馈上,不管是有部分同学使用同伴反馈的 15 级还是没有使用同伴反馈的 16 级,反馈数量下降都很明显。笔者在平时的写作评改和反馈中,只对语言表层的浅显错误采用直接纠错,也就是说只对比较明显的拼写、词汇、语法等错误直接修正。其他涉及比较复杂的语言现象的错误,如复杂的语法、句法结构、逻辑组织、文章架构、思想内容等方面,都是采用间接纠错性反馈或非纠错性反馈方式。所以关于表中间接纠错性反馈数量的明显下降（特别是在最后一次作文词数成倍增加的前提下），笔者有理由相信经过一年的写作学习和训练，学生在整体把握写作架构和思想内容、写作的逻辑性、语篇能力等方面有较大的提升。笔者在收集数据的过程中也发现，15级和16级最后一次写作作业在语篇结构、内容组织、文章条理、上下文承接与过渡等方面跟第一次作业相比都有了很大进步。

当然，这些数据收集的方法不够科学，影响数据的变量也没有排除，所以并不能证明笔者所采取的反馈方式和具体反馈内容一定行之有效。结合下面来自笔者实践中的具体反馈案例，希望能给写作研究者们提供一定的参考。

4. 教师反馈实例

A. 纠错性反馈

笔者对学生习作采取的纠错策略是直接纠错和间接纠错相结合，视错误类型和学生语言水平而定。除了局部的、细节的反馈，每篇习作最后都会有关于文章思想、内容、结构、逻辑、语言等的综合性评价（实例见B部分"非纠错性反馈"一节）。

1）直接纠错性反馈

用于只出现一次的拼写错误（同一个词多次出现同样的拼写错误时，结合非纠错性反馈进行补充说明）或简单的语法错误。

- 实例1：We <u>become</u> friends because we <u>have a</u> same interest, which is
  　　　　　 became　　　　　　　　　　　had the
Gu Feng tone, a kind music represented by flowery rhetoric.
　　　　　　　　　　　^of

- 实例2：I did something harmful to <u>me</u>. For instance, I didn't review
　　　　　　　　　　　　　　　　　　　　　myself
the lessons until the final exam, which <u>leading</u> to the disappointing result in the
　　　　　　　　　　　　　　　　　　　　　led
final exam.

- 实例3：In order to <u>debating</u> well, I've been pushed to collect <s>to</s>
　　　　　　　　　　　debate/do debating
information, discuss with my team and make a conclusion logically after that.

- 实例4：Also, I <u>deleted</u> some of my ideas to complete the article. So it
　　　　　　　　　　gave
was not wonderful as I had thought.
　　　^as

- 实例5：After all, we are supposed to face difficulties alone for most of

the times in our lifetime.
                 ∧ the

- 实例6：I had been trying so hard to learn. So when I was informed to make a poster for the new recruit of Youth Volunteer Association, nervousness and uncertainty took over me.
  (recruitment)

- 实例7：When almost all of my competitors already had had partners, I was still anxious to find a partner.
  (anxiously looking for one)

- 实例8：It's difficult for me to write in English because my vocabulary is poor.
  (limited)

2）间接纠错性反馈

- 实例1：I think the ability of contacting with other people is absolutely important, so I think it was the biggest gain in the past.（用词不当）

  教师反馈说明：指出错误，标注错误位置，并给出说明/解释和修改建议。

  Teacher feedback： "Contact" is different from "communicate". If you want to avoid repetition, try "handling interpersonal relationships".

- 实例2：We would meet the style we appreciate through numerous choices and imitate it at the beginning.（名词并列结构）

  教师反馈说明：指出错误，标注错误位置，提供修改建议。

  Teacher feedback： What about "numerous choices and imitation"?

- 实例3：No one will chase behind you to warn you any more or let you be the little prince or princess and do almost everything for you.（中式英语）

  教师反馈说明：指出错误，标注错误位置，并给出说明/解释和修改建议。

  Teacher feedback： Chinglish. Try "push you to learn".

- 实例4：Last year, I confronted myself with a difficult choice. Because I had joined the art club, and at that time, I had to deal with many things.

  教师反馈说明：指出错误，标注错误位置，给出说明和修改建议。

  Teacher feedback： Why "because" here? 因果关系在哪里？学会用英语思维。Change it to "You see/know I joined an art club at that time and had a lot of things to deal with".

- 实例5：Although there is still a lot to be improved, I believe I'll try my best to correct my shortcomings and try to do better in the days to come.

教师反馈说明：指出错误，标注错误位置，给出说明和修改建议。

Teacher feedback：Change it to "overcome/get rid of shortcomings".

● 实例6：So my composition wrote about it to show my true feelings.

教师反馈说明：指出错误，标注位置，说明原因并提供修改建议（搭配错误，导致逻辑也跟着出现问题）。

Teacher feedback：You can write, but your composition cannot write. 改为"My composition was about/I wrote a composition about my true feelings"。

● 实例7：Then I could travel where I cannot actually go, suffer what actually doesn't happen to me and talk to the ones who have passed by.

教师反馈说明：指出错误，说明原因并提供修改建议。

Teacher feedback：①看到这里终于明白你的意思了，是说在书里可以做到这些？表达不够明晰。句子之前宜加上"In the books/With the help of books, I could …"。②pass by 和 pass away 意思不一样。

● 实例8：I'm not confident in my writing. I usually make a draft first, perfect it, correct it, and at last write the last version on the exercise book.

教师反馈说明：指出问题所在，说明原因并提供修改建议。这里三个动词是有内在逻辑上的先后关系的。

Teacher feedback：Which happens first, "correct" or "perfect"? 改为"make a draft first, correct it, perfect it"。

3）重新表述

在学生的写作中，有时候并没有明显的拼写、语法、词组搭配等方面的错误。但从写作的角度来说，语言表达平淡乏味，没有新意，读起来味如嚼蜡，写作水平停留在最基本的阶段，或者表达基本准确但意思晦涩，或者不符合英文思维、写作习惯等。对于这类没有具体错误但是表达欠佳的习作，笔者经常会提出重新表达的建议。

● 实例1：At first, I needed to look up many words in a dictionary, but later I did not need to do it.

教师反馈说明：表达停留在表层，词汇和句型都是最初级的。

Teacher feedback：For the sake of variety, change it to "I was able to manage reading without dictionary/go on with my reading without consulting the unknown words".

• 实例 2：I taught her Chinese twice a week <u>except either of us have another plan</u>.

教师反馈说明：表达能让人理解但不够准确，不符合英文的表达习惯。

Teacher feedback: Change it to "unless we were otherwise occupied".

• 实例 3：<u>From day to day, when final exams came</u>, I stayed up for reviewing English for several days the same as others.

教师反馈说明：表达不够清晰，给读者造成理解上的困难。

Teacher feedback: Make it clear: This continues from day to day, until the final exams came.

• 实例 4：When I was aware of my fault, <u>I learned a lesson and practiced groping and changing</u>, which also helped me understand the importance of hearing my voice.

教师反馈说明：语义表达含混，给读者造成理解上的困难。

Teacher feedback: Not clear. Change it to "I groped my way along, practiced and sought for changes".

• 实例 5：I looked down to the way which I came from, <u>only to</u> find that it was beautiful, giving me a sense of well-being.

教师反馈说明：这里重新表达结合了间接反馈进行解释和说明。

Teacher feedback: only to 一般指不太好的结果。这里的句式可以改变一下，不一定非要用复杂句，可以用短句，可以用感叹句强调当时的情感，如 I looked down to the way where I came from. What a view! I didn't realize until now that it was such a beautiful road, full of … + 细节。

• 实例 6：It was just like a <u>splint</u> began from the core of your heart and then spread all over your body.

教师反馈说明：这个词不够确切。这里是要形容有某种东西把心撕裂开来，这种撕裂的痛又蔓延至全身。

Teacher feedback: It was just like a sharp knife stubbing hard at your heart/tearing your heart open, and the pain then spread all over your body.

• 实例 7：After a day of busy study, I got a call from my mum. She just kept asking me to calm down in tears. It was very noisy in the canteen but I just could not hear other voice for several seconds. I knew this day would come after dad was ill.

教师反馈说明：在经过对记叙文的详细讲解后，学生的叙述还是没有按照要求来完成。故事本身不太寻常，可以用更多的细节来突出心理状态。

Teacher feedback：You have an unusual experience. It can be made very impressive. The following beginning is an example：

It was a busy day of study. At 5 pm, like always, I was sitting in the school cafeteria, ready to fill my stomach with food. The phone rang. It was my mother.

I picked up the phone. Mother's sobbing broke in. She was crying. My heart sank.

"Mom, what's wrong?"

B. 非纠错性反馈

1) 非纠错性反馈主要针对作文形式（format）、思想内容（idea）、逻辑性（logic）、语篇组织、词汇误用及其他需要学习者思考的语言现象提供反馈和建议。

- 实例1：Time <u>floated</u> like running water …

教师反馈说明：标注错误位置，不纠错，提供修改方向。

Teacher feedback：Check the usage of "float" in your dictionary.

- 实例2：As to me, writing is a kind of <u>expressing my emotions</u> and <u>talking to myself,</u> by the way <u>recording my life</u>.

教师反馈说明：指出句子存在逻辑错误，提供修改方向。

Teacher feedback：A little confusing here … are the three expressions of equal weight?

- 实例3：Besides above, I also wasted a lot of time on something boring during my process of exploring my interests.

教师反馈说明：与上下文结合起来看，这一句出现得比较突然。

Teacher feedback：前文都很通畅自然，到这里额外加一句。What is the purpose? If you say "although I wasted a lot of time …, I learned that …", it will make sense.

- 实例4：A man will grow up three times in his life. The second time is when you find no matter how hard you've tried, there's still something that can't be helped.

教师反馈说明:没有语言或语法错误,但从句子逻辑结构和文章内容来看,中间缺乏过渡。没有 the first time,直接跳跃到了 the second time。

Teacher feedback: The first time is? (不能想当然地认为这是一个显而易见的事情或者读者肯定能理解就不说了)

• 实例 5: However, due to the schedule of the teacher, we only practiced together twice before the competition, That's why I was so worried before going to the stage.

教师反馈说明:学生习作常见的一个问题:习惯用直白的语言浅显地 tell,而不是用细节去 show(在写作课堂曾讲解过的写作技巧:描述/叙事时要 show, not tell)。

Teacher feedback: To impress your readers, you can give more details about "how worried" you are …

• 实例 6: In recent few days, we have seen the freshman came to our university and started their college life, which let me think of my experience of that time.

教师反馈说明:此句有两句错误,第一处没有直接纠错。第二处标注了位置,给出问题让学生思考。

Teacher feedback: ① see sb. do/doing/done 这里用什么比较好? ② Think why I put a comma here.

2) 鼓励性评价反馈

鼓励性评价在每一篇学生作文、每一次作文的课堂讲评中都会涉及。笔者的做法是从每一个学习者的每一次习作中找出可以鼓励和肯定的地方。特别好的词汇用法、句子结构或文章会与全班同学分享。这里只是选择几个作为示例。

• 实例 1: I've come to realize that there never exists the so-called right choice. It's your action that makes your choice become right.

教师反馈说明:记叙文最后一句话画龙点睛,点题(一般用波浪线画出精彩的词汇用法或句子)。

Teacher feedback: Good point!

• 实例 2: The cool breeze flew by my face and blew away some of my fatigue, and the mild moonlight streamed through the branches of the streets lining the road, a few countable stars twinkling in the sky.

Teacher feedback: Beautiful!

● 实例3: With unfailing childlike appetite for the joy of game, she suddenly would like to tell me more about the girl living in the opposite bank.

Teacher feedback: Like it!

3) 总体性评价反馈

笔者对学生每一篇习作进行评改反馈后,都会在文末做总体性评价。评价涉及写作的用词、语法、句法、内容结构、逻辑论证等。纯负面的反馈容易让学生产生沮丧和抵触写作的心理,所以笔者在教师反馈时通常都会先对作文中好的地方进行鼓励和肯定,然后针对问题进行评述,并提出今后写作努力的方向。

● 实例1: 这是一位总体写作水平偏弱的学生,但是在努力地提高自己写作水平,比如,尽量丰富自己写作的词汇和句子结构。但是由于语言基础薄弱的原因,用词不准确,句子结构为了变而变,语法错误较多,经常出现中式英语。教师总体性评价如下:

Teacher feedback: I can see you are trying your best to achieve variety in vocabulary & sentence structure. Some of them are well put, some not. But it's always good to try.

You already know how to express yourself. You are just looking for the best way to do it. Beautiful words/sentences don't just come. They need a lot of reading, remembering and copy writing as well. Before that, use the vocabulary/expressions you are sure of. Clarity comes first before variety.

Keep working, and you will see progress.

● 实例2: 这位学生的写作水平高于班级平均水平,但是离优秀还有一段距离。他写作态度非常认真,每次写作都会尽量按老师要求完成。为了追求词汇的精美和句子的复杂,有时候会牺牲行文的简洁流畅。教师总体性评价如下:

Teacher feedback: You have a good variety in vocabulary & sentence structure, which is great. Some of your word choices don't seem to fit in the right context and so are awkward to read … Remember, don't sacrifice brevity and conciseness for the sake of variety/complicacy. 写作中使用高端词汇或复杂句型不是唯一目的,用适合的语言清楚、准确地表述主题是最重要的。以你现在的基

础,对所掌握的知识能应用更恰当更熟练的话,离更高的台阶只有一步之遥了。

● 实例3:这位学生的英语基础不弱,但对写作任务比较敷衍,是单纯为了完成任务而应付式地写作。文中有很多非常简单的拼写和语法错误,稍加留意或者写完草稿后稍做修改就可以避免。教师总体性评价如下:

Teacher feedback: You made your idea clear with the right organization.

Could you spend a little time checking or revising your work after drafting it to get rid of the unnecessary minor mistakes? And then, add variety to vocabulary & sentence structure, if you can.

Pay attention to the consistency in tense(时态一致).

● 实例4:这位学生对英语写作有基本的了解,语篇结构完整,语言表达清楚,但是对作文题目审题失误。教师总体性评价如下:

Teacher feedback: A good organization and clear structure, you certainly communicated your ideas successfully to the readers.

But look at the title, you are supposed to focus on the BIGGEST GAIN, which is one, and only one. TO AVOID digression/straying away from the topic, you can actually combine the three things you covered together, make it into one (= English learning) and elaborate from three aspects …

● 实例5:这位学生有很好的语言基础,写作能力在班级名列前茅。每次的写作作业也都能高质量地完成。写作时用词精准、妥帖,句子结构精巧,思想内容富有创意,但偶尔会忽略读者立场,使得叙事逻辑上出现问题。教师总体性评价如下:

Teacher feedback: Very good design and good thinking! Good variety in vocabulary and sentence structure. I feel you can make this a great story if more details are given. Otherwise, it seems your readers have to guess what happened here or there, which may lead to confusion.

● 实例6:这位学生对写作的内容和结构有基本的了解,写作构思有新意,但是对句与句之间的过渡把握不好。教师总体性评价如下:

Teacher feedback: You had a very good and clear beginning, and the developing in the first half of the body part is OK too, but the last few sentences in the body part lack cohesion and transition. I didn't quite get your point there.

It can be easily made better with a little more work.

● 实例7:这位学生基础较弱,英语写作句型千篇一律,80%的句型都是简单的主谓宾(主语为第一人称)。这种类型的作文在语言能力较弱的学生中比较具有代表性。笔者在批改时在这些句型下面加了下划线。教师总体性评价如下:

Teacher feedback: You communicated your ideas successfully to the readers. That's good.

But vocabulary and sentence structure can be further improved. Look at the underlined sentences. They are oversimplified and monotonous. How many of them can you improve?

● 实例8:这位同学语言水平较弱,写作过程中也并没有花时间去打磨语言,除了很多小错误以外,对词汇的误用较多。教师总体性评价如下:

Teacher feedback: Thank you for sharing. This is a big gain.

As for the writing, you communicated your ideas well to the readers.

For revising, avoid minor mistakes like grammar, tense …; be more careful with word choices, some of the misusage can be terrifying (like the word "boil"…); try as much as you can to increase variety to your vocabulary & sentence structure.

● 实例9:这位同学是本部分实例里唯一一篇选自最后一次写作作业的文章,非常具有代表性。词数达到1 787字,全文设计精妙,悬念铺垫得非常成功,也成功地达成了写作的目的。

Teacher feedback: Oh my god, is this a true story? I was totally drawn to it and felt extremely sorry (for the little girl) and furious (for the evil man). If it is true, you are very brave to open your heart and share this with me … (big hug). I admire your courage and positive attitude. If it's not (hope not), then you have very successfully composed a narrative! You nailed it! The opening, the development, the twist and turn … all were cleverly done! Very successful narrative, I get goose bumps when reading it!

4) 分享、范文

每次对学生习作评改、反馈完后,笔者会把学生所有的共性错误进行总结分析,并制成PPT,然后在写作课上进行作文反馈与讲评。通过强调共性错误,帮助学生避免再犯类似的错误。讲评的重要一部分是摘录学生习作中的闪光之处,如精准的用词、精彩的句型结构、巧妙的构思、优美的语言等。实践中笔者也发现,这种正面反馈能带给学生成就感,特别是对于写作能力相对较弱的学生。在大屏幕上看到自己的名字和作品出现,这种自豪感有助于克服学生的写作倦怠心理，进一步激发学生的写作兴趣。对于写作驱动力强的学习者，看到别的同学能写出这么好的句子或文章，会对自己提出更高的要求。本书选取其中一小部分作为实例分享。成篇的范文分享请见本书第八章。

Descriptive writing: Space Development

实例1：Decorated with soft light, surrounded by the tender night, and accompanied by peers who are absorbed in studying, the library brings me a sense of safety and ease. I value these feelings as well as I value the library itself.

实例2：Stepping onto the path, we are at the entrance to a secluded world. The stone path, scattered with ginkgo leaves, winds its way northward, leading to a semicircular platform. Right to the platform, a tall arch bridge divided the lake into two parts. The road curves as we come off the bridge, and the chirping of the birds summon us onto a narrower serpentine path.

实例3：Casting your eyes a little further on the surface of the river, you will find a small bridge made of peculiar stones, which connects two lawns. With each part of it harmoniously combined, this little world is a splendid place for you to escape from your daily routines.

Expository writing: Comparison & Contrast

实例1：Though both Halloween and the Ghost Festival are the days for people to honor the memory of their ancestors, they differ from each other in many facets. How children behave at the two festivals is a case in point.

实例2：Unlike the past, with concentrated skyscrapers standing everywhere, neon lights shining upon the intoxicated and colorful world, the raucous riot of commerce pervades every corner of Shanghai, washing the historical sediment away. In the past, many people yearned for living or working in Shanghai and spared no efforts to strive for even one slender chance because it was tremendously ahead of other cities, whereas many people begin to hate the hustle and bustle and the huge competitive pressure here now.

Argumentative writing: On Microblog/Phubbing

实例1：The time we spend on Microblog is not proportional to what we can actually get from it. What we are scanning on microblog are mostly fast-food materials that pass through our mind and ultimately leave nothing, for the majority of the posts, such as headline news, funny jokes, photographs of celebrities, merely aim at getting more views or likes, whose contents are therefore incomprehensive and meaningless.

实例 2: It is true that the Weibo is suffused with cynicism, negative criticism and violent remarks. However, it is unfair to condemn microblog as a Pandora Box which brings all the malice and evil. What microblog does is to reveal, rather arouse, the darkness of the society that has existed long before the birth of microblog.

实例 3: Second, microblog is conducive to the development of people's originality. On the microblogs, the 140-character limit puts civilians and Shakespeare on the same level, which has led to an explosion of original content being produced.

实例 4: Moreover, microblog is a serviceable platform to release emotion. It provides us with the right to give vent to our innermost thoughts, by which the bad mood and loneliness may fly away. If we are fortunate enough, we can even acquaint ourselves with some famous figures in other circles.

实例 5: "The furthest distance in the world is not between life and death, but when I stand in front of you, you are still playing cellphones." Certainly, when we are phubbing, we may tend to focus on something far away from us rather than what are around us.

实例 6: Whether because of the unwillingness to hear others' boring bits or the wish to escape an awkward situation of no topics to talk about, real life conversation has been replaced by WeChat, video games or something else in phones. Consequently, we are getting used to a new relationship mode of being alone together.

Narrative writing:

实例 1: I used to stand under the tree, looking up through its lush leaves and intricate branches and smiling. I saw the sunlight pouring in the tree and flowing on those leaves. The lovely light spots are like lively sprites jumping up and down, left and right, tickling the green leaves into giggling laughter. I observed the gentle and caring touch of the wind, caressing the head of the tree and whispering to it in a mothering tongue. I stood there, hair flying, arms spreading, head raising, content with just being indulged in such peace and pleasure.

实例 2：When I raised my head, I saw a small shadow on the roof of the shopping mall across the road, sliced by the blinding sunlight, like a flimsy sheet of paper. A few seconds later, I realized that it couldn't be a piece of paper because no paper fell at that speed.

实例 3：The dawn crept stealthily and the solid walls of the black forest softened to grey. The temperature was still very low but my heart was lighted by excitement and amazement. When the sun jumped into people's eyes, the hurrah broke out. All was soft and beautiful and enchanting. The sun distributed a pink light and a powder of gold yonder. The color of sky turned from blue to golden yellow and at last became brilliantly white.

实例 4：The sunset was shining, softly enlightening her face, skirt and skin. Her pin was shining in orange. Her tassels beside legs were swaying in breeze. Stars were glimmering in the dark blue sky east.

And she smiled, with all the petals came dancing in the melody of the wind.

实例 5：With ceaseless rain sweeping away wildly the long and lamentable blast outside, a breath of chill wind penetrated into the house as if to take a furtive glance at the scene inside. The patter of rain, the rustle of wind and the tick of the clock were reminding me that it was time to leave.

实例 6：The beautiful, big blue ocean waves were crashing against the cliffs and drenching the idyllic beach. I was trying to pick up a gorgeous, shiny shell; suddenly, the alarm clock went off, pulling me back to reality. Seconds later, a message flashed on my phone screen, "Your flight to Bali will take off in one hour." One hour!

5. 小结

写作评改反馈在很大程度上是语言能力强者向语言能力相对弱者提供文章修改建议和改进的过程。写作教师作为传统的语言能力强的一方，她们的评改反馈在提高学生写作能力的过程中有着不可替代的作用（金晓宏，2016）。语言准确性、流利性、复杂性和作文质量的提高与作文的反馈和修改有着密切的关系,笔者在多年的写作教学实践中,也发现与同伴互评、在线反馈等形式相比,学习者更欢迎教师的评改反馈,尤其是教师提供补充说明和解释的间接纠错反馈,这一点也在很多研究中得到证实(李竞,2011;王颖、刘振前,2012;金晓宏,2016)。但是单向的教师反馈并不是唯一的反馈途径。尤其是在大数据时代背景下,智能化的自动写作评改系统已经被大范围使用,它和同伴反馈一样,是教师反馈的有益补充。在教学过程中把教师反馈、同伴反馈、在线反馈三种形式结合统一起来,根据学生的特点和不同写作任务的需要灵活使用,既能减轻写作教师的负担,又能最大限度地发挥每种反馈方式的优势,从而最大可能地为学生写作能力的提高发挥作用。

第三节 同伴反馈与案例分析

一、同伴反馈

同伴反馈的英文表达方法有很多种:peer response, peer review/revision, peer feedback, peer editing, peer evaluation 等。它对应的中文译法也有多种:学生互改、同伴互评、同级反馈。Liu 和 Hansen(2002:1)把同伴反馈定义为"用学习者作为信息来源,通过学习者承担传统意义上教师或导师角色,对同伴的文本进行口头和书面的评价和反馈的交互过程"。从 feedback 的内涵上来说,作为教师反馈的补充,同伴反馈不仅包括了学习者之间对彼此文本的修改、检查等否定性的意见和建议,也包括正面的肯定性评价和反馈。因此,与教师反馈的概念相对应,笔者用同伴反馈来指代写作过程所有基于同伴之间的互评、互改等互动。

同伴反馈是伴随着过程写作法的盛行而出现的,并且成为过程写作法的一个有机组成部分。过程写作法包括一系列循环反复的过程:写前准备、草稿、修改、反馈、重写、再反馈、修改……它强调写作的过程而不是结果,反馈是这个流程里非常重要的一环。反馈可以来自不同的渠道,除了教师,还有自己和同伴。同伴反馈在二语/外语教育领域的应用和实践,是教师反馈的一种有益补充,它丰富了写作文本的反馈方式和写作活动的互动性。近些年来,研究者们对同伴反馈的关注持续上升,但同伴反馈在研究和实践领域一直是褒贬俱存的写作教学策略,研究者对同伴反馈的作用和有效性也存在不同的看法。支持者们认为它是写作课堂的一种有效尝试和补充（Villamil & Guerrero，1996；Tsui & Ng，2000；Hansen & Liu，2005；Hyland & Hyland，2006；龚晓斌，2007；邓鹂鸣、岑粤，2010），同伴反馈能促进学习者学业成绩的提高（Fuchs et al.，2000）及社会情感策略的增强（Tsui & Ng，2000）。此外，同伴反馈对培养学生的批判思维能力、分析和解决问题的能力有所助益，能帮助学生降低写作焦虑，更好地激发学生写作兴趣（Rollinson，2005；Hu & Lam，2010）。不同于教师反馈的权威感和距离感，同伴反馈的对象是自己的同学，在进行互评互动的过程中能够更放松、更真实、更直接地看到写作中的优点和缺点。

同伴反馈的研究涉及方方面面：关于反馈的视角和有效性的研究、反馈中学生角色和作用的研究、同伴反馈策略研究、同伴反馈的影响因素研究、和其他反馈方式的对比分析研究等。很多研究者们把目光聚焦在写作的最终文本上，来探讨反馈的方式类型及在反馈过程中的学生互动对最终写作能力的影响。对于同伴反馈的双方谁更受益的问题，Lundstroms 和 Baker（2009）认为提供反馈的一方和接收反馈的一方相比，如果不是受益更多的话，至少是能同样受益。但是同伴反馈的互评者双方的语言能力显然对反馈的效果会有直接的影响。如果写作者语言能力不如评阅者/反馈者，那么对于反馈者来说，这个过程对于他们自己学习能力的提高并没有帮助（Lundstroms & Baker，2009）。目前关于同伴反馈中反馈者角色的研究并不多见（Rouhi & Azizian，2013）。

越来越多的研究关注同伴反馈中学习者的态度：他们是否接受这种反馈模式？这种同伴反馈对学习者的帮助到底有多大？研究发现，并不是所有的学生都对同伴反馈持欢迎态度（Mangelsdorf，1992；Rollinson，2005）。有些学生不相信同伴提供的反馈能与教师反馈一样有效，也就无法去了解到同伴反馈的益处。有的学生不愿意参加同伴反馈，因为他们对自己的语言水平和写作能力不自信，对要给他人提供写作反馈和意见感到焦虑不安。还有学生则担心在同伴反馈过程中分享习作会带来反效果，因为同伴读完他们的习作草稿后可能会抄袭他们的想法（Hislop & Stracke，2017）。学习者们显然还需要增加对同伴反馈优势的了解，和教师反馈相比，同伴反馈可以是一种"less threatening, less authoritarian, friendlier, more supportive"（Rollinson，2005：24）的模式，比教师反馈更能减轻写作焦虑和压力。

同伴反馈的反馈质量也是学者们关注的热点之一。Hyland（2000）认为，二语学习者可能缺乏相应的技巧和语言能力去提供有效的反馈，在评阅文章、检查错误和修正错误时遇到困难。要提高同伴反馈质量，这些参与互评和反馈的学习者们需要树立为反馈负责的意识。另一方面，写作教师们在同伴反馈发生前应该提供系统的指导和培训,让学习者知道如何有效地参与互动反馈过程(Berg, 1999a, 1999b; Hansen & Liu, 2005; Hu, 2005; Rollinson, 2005; Hyland & Hyland, 2006; Lam, 2010; Min, 2006; Rahimi, 2013)。Berg 基于自己的课堂教学实践经验,也参考了写作研究者们关于同伴反馈训练的建议,经过多年的实践研究,自己逐渐建立了一套行之有效的训练方法。在1999 年的实验研究中,Berg 比较了美国一所大学四个英语写作班级(ESL learners)的同伴反馈效果。她把学生分成四组:两组接受同伴反馈培训,两组没有任何培训。结果发现,接受过同伴反馈训练的组能做出更多的意义类型的修正(meaning-type revision)。跟没有接受过培训的组相比,接受过同伴反馈培训的组能提交更高质量的二稿。同样的,Min(2006)对一年级写作课的学生进行的调查表明,接受了同伴反馈培训的学生给出的反馈质量更高,给同伴提供的反馈更有针对性和关联性。Min 的培训包括一个 4 小时的课内教学示范,由教师用有声思维的方法向学生示范如何弄清楚写作者意图,如何发现文本问题、理解问题及给出建议。培训还包括与每个学生进行的一个小时的师生对话,来进一步帮助学生熟悉同伴反馈的内容和技巧。不过,也有学者认为同伴反馈的培训不用太宽泛、太花时间,有些培训活动只要在写作课前 5~10 分钟内快速进行,耗时长的培训内容可以融入写作课堂教学内容中,比如,对一篇范文的同伴反馈示范就可以融入过程写作教学内容中(Hislop & Stracke, 2017)。

　　同伴反馈训练能解决学习者们在实践过程中的一些问题,但是仍然有学生觉得同伴反馈的协作本质(collaborative nature)难以达成(Rollinson, 2005)。这也就意味着接受了同伴反馈培训后的同伴反馈质量不一定能达到培训者期待的效果。为此,Rollinson 提出了反馈培训应该包含的三个主要内容:awareness raising, productive group interaction 和 productive response and revision (2005: 27)。awareness raising 旨在让学习者熟悉同伴反馈的原则和目的;productive group interaction 让学生理解协作、同伴支持、技巧、礼节等概念;productive response and revison 训练基本的反馈步骤、有效的点评方式、作者—读者如何对话及有效评改反馈。关于第三个方面的培训内容,研究者们建议使用一个同伴反馈量表,量表能清晰地表明同伴反馈的目的,模拟反馈进度,教给学生适合用于点评的语言表达及如何问合适的问题。

　　总而言之,同伴反馈作为写作教学领域的一个研究热点,作为教师反馈、在线反馈的一种有益补充,共同丰富了英语写作教学的内涵。相关的研究和教学实践,对进一步完善同伴反馈模式、促进学生写作能力的提升和自主学习能力的发展有着重要的意义。

二、案例分析

同伴反馈是笔者在写作教学中一直结合教师反馈同步进行的尝试。在学生进行同伴反馈前,教师没有专门安排时间进行同伴反馈培训,但是在平时的写作课上对写作过程有详细的要求。明确学生要按照要求的流程完成写作练习:写前准备、草稿、自我修改、同伴反馈、定稿、上交作业。对于同伴反馈的内容和形式,教师只要求至少找到同伴作文中 3 处可以修改或值得肯定的地方并点评。对于怎么修改作文,教师在写作课堂上讲到写作过程时,强调过应该从哪些方面修改,不管是自我修改还是同伴互改,并提供了一个列表给学生修改和反馈时思考、对照。列表以丁往道、吴冰《写作基础教程》中相关内容为模板(2011:136 – 137),内容如表6.4。

表6.4 英语写作修改、反馈对照表

CHECKLIST FOR REVISION & PEER FEEDBACK
1. CONTENT LOOK AT THE PAPER AS A WHOLE
A. What is the topic? Does the draft fulfill the assignment? B. Is the thesis clear? Is it supported by enough facts? C. Are there irrelevant materials that should be removed? D. Is the logic sound? Are there gaps in the logic?
2. ORGANIZATION
A. Does the introductory paragraph lead to the main point of the paper? B. Does each paragraph have a separate central idea? Does it relate to the paper's main idea or to the previous paragraph? Are there proper transitions between sections? Are the paragraphs arranged in climatic order? C. Does the concluding paragraph give the readers a clear impression of what the paper intends to say?
3. SENTENCES
A. Is each sentence clearly related to the sentence before it and to the sentence after it? B. Are there unnecessary sentences that may be removed? C. Are there structural mistakes? D. Are there wordy and redundant sentences? E. Is there variety in the sentence type?

(续表)

CHECKLIST FOR REVISION & PEER FEEDBACK
4. DICTION
A. Are there words that are not appropriate for the topic or the style of the whole paper? B. Are there words or phrases which are directly translated from Chinese but which may mean something different in English? C. Are there collections which may be correct because they are taken from Chinese?
5. MECHANICS
Mistakes in grammar, spelling, punctuation, and other mechanics.

在实践中,笔者发现学生不一定会按表格里的内容和问题一一对照思考、修改和反馈,所以并不强求每个人都按表里的要求做到位,但是在课堂上反复强调一点:修改和反馈不是只检查拼写、语法、句子等语言表层的错误,首先要考虑的是文章思想内容的表达和组织架构是否切题,逻辑是否通顺,是否有自然的过渡,等等,最后一步才是检查拼写、语法等细节错误。

除此以外,笔者前几次作业没有要求学生进行同伴反馈,而是要求学生自己修改,再由教师反馈。通过自己修改和模仿教师反馈的格式,学生慢慢建立同伴反馈的概念。在接下来的每次作业中,笔者都要求学生按照写作过程的要求进行写作和同伴反馈。笔者在实践中发现,大部分学生都能按照反馈列表中的几个大类进行评改和反馈,尤其是学习动力强、有自主学习能力的学生,在经过同伴第一次反馈后,会进行修改重写,再重新做同伴反馈,在这个反馈基础上进行第二次修改形成第三稿,直至最后的定稿。相反,少部分语言能力较弱的学生,或者学习自主性差的学生,对同伴反馈相对不太重视,反馈的质量和结果也就流于表面、差强人意。

为了鼓励学生认真参与同伴反馈,笔者会在最后终稿的教师反馈中,酌情对反馈认真和反馈质量高的同伴组进行额外加分。因为写作课作业的分数,也就是平时分占写作课程期末考核的40%,所以加分措施在一定程度上起到了督促和激励作用。教师也会将特别认真的反馈文稿、质量高的反馈互动在班级进行分享、示范。笔者在下面的实例分析中将学生的同伴反馈分为三类:纠错性反馈、非纠错性反馈(总体性评价反馈)、互动评改。

1. 纠错性反馈

不同于教师反馈中的纠错性反馈,在同伴反馈中,学生对于发现的错误或问题很少使用直接纠错,而是采用商量的语气提出疑问,并尝试提出自己的建议。原因可能是对自己的语言能力不是非常自信,对纠错的能力没有把握。事实上，在教师反馈阶段，笔者往往发现学生对同伴给出的建议和反馈非常到位。有些同学即使本身的语言能力偏弱，自己写作的时候存在不少问题，但是作为读者和反馈者时，却能看出同伴在写作中存在的问题。

- 实例 1：Comparison and contrast 段落写作练习，如图 6.1

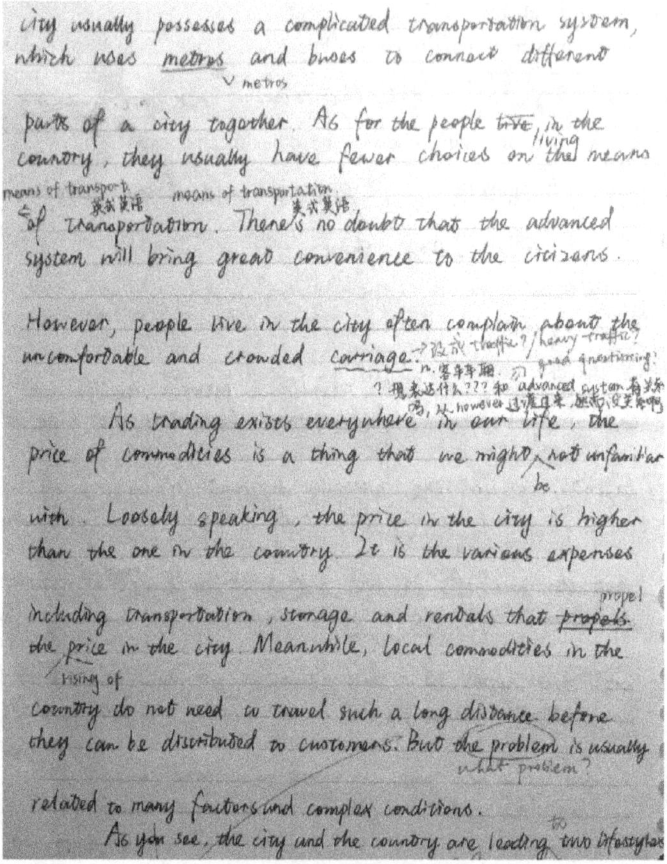
city usually possesses a complicated transportation system, which uses metros and buses to connect different
metros
parts of a city together. As for the people live in the country, they usually have fewer choices on the means
living
means of transport 英式英语 means of transportation 美式英语
of transportation. There's no doubt that the advanced system will bring great convenience to the citizens.

However, people live in the city often complain about the uncomfortable and crowded carriage.
→没说traffic?/heavy traffic? good questioning!
n. 客车车厢
?想表达什么??? 和 advanced system 有关系吗，从 however 过渡而来，然而没关系啊

As trading exists everywhere in our life, the price of commodities is a thing that we might not unfamiliar with.
be
Loosely speaking, the price in the city is higher than the one in the country. It is the various expenses including transportation, storage and rentals that propels the price in the city.
propel
rising of
Meanwhile, local commodities in the country do not need to travel such a long distance before they can be distributed to customers. But the problem is usually related to many factors and complex conditions.
what problem?
As you see, the city and the country are leading two lifestyles

图 6.1 同伴反馈实例 1

如图 6.1 所示，在这个同伴反馈中，反馈者做了三个层面的反馈。①对比较表层的语言错误，如拼写、语法等做了直接纠错，如 propels→propel；as for the people live in the country→as for the people living in the country；the price→the rising of price；等等。②深层语言特征：对于作者 carriage 的用法，反馈者给出词汇定义再提出疑问：想表达什么??? 和 advanced system 有关系吗？从 however 过渡而来，然而没关系啊。这是就文章内容的逻辑性和组织结构的反馈。③语际间反馈：对于作者 means of transportation 这个词组的用法，反馈者给出英式英

语和美式英语的不同,给作者提供思考的空间。
- 实例2: Comparison and contrast 段落写作练习(草稿和定稿)(如图6.2)

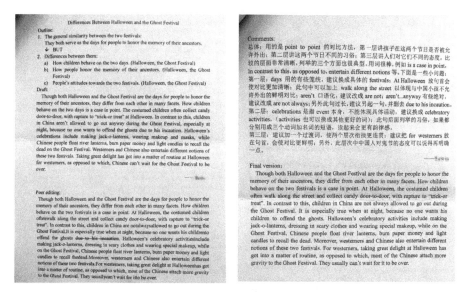

图6.2 同伴反馈实例2

如图6.2:段落写作中的"比较与对比"练习。同伴直接纠错,然后在最后总体评价中对前面的直接纠错给出理由。

这也是一个质量比较高的同伴反馈,反馈内容涉及了语言的表层特征的纠错(如 aren't→are not),但更多的是深层次的语言特征的反馈——词汇的选择(如 days 还是 festivals, clebration 还是 celebratory activities)、句子结构(如建议增加 at Halloween, for Westerners 在句首,增强对比性)、语篇逻辑(建议增加衔接过渡词)等。

- 实例3: Spade development 段落写作练习(如图6.3)

图中的同伴反馈包括两种反馈方式:直接纠错和间接纠错。直接纠错针对语法错误等表层特征,如 in→out of; a→the; made→make; besides→beside; there is a road ... to ...→there is a road ... extending to;删除多余的词 are;增加介词 on;等等。同时,反馈也涉及语篇内容和句法结构,如"个人觉得不用介绍,不是重点""前面未出现,较突兀""插入地点后作修饰语""较突兀,可以在前面加 taking back"等。原作者也对此做出了反馈和互动(互动评改会在后面专门介绍,这里不重复)。反馈者给出的点评是:

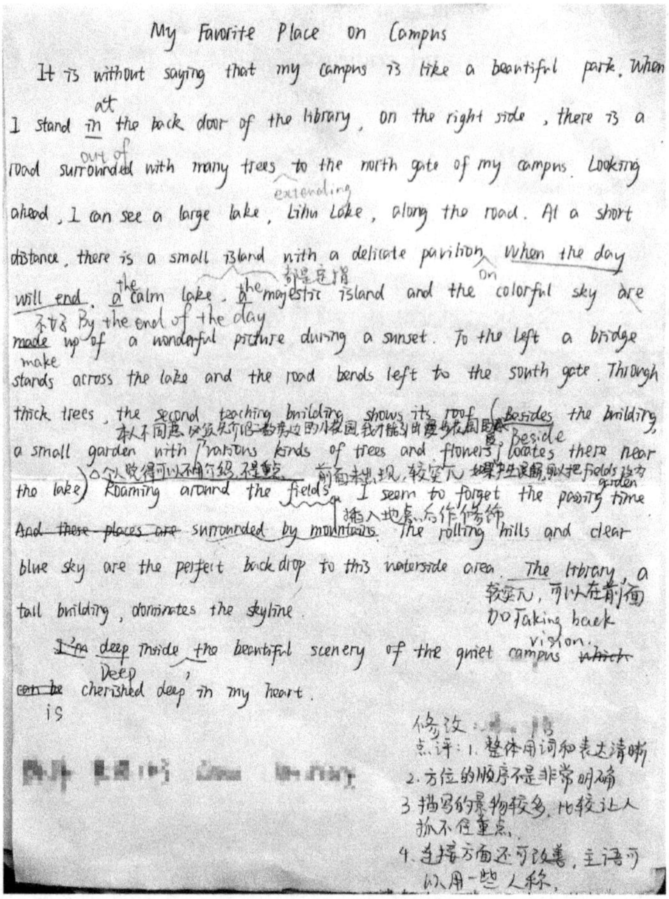

My Favorite Place on Campus

It is without saying that my campus is like a beautiful park. When I stand in (at) the back door of the library, on the right side, there is a road surrounded with (out of) many trees to the north gate of my campus. Looking ahead, I can see a large lake, Lihu Lake, along (extending) the road. At a short distance, there is a small island with a delicate pavilion. When the day will end, a calm lake, the majestic island and the colorful sky are made up of a wonderful picture during a sunset. To the left a bridge stands across the lake and the road bends left to the south gate. Through thick trees, the second teaching building shows its roof. (Besides the building, a small garden with various kinds of trees and flowers locates there near the lake) Roaming around the fields, I seem to forget the passing time. And these places are surrounded by mountains. The rolling hills and clear blue sky are the perfect backdrop to this waterside area. The library, a tall building, dominates the skyline.

I'm deep inside the beautiful scenery of the quiet campus which can be cherished deep in my heart.

修改：
点评：1. 整体用词和表达清晰
2. 方位的顺序不是非常明确
3. 描写的景物较多，比较让人抓不住重点，
4. 连接方面还可改善，主语可以用一些人称。

图 6.3　同伴反馈实例 3

①整体用词和表达清晰。②方位的顺序不是非常明确。③描写的景物较多，容易让人抓不住重点。④连接方面还可改善，主语可以用一些人称。

该同伴反馈从语篇、内容、句子结构、语法、用词等方面比较全面地进行了反馈，并与作者成功进行了互动交流，值得肯定。

- 实例 4：Spade development　写作练习（图 6.4）

同伴反馈在这一组是用电脑的审阅模式进行评改，然后打印出来交纸质版给老师。反馈内容包括直接纠错、间接纠错、总体评价等。直接纠错如 path→place；westward→westwards；spreading→sheding；beautiful→beautiful scene 等。间接纠错同样关注句法等深层次的语言特征，如把 in my opinion，on campus 顺序调整，改为 on campus，in my opinion，以跟前文承接更自然，整句调整后变成 "… you will enjoy the most beautiful view on campus，in my opinion"。对指代模

糊的代词 it 提出疑问"refert to what? Might cause confusion in the reader, you can use 'the scene'"。最后用英文给出总体性评价,总体评价既肯定了作文的优点,也指出了不足,并提出了改进的建议。同时同伴反馈里比较容易出现而教师反馈不太会涉及的,就是反馈者作为读者的直观感受(第一句)。这也说明了同伴反馈中作者和读者(互评者)因为身份的对等,更能从作者的角度理解文本,并做出反馈。这也在一定程度上证明了同伴反馈在实践中的交际互动功能。

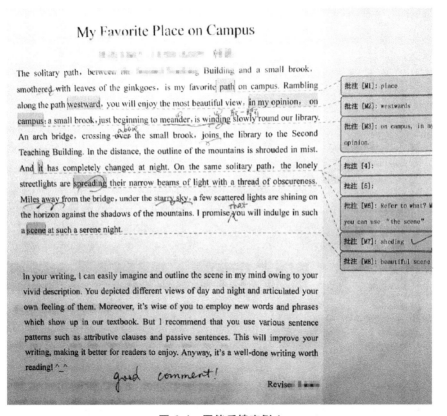

图 6.4　同伴反馈实例 4

- 实例 5：Spade development　段落写作练习(图 6.5)

在这个同伴反馈里,读者/反馈者清晰地给出了 5 条纠错建议,从用词、文章条理性、内容等方面进行反馈。有的是直接纠错,有的是间接纠错。直接纠错如 link→links(第三人称单数);inside of the two buildings are→inside the two buildings are(删除多出来的 of)。增加词汇让句子完整,如 you'll/you'll find(a large pool in the middle of the pond);there is(a five-floor building);等等。针对

句子内逻辑和简洁度及文章流畅性给出的间接纠错性反馈,如 the library in our campus→our school library,理由是 in our compus 跟同一个句子中最后的 on campus 重复;of the university 建议用其他表示 area 的词替换,因为前面已经写了 our school,再出现 of the university 略显啰嗦。

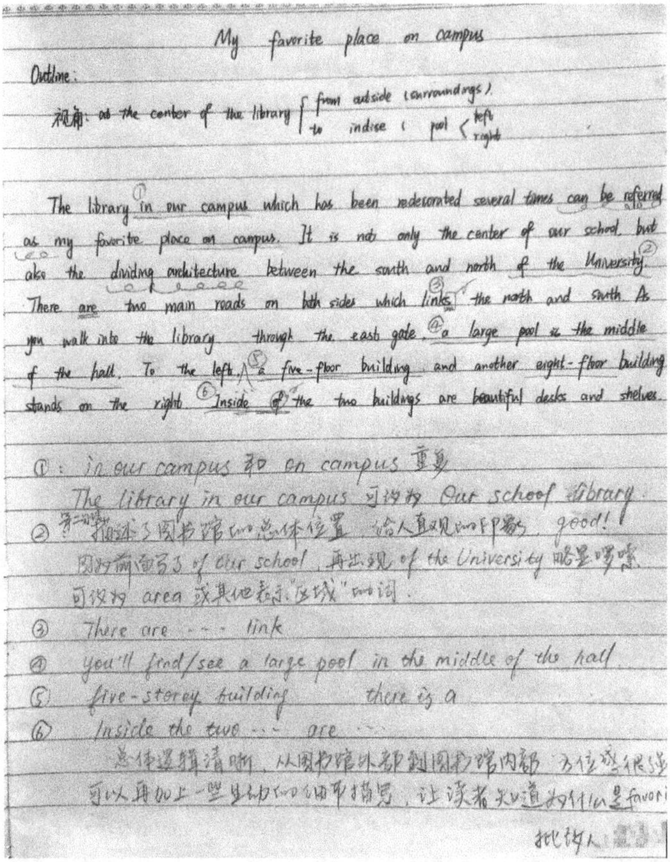

图 6.5 同伴反馈实例 5

最后总体性评价如下:总体逻辑清晰,从图书馆外部到图书馆内部,方位感很强。可以再加一些生动的细节描写,让读者知道为什么是 favorite place。

- 实例 6:Comparison and contrast 段落写作练习(图 6.6)

本篇实例里的反馈全是直接纠错性反馈,但是反馈的内容从表层语言特征到深层的句子结构、篇章内容等都包括在内。表层特征如把 However→However,(加上标点符号);reflects→reflect(动词第三人称单数);culture value→culture values(复数形式);simple and fast→quick and convenient;等等。深层

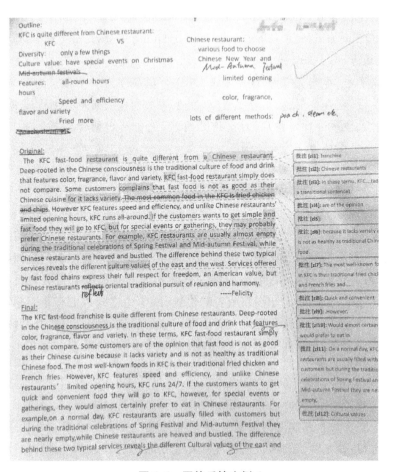

图6.6 同伴反馈实例6

语言特征的纠错比较多,从词汇选择到句子逻辑性再到文章流畅度,都进行了一些纠错。如complains→are of the opinion;增加in these terms,使上下文过渡更自然;从句的使用,如for it lacks variety→because it lacks variety and is not as healthy as traditional Chinese food;用词的精准度the most common food→the most well-known food;may probably prefer Chinese restaurants→would almost certain/would prefer to eat in Chinese restaurants。

有一个非常精彩的反馈是关于句子内部逻辑性的修改:

原句:For example, KFC are almost usually empty during the Chinese traditonal celebrations of Spring Fesitval and Mid-autumn Festival, while Chinese restaurants are heaved and bustled.

修改建议：On a normal day, KFC restaurants are usually filled with customers but during the traditonal celebrations of the Spring Festival and the Mid-autunm Festival, they are nearly empty.

可以看出，原句用了举例的方式，把这个现象作为一个细节对观点进行支持。修改后，还是举例，但用得更自然，跟上下文衔接更流畅。把句子原来比较的两个对象顺序进行调整后，对比得更明显，更能突出两者在不同节日的显著不同，是个很成功的同伴反馈例子。

2. 非纠错性反馈（总体性评价反馈）

跟纠错性反馈相比，同伴反馈中的非纠错性反馈更多一些。就算是使用纠错性反馈的建议中，也常常结合非纠错性的说明或解释（可参见上面实例）。究其原因，一方面是学习者比较谨慎，面对同伴时不好意思直接明白地纠错；另一方面，学习者对自己的语言能力或某一方面知识的掌握没有百分之百的自信。在教师反馈中，教师处于知识权威者的位置，跟学生之间也更有距离感，给出的反馈更客观、确切。同伴反馈则会有更多因素的影响，除了自身的语言能力，也会更多受同伴关系等其他因素的影响，所以非纠错性反馈和鼓励性评价更常见。

- 实例7：Comparsion and contrast　写作练习（图6.7）

尽管在文中也有少量的纠错性反馈，但这篇文章的反馈者更多地采用了非纠错性反馈：她把她认为有疑问的地方标注出来（1，2，3，4处），以讨论、协商的语气把看法和修改建议提供给原作者。

该篇反馈关注文章的深层语言特征，对文章的结构、篇章内容、条理和逻辑等做了比较全面的反馈，是同伴反馈里比较负责任的。尽管只是标注了要修改的出处，没有直接给出修改示例，但是会尽量引用权威渠道的知识点支持自己的观点，如反馈建议中提到的"综合英语教程第三册 Unit 11"。笔者在教师评改中也对此做出了肯定。

有趣的是，这篇反馈也体现了作者和读者/反馈者之间的一个互动协商过程：针对反馈中的第4点建议，作者表示了反对，并给出反对的原因：在突出存在的差异之后，指出教师的本意是为了更好地教育学生，增加读者赞同感和熟悉感。经过协商互动反馈后，两人最后保留了原作的写法。这种协商互动也是笔者实施同伴反馈喜闻乐见的。

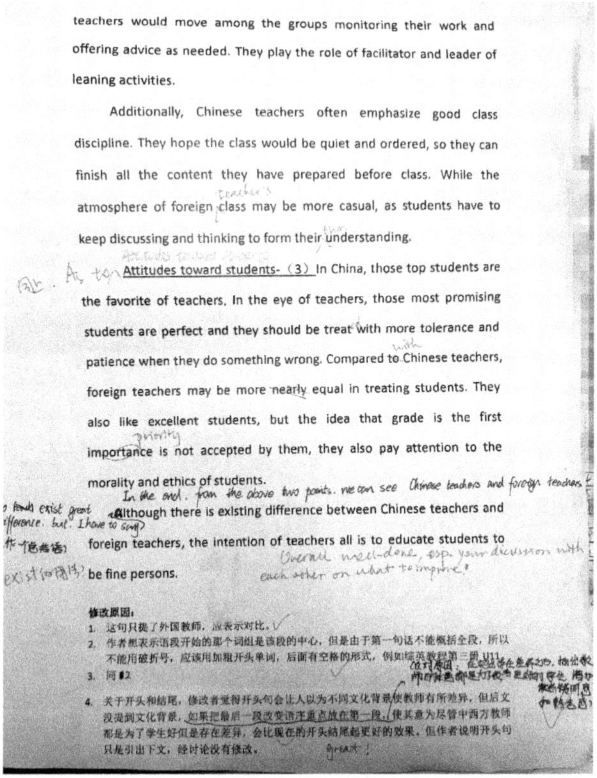

teachers would move among the groups monitoring their work and offering advice as needed. They play the role of facilitator and leader of leaning activities.

Additionally, Chinese teachers often emphasize good class discipline. They hope the class would be quiet and ordered, so they can finish all the content they have prepared before class. While the atmosphere of foreign class may be more casual, as students have to keep discussing and thinking to form their understanding.

Attitudes toward students-（3）In China, those top students are the favorite of teachers. In the eye of teachers, those most promising students are perfect and they should be treat with more tolerance and patience when they do something wrong. Compared to Chinese teachers, foreign teachers may be more nearly equal in treating students. They also like excellent students, but the idea that grade is the first importance is not accepted by them, they also pay attention to the morality and ethics of students.

Although there is existing difference between Chinese teachers and foreign teachers, the intention of teachers all is to educate students to be fine persons.

修改原因：

1. 这句只提了外国教师，应表示对比。
2. 作者想表示语段开始的那个词组是该段的中心，但是由于第一句话不能概括全段，所以不能用破折号，应该用加粗开头单词，后面有空格的形式，例如综英教程第三册 U11
3. 同 2
4. 关于开头和结尾，修改者觉得开头句会让人以为不同文化背景使教师有所差异，但后文没提到文化背景，如果把最后一段改变语序重点放在第一段，使其意为尽管中西方教师都是为了学生好但是存在差异，会比现在的开头结尾起更好的效果。但作者说明开头句只是引出下文，经讨论没有修改。

图 6.7　同伴反馈实例 7

- 实例 8：Comparsion and contrast　写作练习(图 6.8)

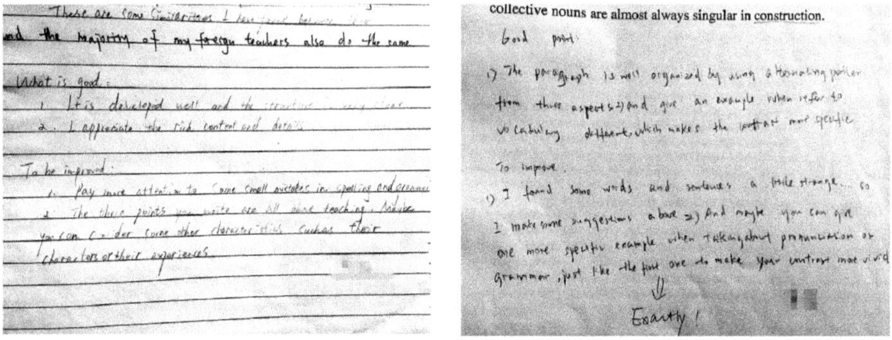

图 6.8　同伴反馈实例 8

这是同伴反馈中两个同伴之间的相互反馈。

反馈者 A：

What is good：

1) It is developed well and the structure is very clear.

2) I appreciate the rich content and details.

To be improved:

1) Pay much attention to some small mistakes in spelling and grammar.

2) The three points you write are all about teaching. Maybe you can consier some other characteristics such as their characters or their experiences.

反馈者 B:

Good point:

1) The paragraph is well organized by using the alternative pattern from three aspects.

2) And give an example when refer(应为 refering,笔者注) to vocabulary different(应为 differences,笔者注) which makes the contrast more specific.

To improve:

1) I found some words and sentences a little strange …, so I make (应为 made,笔者注) some suggestions above. 2) Maybe your can give one more specific example when talking about pronunciation or grammar, just like the first one to make your contrast more vivid.

可以看出,同伴会对彼此的反馈方式和内容产生影响。图6.8中两位同伴的反馈内容遵循一样的格式,内容彼此对应:都是先肯定优点,再指出不足。优点都是对作文的结构和内容进行肯定性评价,不足的地方提出建议:第一点都涉及语言浅层的特征(拼写错误、语法错误等);第二点是关于文章的内容或结构方面。这些表明同伴反馈能够起到互相影响、互相促进的作用。同伴会学习彼此的优点,关注彼此的不足并尽可能在写作中避免类似的错误。

- 实例9:Spade development 写作练习(图6.9)

图6.9中的同伴反馈实例非常有趣。在文中做出一些直接纠错性反馈后(如 step→sneak; right corner→northwester corner; left corner→other corner; the front wall→the east wall),增加让方位更明确的表达(如 in the middle of the west wall),反馈者发现原文在进行空间顺序的描述中,可能对方位的介绍有误,表达不清晰,在文后的总结性评价处做了点评后,为了进一步让原文作者明白自己的观点,也更清楚地展示方位,在反馈评价后画了一张空间方位图(如图6.9)。

This is a complete writing with an attractive beginning and an echoing ending sentence. The author has a good use of vivid verbs and figures of speech. But it seems that the description of the rehearsal room doesn't follow a specific space order,

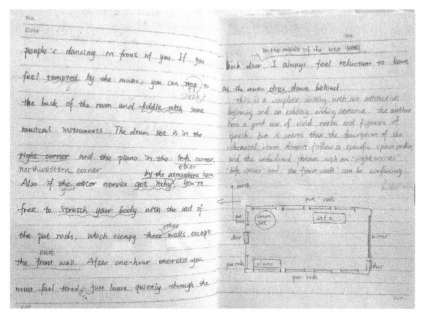

图 6.9　同伴反馈实例 9

and the underlined phrases, such as "right corner" "left corner" and "the front corner" can be confusing.

这种反馈模式无疑是学生所独有的。作为学习伙伴,他们不仅更能理解同伴所描述的内容,而且对被描述的对象更熟悉,因此也更容易发现同伴写作中内容或表述上的问题。

3. 互动评改

同伴反馈最大的特点之一,也是教师反馈无法拥有的优势就是它的互动性。如果说教师反馈是单向的,那么同伴反馈就是双向的。这种互动的交流与反馈,一方面因为可以从学习者角度对同伴的写作进行评阅,在评阅的过程中熟悉、了解其他学习者的优点和缺点,增强纠错能力,从而学会避免在自己写作时触碰"雷区";另一方面还可以降低学生的写作焦虑感,激发写作兴趣。更重要的是,在同伴反馈过程中,学习者通过与同伴的交流、讨论、协商等互动形成最终文稿,逐步完成并优化写作任务,学习者在学习中的主体作用得到了充分的发挥,从而真正促成以学生为中心的自主和自助的交际法写作模式的养成。

学习者出于对自己语言能力的不自信和对同伴的尊重,在反馈中较少使用直接纠错,更常见的是间接纠错性反馈或非纠错性反馈。很多时候,反馈者对有疑问的地方都是从学习者同伴的角度，以读者的身份发出质疑。而作为同伴的学习者，也会就问题进行回答、协商，通过这种互动达成评改的最优化。

- 实例10：（图6.10）

make
stands across the lake and the road bends left to the south gate. Through thick trees, the second teaching building shows its roof. (Besides the building, a small garden with various kinds of trees and flowers locates there near the lake.) Roaming around the fields, I seem to forget the passing time. And these places are surrounded by mountains. The rolling hills and clear blue sky are the perfect backdrop to this waterside area. The library, a

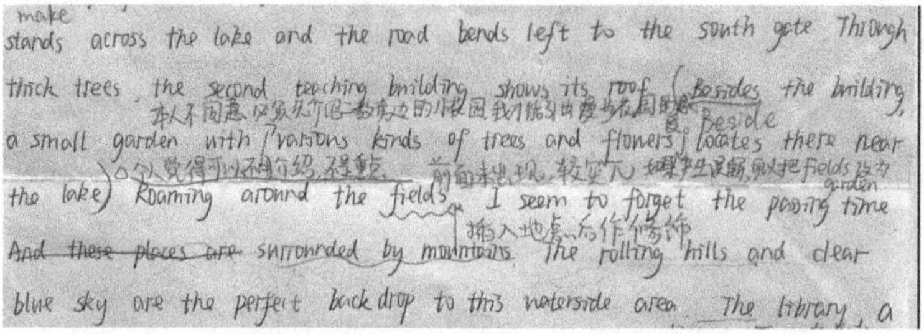

图6.10　同伴反馈中的互动评改实例10

在同伴反馈中，评阅者对文中句子（“besides the building, a small garden with various kinds of trees and flowers locates there near the lake”）提出个人理解：个人觉得可以不用介绍，不是重点。作者表示：本人不同意，必须先介绍二教旁边的小花园，我才能引出漫步花园的感受。第二个互动的地方是下文中的 fields，反馈者认为这个概念前面未出现，较突兀，作者回答：如果产生误解，可以把 fields 改成 garden。这种对话在反馈中能增进交流，帮助读者弄清作者意图，也帮助作者厘清自己的想法。

- 实例11：图6.11

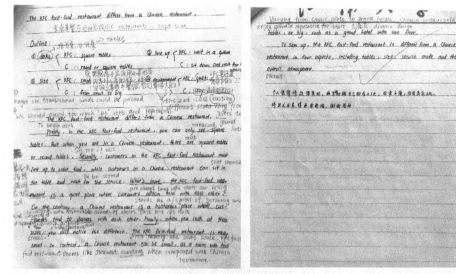

图6.11　同伴反馈中的互动评改实例11

同伴反馈在一些研究中被认为不如教师反馈有效，学生对于来自同伴的评价不信任、不接受，但是这篇同伴反馈的互动是对同伴反馈形式和效果非常有力的支持。反馈者从词汇、句法、语篇结构、思想内容等方面，对原作者文稿进行了修改并给出了建议。原作者在阅读过反馈者的修改和评价后，真心地发出这样的感叹：个人觉得修改得真好，我写的初稿自己都看不下去，非常平庸，没有出彩之处。修改之后显得很有格调。谢谢搭档！

- 实例12：图6.12

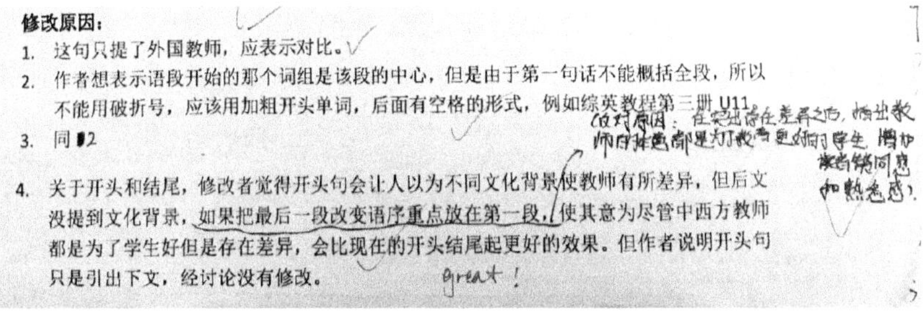

修改原因：

1. 这句只提了外国教师，应表示对比。
2. 作者想表示语段开始的那个词组是该段的中心，但是由于第一句话不能概括全段，所以不能用破折号，应该用加粗开头单词，后面有空格的形式，例如综英教程第三册 U11
3. 同2
4. 关于开头和结尾，修改者觉得开头句会让人以为不同文化背景使教师有所差异，但后文没提到文化背景，如果把最后一段改变语序重点放在第一段，使其意为尽管中西方教师都是为了学生好但是存在差异，会比现在的开头结尾起更好的效果。但作者说明开头句只是引出下文，经讨论没有修改。

图6.12　同伴反馈中的互动评改实例12

在本篇反馈的总体性评价中，同伴反馈者基于语篇结构和逻辑性上的考虑，提出“把最后一段改变语序重点放在第一段，使其意为尽管中西方教师都是为了学生好但是存在差异，会比现在的开头结尾起更好的效果”。对此，作者表示反对，澄清自己的意图是“在突出存在差异之后，指出教师的本意是为了教育更好的学生，增加读者赞同感和熟悉感?”最后的问号也是一种商榷的语气。最后同伴之间经过讨论（没有体现在图中的反馈里），保留了原来的写作方式。这样基于语言细节进行的同伴间的互动和讨论，无疑可以增强学生对文本的理解，使学生更熟悉写作方式和方法，语言的交际功能也因此得以体现。

- 实例13：图6.13

图6.13中的同伴在评阅过程中遇到了理解困难，于是提出：“It's a little difficult to understand. Could you make the sentence more concise?”作者对自己的意图做出解释：“中文是指他们父母从不说破，唯恐惊扰了这份纯真的感情。可能翻译过来后我又加了 lest 有点难懂。”在这个互动过程中，同伴反馈者从读者的立场和感受提出建议，促使作者思考自己语言表达的精准性。如果反馈者出现理解困难，这就意味着别的读者可能也会遇到同样的困难。也就是说，写作中强调的 communication between writer and reader 没有成功实现。而正因为反馈者是学习者同伴，语言能力在读者群中有代表性，因而对作者来说这样的同伴反馈更真实，更有参考价值。

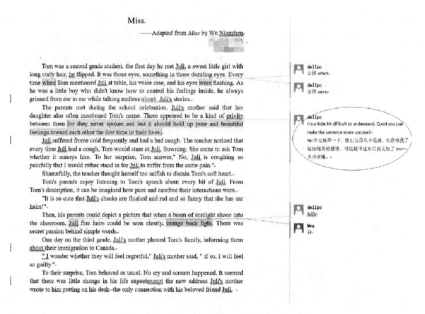

图 6.13   同伴反馈中的互动评改实例 13

- 实例 14：图 6.14

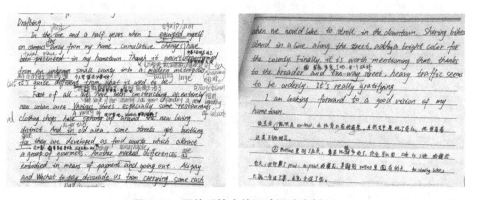

图 6.14   同伴反馈中的互动评改实例 14

这篇同伴反馈的文章有两个评改者/反馈者,因此发生了很有意思的互动反馈。文中多次出现了第一个修改者进行修改后,第二个修改者提出质疑和表示否定。如第一位反馈者把首句中的时态改成一般现在时,第二位反馈者直接质疑"如果上面时态改了,下面的为啥不改?"第二次质疑是关于原文句子中 but 关联词的使用:**Though** it wasn't transformed from an unkown small country into a modern metropolis, it's quite different from what it used to be。第一位修改者建议去掉though，在句中增加but。修改前和修改后的句子意思大致相同，但是强调的部分有细微的不同。对此，第二位修改者表示不赞同："个人觉得完全没有必要啊。though或者but达到的效果是一样的。"第三次互动是关于various和a variety of的用法：第一位修改者把various stores改成a variety of stores。第二位修改者再次提出质疑："没必要吧，various用得已经够了。"第四次互动是针对句子里把since改成for的修改。原文是：And in old area, some streets get bustling **for** they are developed as food courts which attract a group of goumets。第一位修改者把for换成了since，第二位修改者再一次指出："没必要，要表示因果关系，还可以用'in which'。"最后的总体性评价由第二位反馈者给出：

①既然是contrast，应该有以前的前景。虽然文中展现了变化，但我看着还是不够明显。②outline里列了5点，算是比较多的了。完全可以用side to side的模式行文，但用了point-to-point的模式，导致outline里有的点，如sharing bikes只能一句话了事，未免仓促了些。

这是一个非常有趣的互动评改实践。从语言的细节可以推测出两位反馈者，尤其是第二位反馈者在这个过程中所扮演的角色和所起的作用。第一位反馈者评改的时候用的是铅笔，第二位反馈者用的是钢笔。相比之下，铅笔可以轻松擦除，钢笔却不能擦除。此外，第二位反馈者在互动质疑的过程中，虽然始终有理有据地提出不同的看法，但语气有微妙的变化：从"个人觉得没必要啊"到"没必要吧"到"没必要"。第一次用了"个人""吧"等词，相对而言，是3次中语气最不确定的，是协商的语气；第二次去掉了"个人"，保留了"吧"，仍然是协商的语气，但是角色中开始显示更多确定和更自信的立场；第三次直接用了"没必要"，带有协商意味的"吧"去掉了，表明第二位修改者经过前面两次反馈的修正，更加确信了自己的评改判断。最后的总体性评价由第二位反馈者给出，从语篇结构和内容方面指出了文章中存在的问题。至此，互动反馈完成，也证明最后经过讨论协商，第二位反馈者的建议被接受。

4. 小结

从上述同伴反馈的实例中可以发现，尽管有些研究认为同伴反馈存在不足，如学生的语言能力发展不一致，导致有些反馈缺乏实用价值和有效性，进而影响学生对同伴互评的信任度及重视度；或者同伴反馈中关注的是语言的微观维度，而不是在文章结构与思想内容等宏观维度（曾永红、梁玥，2017）。但是笔者在教学实践中发现，同伴反馈中绝大部分学习者不仅会关注浅层的或微观的语言特征（如拼写、语法等错误），也会（如果不是更会）关注文章的深层语言特征。几乎所有的同学,在进行纠错性反馈或非纠错性反馈中,对文章内容、结构、句法、逻辑等方面都会提出看法或建议。虽然不是每一位同伴反馈者提出的建议都是正确或有效的,但笔者发现,学习者们也许不能明确发现自己作文中的错误,可作为读者和评改反馈者时,却能准确地发现别人文章中的问题和不足。同伴反馈模式的实践,在一定程度上缓解了教师批改作业的负担,也让学习者们在反馈和互动中更好地学习同伴的优点。通过发现别人的缺点和不足,进行纠错和反馈,提醒自己不要犯同样的错误。在语言细节方面进行的协商和讨论,能减缓学习者的写作焦虑,增强写作的信心。更重要的是,在这个过程中提升语言能力,促进自主学习能力的养成。

第四节 在线反馈与案例分析

一、在线反馈

在线反馈是随着信息化技术的发展而发展起来的。计算机技术、网络、自然语言处理技术的相结合促成了英语写作在线反馈方式的产生,大数据的背景进一步加强了在线反馈的可行性、可靠性和流行度。在线写作反馈基于自动写作评改系统和大数据,从各种维度对比学生提交的写作文本和语料库中标准文本,进行打分,给出修改和建议。并对写作的错误分布、相似统计、词频、搭配、等进行数据分析。

在线反馈方式得以产生的前提是各种自动写作评估系统的产生(前文已经做过介绍,不再赘述)。经过多年的发展,国内外的各种 AWE 系统已经颇具规模,各自拥有一批用户群。国外的自动评估系统比国内开发得早,类型更多,相关的研究也更丰富多样。对于自动评估系统的开发研究最早可见于 20 世纪 60 年代由 Ellis Page 教授团队开发的写作自动评分系统 PEG。随后,更多的自动写作评估系统如 IEA, E-rater, BETSS, IntelliMetri, Criterion, MyAcess 等十几种 AWE 系统先后成功开发。国内的自动写作评估系统开发相对较晚,数量也更少。使用最为广泛的是句酷批改网,简称批改网,于 2010 年正式上线,拥有国内高校规模庞大的用户群,目前批改篇次已达到 4.4 亿次(数据截止到 2018 年 7 月)。除了句酷批改网,还有一种基于智能平台(体验英语——写作教学资源平台,Teaching Resources Platform, TRP)的在线反馈方式,使用受众数量相对少一些。这种在线反馈方式一般是由高校的写作教师团队引导,在平台上进行互动反馈和评价。

国内外学者们对这种基于大数据技术的在线自动评改模式做了诸多研究,有褒有贬,研究涉及各个方面。有基于 AWE 系统在写作测试场景可靠性的研究(Attali et al., 2013; Attali & Burstein, 2006; Elliot, 2003; Shermis & Hamner, 2013; Ware & Warschauer, 2006),这种可靠性得到了研究人员的肯定。更多的研究者关注自动评改系统在教育领域的运用和价值,通过基于写作课堂的实证研究来探索在线自动评改系统对教学的积极影响。这些研究证明了在线反馈模式的合理性和其他反馈方式对比存在的优点:如能够给学生提供比较合理的语言质量反馈;能够促使学习者更多地修改文稿、进行写作练习(Attali, 2004; Choi & Lee, 2010; Kellogg et al., 2010; Li et al., 2015; Moon & Pae, 2011);能够允许学生更自由地控制写作反馈的时间,不管是在写作过程中还是在写作全部完成后,从而使反馈更便捷,加速有效的反馈循环(Foltz et al., 2013; Kellogg et al., 2010)。Lai(2010)把关于在线反馈有效性的研究分为三类:第一类是在线反馈对学生写作结果的影响(如分数、错误率、文本长度);第二类是对学生写作过程的影响,如修改所用时间、错误修改率、写作花费时长;第三类是在线反馈的有用性。相对来说,第一类研究最多,对写作过程的研究较少,尤其是关于写作过程中学生和在线系统的互动研究。Zhang(2017)、Zhang 和 Hyland(2018)基于学生对在线反馈的参与度做了调查研究后发现,参与度高的学生会花更多的时间来消化、吸收在线反馈的内容,运用更多的修改策略,拥有更积极的写作态度。在线反馈对学生的有效性取决于每个学生和系统如何实现行为上、情感上和认知上的互动。

当前国内对在线反馈的研究主要集中在两个方面:关于在线反馈有效性的实证研究;对比在线反馈与教师反馈、同伴反馈等其他反馈方式的比较研究。在线反馈基于对大量语料的分析和总结所归纳出的语法错误,具有较高的可信度。英语写作的在线反馈,对于英语写作教学实践也有积极的作用(石晓玲,2012;何旭良,2013;蒋艳、马武林,2013;杨晓琼、戴运财,2015;黄礼珍,2017;Lv, 2018)。基于批改网的在线反馈,能即时给提交的作文打分,并同时在语法、词汇、表达规范性等方面给予修改建议。写作教师也可以随时对学生的作文进行人工评阅、布置学生进行在线同伴互评和群批。笔者在实践中发现,由于批改网在线反馈的即时性和便捷性(批改网的宣传语是"秒批作文"),学习者提交作文后会立刻得到评分与反馈。如果得到的评分不理想,绝大部分学生会按照系统语料库的建议,修改自己作文里的用词,调整句子结构等,再提交,得到作文修改后的评分。如果还是不满意分数,再修改,再提交……直到得到自己相对满意的评分。笔者的学生里修改次数最高的达到83次。这种高达几十次甚至上百次的作文修改和对语言的提炼,无疑对学生语言能力的提高是有帮助的。笔者认为,这也是在线反馈最大的功能之一,这种观点在其他研究中也能得到证实(Ware & Warschauer, 2006)。从写作教师的角度来说,这种促使学生进行反复修改的在线反馈,能解决学生作文里的浅层语言错误,如拼写、大小写、基本语法、标点等错误,从而在一定程度上缓解写作教师批改评阅作文的负担,使教师们能够节省下修改表层语言错误的时间,更多地关注学生习作中的深层语言质量,如语篇结构、思想内容、逻辑性、条理性等。在Wilson和Czik(2016)的研究中,写作教师结合在线反馈以后进行的习作评改,跟单一的教师反馈模式相比,节约了约1/3到1/2的时间。

当然,在线反馈作为一种新兴的写作反馈模式,又是基于计算机和网络的机器修改,虽然大数据给这种基于机器的反馈方式提供了保障和成功实施的条件,但还是存在诸多不足。国内外学者对在线反馈有效性的研究发现,由于系统的技术发展还有欠缺,系统给出的关于语言质量的反馈比较表面化,不能提供更高质量和更深层次的建议(Fang, 2010;Weigle, 2013;何旭良,2013;蒋艳、马武林,2013;杨晓琼、戴运财,2015),尤其是与人工评改相比,不能评估文章内容切题与否,过于关注学术性词汇,对文章修辞特点没有反馈,尤其对文章的内部逻辑和关联性、文章的流畅性无法给出反馈,等等。有时候学生按照系统提示修改,成绩反而比前一次低。在学生和在线反馈方式的相互作用方面,研究发现学生的参与度相对同伴反馈和教师反馈而言有所欠缺(Warden, 2000;Attali, 2004;Grimes, 2005;El Ebyary & Windeatt, 2010;Zhang & Hyland, 2018)。Grimes(2005)指出,学生对于在线反馈的互动仅停留于表面,学生通常在提交第一稿后,根据在线反馈,迅速修改掉几处错误,然后立刻提交第二稿,没有留出太多时间对语言错误进行深度的思考。还有学者(Attali, 2004;El Ebyary & Windeatt, 2010)提出,有相当一部分学生(半数或2/3以上)在收到在线反馈后不修改、不提交二稿。

综上所述,国内外研究者们对基于技术支持的在线反馈的调查研究有一个共识:基于AWE写作评估系统的在线反馈确实能给写作教师和学生带来便利,于教师而言,节省了批改作文的时间,可以把更多精力用来培养学生其他方面的写作能力;于学生而言,在线反馈能减轻写作焦虑,增加自信心,促进自主学习能力养成等。但不可否认的是,由于在线反馈方式在很多方面还存在不足,准确性与灵活性有待进一步提升。基于在线写作反馈的智能系统在写作内容、结构、文章连贯性和思想性等深层语言特征方面给出的建议和反馈都比较有限。在线反馈丰富了写作评改和反馈方式的内涵,是教师反馈和同伴反馈的一种有益补充,却不能用来替代教师的人工评价和反馈。最有益于学生写作能力发展的评价与反馈是自动在线反馈与写作教师的人工反馈相结合的模式(石晓玲,2012;何旭良,2013;蒋艳、马武林,2013;Wilson & Czik,2016;李奕华,2015;黄礼珍,2017;Zhang & Hyland,2018)。因此,在教学实践中,写作教师应根据教学任务,灵活设计多元的英语写作反馈模式,使各种反馈方式能够相互补充,从而最终促成学生写作能力的发展。

二、案例分析

1. 背景介绍

我校(江南大学)教师自批改网 2010 年上线起就开始使用。截止到 2018 年 6 月 1 日,江南大学共有 149 位老师和 28 642 名学生注册使用批改网。学生提交的作文数量达到 119 281 篇,其中教师布置的作文数量为 102 323 篇。数据如图 6.16。在注册的 28 642 名学生中,有 26 338 名学生提交了教师布置的作文,占学校总注册人数 91.96%。学生共提交作文 11 9281 篇,其中教师布置的作文 102 323 篇,自主提交系统进行反馈的作文 16 958 篇。学生共修改作文 662 052 次,平均每篇作文修改 5.550 次。

截至2018年6月1日,江南大学共149位老师和28642名学生注册使用批改网,学生共提交作文119281篇(其中提交教师布置的作文102323篇)。本学期使用数据如下所示:

时间	教师数量	教师布置作文数量	提交作文学生数量	学生提交作文数量
2014-01-01	110	618	13532	52274
2014-04-01	115	659	14474	54858
2014-07-01	116	712	14844	60171
2014-10-01	120	759	17247	63033
2015-02-01	123	849	18707	75133
2015-05-01	125	885	18865	78086
2015-08-01	128	903	18943	81023
2015-11-01	128	939	20903	84556
2016-03-01	130	998	21475	89226
2016-06-01	131	1029	21818	92595
2016-09-01	133	1034	21921	93571
2017-01-01	137	1117	24629	102283
2017-04-01	138	1139	24988	103905
2017-07-01	139	1150	25151	106732
2017-10-01	140	1170	26693	109040
2018-03-01	144	1265	28066	115443
2018-06-01	149	1305	28642	119281

图 6.15 江南大学教师批改网使用情况

(数据来源:批改网)

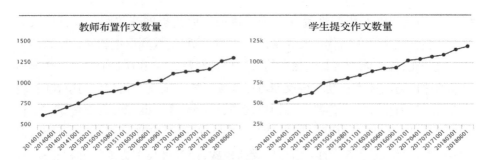

图6.16　江南大学教师布置作文和学生提交作文情况

（数据来源：批改网）

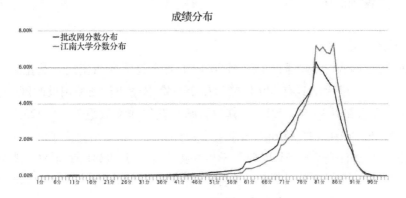

图6.17　江南大学学生批改网成绩分布

（数据来源：批改网）

笔者于2011年正式开始使用批改网,截止到2016年6月,共布置写作任务26次,收到学生作文641篇。笔者基于批改网的在线自动反馈模式,给学生发布写作任务,设定写作要求和截止日期,在截止日期后发布互评任务,读取在线反馈和互评数据,进行习作点评和总反馈。考虑到在线反馈更多的是针对学生的表层语言特征提出修改建议,如拼写、语法、大小写错误等,笔者一般会根据写作任务的需要,对已被机器批改的学生习作进行人工批阅,修正在线反馈可能出现的失误,也给学生提供更有针对性的、个性化的写作建议。出于学生练笔目的发布的写作任务,如英语读书报告,教师没有进行人工评阅。

2. 案例分析

1）概况

笔者选取批改网的8篇学生习作（有3篇作文题目一样,但是学生不一样）,进行数据对比。作文体裁包括英语说明文和议论文（作文题目和编号参见

表6.5)。除了作文1和2,其他写作任务都和综合英语教程的课文内容有相关性:一篇模仿写作(copy writing,作文6、7、8),作文3、4、5是对课文内容的拓展和延伸讨论。这也就意味着学生写作前对写作材料有一定的了解和准备。

在批改网发布的作文任务要求,除了作文4和5只给出题目背景知识和讨论之外,其余作文要求均参考大学四级或专业四级考试写作部分的格式,明确要求三段式作文,对每一段有具体的要求。同时在批改网的"附加选项"选择打分公式、字数范围、期待的平均分、最低分和最高分。批改方式选择"系统多次性+教师一次性批改"。按句点评模式开启中式英语、学习提示、高分表达、搭配统计。8篇作文在系统里发布的要求如下。

- 作文1:

题目:The Dragon Boat Festival;词数150左右,超出词数范围不扣分。

第一段,谈谈你对端午节的认识;第二段,端午节都做些什么,如何庆祝端午节;第三段,保留端午节传统的必要性。

- 作文2:

题目:My opinion on intellectuall dishonesty;词数150左右,超出词数范围不扣分。

Write 150 words or so on the topic, at least three parts:

In the first part, state specifically what your view is. In the second part, support your view with evidence and examples. In the third part, bring what you have written to a natural conclusion or summary.

- 作文3:

题目:What is happiness? 词数200左右,超出词数范围不扣分。

In the first part, define the word "happiness". In the second part, support yourself with details and evidence. In the third part, bring what you have written to a natural conclusion.

- 作文4:

题目:Is an only child a lonely child? 词数150—200,超出词数范围不扣分。

Ever since the adoption of the "One Couple, One Child" policy, China has succeeded in slowing down the rapid expansion of her population. But every coin has two sides, and so does China's population policy. Talk about the advantages and disadvantages of being the only child at home.

- 作文5:

题目：To forgive or not to forgive：词数不少于 200，超出词数范围不扣分。

We are often self-contradictory. On the one hand, we have this "an eye for an eye, and a tooth for a tooth" brand of justice on which we base our laws. A criminal is punished for his crimes; and we tend to hurt others just because they hurt us. On the other hand, we also believe that "to err is human; to forgive, divine". That means forgiveness is considered a great virtue though it is difficult to acquire. Write a composition with the given title.

- 作文 6，7，8：

题目：The virtues of being young：词数 200 左右，超出词数范围不扣分。

Copy writing：Copy the structure and writing techniques of Unit 2 (Text I).

Part I：Present your viewpoint. Part II：Support your idea with examples and evidence, using comparison and contrast if possible. Part III：Bring what you've written to a natural conclusion.

目前没有研究来证明在线反馈给出的评分是否与作文的具体要求有相关性，但是从批改网对这 8 篇作文打出的作文平均分来看（以每次作文提交的班级为单位），教师设定的作文要求选择似乎和打分是有相关性的。得分最低的两篇为 My opinion on intellectual dishonesty（作文 2）和 The virtues of being young（作文 6，11 级），打分分别为 77.9 分和 82.7 分。其中 My opinion on intellectual dishonesty 打分公式选择本科—专四打分公式，The virtues of being young（11 级）选择大学—四级打分公式。其他 6 篇作文选择默认打分公式。默认公式里分四个维度进行打分，其中词汇占 43%，句子占 28%，篇章结构占 22%，内容相关占 7%。也就是说，选择英语专业四级打分公式的作文得分最低，大学英语四级打分公式的得分次之，与默认公式趋向一致。这也说明，教师在发布作文任务要求、选择打分公式及其他具体细则时，要充分考虑到学生的语言背景和写作能力。同一篇作文的打分公式稍有不同，可能分数会相差比较大。这种偏于机械化的在线反馈打分，和灵活的教师反馈方式相比，是有改进的空间的。

在学生作文的错误统计方面，根据 8 篇作文的数据对比，可以看出排名前三的错误分别是拼写错误、主谓一致、句子成分。不同作文排名前三的错误稍有不同，但是排名最前的，无一例外都是单词拼写错误，而且错误率显著高于第二项、第三项。对 8 篇作文的错误排名前三的对比统计如表 6.5。

表 6.5　批改网作文错误统计对比

作文题目	平均得分	第1位（占比）	第2位（占比）	第3位（占比）
① The Dragon Boat Festival	82.8	拼写错误（24%）	搭配错误（14.7%）	主谓一致（11.1%）
② My opinion on intellectual dishonesty	77.9	拼写错误（38.3%）	主谓一致（9.4%）	句子成分（8.5%）
③ What is happiness?	83.8	拼写错误（22.8%）	句子成分（12%）	主谓一致（10.4%）
④ Is an only child a lonely child?	84.2	拼写错误（33.8%）	主谓一致（11.5%）	句子成分（10.7%）
⑤ To forgive or not to forgive	83.5	拼写错误（25.7%）	句子成分（14%）	主谓一致（13.4%）
⑥ The virtues of being young（11级）	82.7	拼写错误（18%）	句子成分（12.2%）	搭配错误（10.5%）
⑦ The virtues of being young（12级）	85.9	拼写错误（19.4%）	主谓一致（13.5%）	句子成分（11.8%）
⑧ The virtues of being young（15级）	84.5	拼写错误（28%）	句子成分（13.7%）	句子结构（12%）

2）以词为单位的在线反馈

批改网在线反馈的错误类型分为拼写错误、搭配错误、主谓一致、句子成分、名词错误、动词错误等16项。大部分如拼写、词性、搭配等属于比较表层的语言特征。通过对学生作文的评改建议和错误分析，可以得出结论：在线反馈能比较精准地检测这些微观维度的错误，尤其是以词为单位的拼写错误检查，准确率很高。

表 6.6　拼写错误误判率

作文题目	拼写错误误判个数/个	误判率/%
① The Dragon Boat Festival *	17/80	21*
② My opinion on intellectual dishonesty	3/175	1.7
③ What is happiness?	0/72	0
④ Is an only child a lonely child?	0/126	0

(续表)

作文题目	拼写错误误判个数/个	误判率/%
⑤ To forgive or not to forgive	1/46	2.2
⑥ The virtues of being young（11 级）	3/73	4.1
⑦ The virtues of being young（12 级）	0/46	0
⑧ The virtues of being young（15 级）	2/51	3.9

* 打星号的数字异常，具体说明见下文。

笔者在对样写错误的复核中发现，学生出现拼写错误的原因只有一小部分是不熟悉单词。很多一大部分学生的拼写错误是电脑键盘输入时的失误，因为在交纸质版作文时这种拼写错误率很低。比如：多出或者漏打字母（如"enormous"打成"enomous"；"recently"打成"rencently"）；或者单词和单词之间没用空格键或者多出来空格键（如"decorative"打成"de corative"；"forever"打成"for ever"；"therefore"打成"there fore"）。在平均打分最高的作文 7 里（The virtues of being young—12 级），拼写错误的比例是相对比较低的（19.4%，总计 237 个错误里有 46 个拼写错误）。在这 46 个拼写错误中，绝大部分都是单词拼写时漏了字母或添加了字母。如：

• 拼写错误例 1：Only if in your youth you have experienced many setbacks, you can feel the power of the <u>stuggling</u> that happened when you were young.

点评：请检查 stuggling，确认拼写正确。

错误类型：拼写错误。

标题：The virtues of being young ｜学生：丁同学

• 拼写错误例 2：<u>Chanllenges</u> exist everywhere and anytime.

点评：请检查 chanllenges，确认拼写正确。

错误类型：拼写错误。

标题：The virtues of being young ｜学生：范同学

• 拼写错误例 3：There is no <u>dennying</u> that being older occurs to everyone.

点评：请检查 dennying，确认拼写正确。

标题：The virtus of being young ｜学生：缪同学

（注：下划线为笔者添加）

笔者的复核证实了在线反馈方式对拼写错误的误判极少,比例只有百分之几或零。但在表6.6里,作文1(The Dragon Boat Festival)的拼写误判达到了21%。笔者在复核的过程中,发现其中相当一部分拼写错误如果换成人工批改,教师不一定会判为拼写错误。作文1是关于中国的传统节日端午节的说明文。这篇作文涉及一些中国特有的词汇,比如粽子、雄黄酒、艾叶等。自动评改系统在进行在线反馈的时候,显然无法结合文化背景来进行评判。在所有检测到的322个错误中,判定的拼写错误有80个,其中zongzi(粽子的拼音)因为没有大写,被判定错误17个(有6个是来自分开写的zong zi),还有3个tsung-tse的拼写错误,这是粤语粽子的拼音,在很多字典里被认可为正确的英语拼写。其他专有名词如雄黄酒的拼音,省份拼音英译因为没有大写,判定错误4个;Chinese没有大写,6个(这些判定不属误判)。其他的拼写错误还包括因为标点符号前后没有按要求大写或小写被判定错误。虽然在线反馈的拼写检查被证明是可靠的,对没有按要求大小写的词判定为错误可以帮助学生认识到写作规范,但这同时也说明,在涉及文化背景和专有名词的判定时,基于语料库的在线批改还是不如人工批改灵活。大数据时代网络热词、新词、流行词汇层出不穷,在线评改系统的语料库也应该时时保持更新,避免把正确使用的流行的、已被收录于词典的新词汇判定为拼写错误。

• 拼写误判例1:During the Dragon Boat Festival, people often eat <u>zongzi</u>, drink realgar wine, and race dragon boats.

点评:确认zongzi大小写是否正确。

标题:The Dragon Boat Festival ｜学生:谢同学

• 拼写误判例2:So people threw <u>tsung-tse</u> into the river in order to calm the dragon down, so they would not hurt Qu Yuan.

点评:请检查tsung-tse,确认拼写是否正确。

标题:The Dragon Boat Festival ｜学生:王同学

(注:下划线为笔者添加)

除了对拼写错误、大小写错误的检测,在线反馈对学生习作中的词性错误、搭配错误等的检查也是比较准确的。虽然误判率比拼写错误要高,但是跟以句子为单位的检测相比,这些以词为单位的反馈相对值得信赖。

3)以句子为单位的在线反馈

研究发现,基于自动写作评改系统的在线反馈模式的最大诟病之一,就是这种在线反馈给出的关于语言质量的反馈比较表面化,不能识别复杂的句子,不能提供更高质量和更深层次的建议(Fang,2010;Weigle,2013;何旭良,2013;蒋艳、马武林,2013;杨晓琼、戴运财,2015)。尤其是与人工评改相比,不能评估文章内容切题与否,过于关注学术性词汇,对文章修辞特点没有反馈,尤其对文章的内部逻辑和关联性、文章的流畅性等无法给出反馈等。纵观批改网提供的16个维度的错误检测,虽然包括了"句子成分、句子结构、语序"等句子层面的分析,但是对文章内容、语篇结构、条理性和流畅性的分类没有处理。而笔者对这些上升到句子层面的错误反馈进行复核时也发现,一旦句子复杂些,系统反馈的误判率也随之增多。笔者把除拼写错误以外"误判"比较多的几项做了对比,如表6.7。

表6.7 句子层面的在线反馈误判率

作文题目	主谓一致误判		句子成分误判	
	数量/个	误判率/%	数量/个	误判率/%
① The Dragon Boat Festival	17/37	45.9	10/25	40
② My opinion on intellectual dishonesty	12/43	27.9	10/39	25.6
③ What is happiness?	11/33	33.3	10/38	26.3
④ Is an only child a lonely child?	12/43	27.9	10/40	25
⑤ To forgive or not to forgive	8/24	33.3	9/22*	40.9*
⑥ The virtues of being young(11级)	12/36	33.3	13/50	26
⑦ The virtues of being young(12级)	11/32	34.4	7/28	25
⑧ The virtues of being young(15级)	5/17	29.4	7/25	28

* 该处错误分析为句子结构

从表6.7里可以看出,在线反馈系统对主谓一致、句子成分、句子结构等的判断失误率最高的达到40.9%,最低的也超过25%。笔者在复核中发现,主谓一致的判定因为是以句子为单位的,所以复杂度更高。在线系统进行评改反馈时还是只能参照系统里的语料库对数据进行比对,难免有误判出现。

排名前三的主谓一致用法错误,大多是由句子中谓语动词与主语的性、数不一致造成的。

• 主谓一致错误 例1:This kind of people <u>does</u> not have a personal standard of morality and ethics that does not sell out to expedience.

点评：请检查 does，确认主谓是否一致。

标题：My opinion on intellectual dishonesty ｜学生：江同学

• 主谓一致错误　例2：They feel happy and relaxed when their teachers <u>trusts</u> them, but when it comes to exams, they will become confused and nervous.

点评：请检查 trusts，确认主谓是否一致。

标题：My opinion on intellectual dishonesty ｜学生：范同学

• 主谓一致错误　例3：It is <u>wisely</u> to forgive because if you don't, you'll make others think you are a mean guy who just <u>take</u> every single advantage and never give up even <u>a little</u>.

点评：请检查 take，确认主谓是否一致。wisely 副词误用为形容词。确认 a little 是否符合语法规范。

标题：To forgive or not to forgive ｜学生：樊同学

• 主谓一致错误　例4：What's more, the only child sometimes <u>depend</u> more on his or her parents, which can make the child less <u>indpendant</u>.

点评：请检查 indpendant，确认拼写是否正确。请检查 depend，确认主谓是否一致。

标题：Is an only child a lonely child? ｜学生：曲同学

上述针对谓语动词单复数形式判断的在线反馈，句子结构相对比较简单，所以反馈准确率也较高。因为主谓一致和句子成分、句子结构等的判定是以句子为单位的，一旦句子变长，结构变复杂，复杂度增加，在线系统进行评改反馈时数据比对还是只能参照系统里的语料库，这样难免有误判出现。笔者在对系统错误分析进行复核时发现，主语是动名词结构，或者从句作主语，或者谓语动词在使役动词之后、在介词 to 之后时，就容易出现误判。

主语一致误判实例：

• 例1：As for myself, I <u>have</u> personally learned to forgive others that <u>have</u> caused injury to my emotions and my physical body.

点评：请检查 have，确认主谓是否一致。

标题：To forgive or not to forgive ｜学生：姚同学

• 例2：On the one hand, too much care and love can make <u>an only child become</u> self-centred, which means that it's difficult for them to make friends with others.

点评：请检查 become, 确认主谓是否一致。an only child 疑似中式英语。

标题：Is an only child a lonely child？ ｜学生：缪同学

• 例3：Boating competitions are held everywhere during every Dragon Boat Festival.

点评：请检查 are, 确认主谓是否一致。

标题：The Dragon Boat Festival ｜学生：陈同学

• 例4：Rumor has it that people of Chu decided to throw food into the river to feed the fish in case that they ate Qu's body and they sat on dragon boats, trying to scare fish away by the thundering sound of drums and the horrible dragon-head in front of the boat.

点评：请检查 scare, 确认主谓是否一致。

标题：The Dragon Boat Festival ｜学生：汤同学

• 例5：When it comes to the Dragon Boat Festival, presumably the first idea which occurs in our minds is that we are going to jump at a statutory holiday.

点评：请检查 is, 确认主谓是否一致。

标题：The Dragon Boat Festival ｜学生：何同学

• 例6：However, as more and more foreign festivals have bought in China, young adults are apt to cerebrate foreign ones rather than our Chinese ones, which, I think, is an unsuitable behavior where they put the cart before the horse.

点评：请检查 is, 确认主谓是否一致。

标题：The Dragon Boat Festival ｜学生：柳同学

• 例7：Hanging branches of wormwood and calamus around the doors of their homes is another custom to drive away misfortune.

点评：确认 drive away misfortune 是否符合语法规范。请检查 is, 确认主谓是否一致。

标题：The Dragon Boat Festival ｜学生：俞同学

• 例8：So from my own perspective, it is actually a need for us to make tradition of the Dragon Boat Festival rejuvenate.

点评：请检查 rejuvenate, 确认主谓是否一致。冠词缺失, 请检查 make tradition of。

标题：The Dragon Boat Festival ｜学生：杨同学

- 例 9：In the end of Warring States Period, the emperor of Chu is very stupid and always <u>listen</u> to hearers. Qu Yuan, <u>an intelligent minister</u> with the high patriotism, cannot <u>get attention of</u> the emperor, in the results of his jumping the Miluo river, and his body with his sorrows of demise of his country sinking in the steam of water.

点评：冠词缺失，请检查 get attention of。an intelligent minister 疑似中式英语。请检查 listen，确认主谓一致。

标题：The Dragon Boat Festival ｜学生：郭同学

- 例 10：<u>The zeal</u> has been missing ever since we said goodbye to our youth, and <u>causes</u> nostalgia eventually.

点评：请检查 causes，确认主谓是否一致。冠词多余，请检查 The zeal。

标题：The virtues of being young ｜学生：吴同学

（注：文中下划线为笔者添加）

上述例句中都出现了频发的主谓一致误判。在例 1 中，在线反馈判定 have 的用法没有遵从主谓一致的原则，但是句子中两个 have 都是遵从主谓一致原则的。例 2（同例 8），make an only child become 中 become 用法正确，没有违反主谓一致原则。an only child 的说法也不是中式英语。例 3、例 7 里的主语是动名词结构，谓语动词用单数形式。例 5 中谓语动词没有紧跟在主语之后，例 6 中主语是从句，如此等等，正确的用法全部被误判成错误。仅在作文 1——The Dragon Boat Festival 里，笔者就在标注主谓不一致的 37 个错误里，找到 17 个被误判的，误判比例高达 45.9%。

同样是在句子层面的错误分析中，针对句子成分和句子结构，在线反馈也显得"心有余而力不足"。在对 8 篇作文的句子成分和句子结构评判中，误判率都在 25% 以上，最高达 40%。

句子成分误判实例：

- 例 1：But wouldn't any person over thirty do anything they <u>could just to</u> slow the aging process?

点评：请检查 could just to，情态动词后面一般接动词原形。

标题：The virtues of being young ｜学生：高同学

- 例2：Young people are passionate enough to stand up again, after brushing down, there would be a new beginning.

  点评：请检查 are | would，疑似双谓语错误。

  标题：The virtues of being young ｜学生：汤同学

- 例3：Being younger is preferable to being older anyway, I think.

  点评：本句语法不规范,请检查。

  标题：The virtues of being young ｜学生：王同学

- 例4：Forgiveness is the key to becoming whole again after a crisis has taken place in someone's life.

  点评：疑似句子不完整,请检查。

  标题：To forgive or not to forgive ｜学生：姚同学

- 例5：But when people learned to forgive, in forgiving, we can move from hurting and hating to healing and reconciliation.

  点评：确认 in forgiving 是否符合语法规范。

  标题：To forgive or not to forgive ｜学生：王同学

- 例6：Doing all of these has a meaning of warding off ill luck and evil.

  点评：本句语法不规范,请检查。

  请检查 ill,该词通常只作表语,不作定语。

  标题：The Dragon Boat Festival ｜学生：闫同学

跟句子成分类似,在线反馈对句子结构的分析和判断常常出现失误,尤其当句子长度和复杂度增加时,句子结构误判率也直线上升。

句子结构误判实例：

- 例1：One of the mothers of victims in 911 and the mother of the terrorist become friends.

  点评：本句语法不规范,请检查。

  标题：To forgive or not to forgive ｜学生：尹同学

- 例2：After all, human fallibility is something that we can not deny and also has been proved inevitable for many times, one that might partly explain why we're all inclined to make mistakes, simultaneously being a wrongdoer who equally doesn't want to be treated to be guilty forever.

  点评：动词 proved 和 inclined 一般不用作被动式。确认 has been proved

inevitable 是否符合语法规范。

标题：To forgive or not to forgive ｜学生：赵同学

• 例3：This definition is a good starting point and we can dig a little deeper from it.

点评：本句语法不规范,请检查。

标题：What is happiness? ｜学生：杨同学

• 例4：I wear beautiful clothes, I can eat whatever I like, I can chat with my friends by advanced technology, I can surf on the Internet and take part in different kinds of activities while my grandparents can only stay at home, watching TV, taking care of their grandchildren and doing some other boring things.

点评：语法错误,can surf on 不规范,建议修改。检查句子中的连词是否缺失。

标题：The virtues of being young ｜学生：薛同学

在以上对句子成分或句子结构的误判中,系统给出的说明通常是语法不规范或双谓语动词错误。如句子成分误判例1:But wouldn't any person over thirty do anything they could just to slow the aging process? 系统给出的错误反馈是"could just to"后面要用动词原形。而原句不仅用了动词原形,整个句子也没有任何语法或句子结构错误。事实上,这个句子是来自教材的原文。同样被判为语法不规范的例4、例5和例6也都是来自课文的转写。系统在对句子进行分析时,对连续出现的两个动词都会机械地判为"双谓语错误",而很多情况下这种所谓的双谓语是因为系统对句子意群的断句出现错误,比如,例1里的意群断句应该是"But wouldn't any person over thirty do anything they could",后面"just to slow the aging process"是另一个意群,但是机器批改无法就此做出准确判断。

4）其他数据分析

A. 词性分析、搭配分布、分级词汇、数据比对

词性分析:在线反馈系统会统计出一个作文号下(即一个作文任务下)各类词性在学生作文中使用的比例、频次、百分比。目前各类词性包括动词、名词、形容词、代词、介词、副词、连词等。写作教师可以通过对学生作文中出现的各种词性比例,了解学生写作练习时较常使用到哪种词性,以及这些词性具体是以哪种形式出现在学生作文中的,从而更好地把握文章的文体特征。

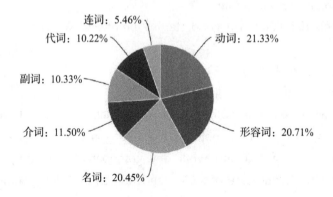

词性	频次	占比(%)
动词	2,863	21.33
形容词	2,780	20.71
名词	2,745	20.45
介词	1,543	11.50
副词	1,386	10.33
代词	1,371	10.22
连词	733	5.46

图6.18 词性分布对比图(作文6)

搭配分布:在线反馈系统会统计出一个作文号下所有文章的搭配使用情况,以及各类搭配出现的频次、百分比。目前批改网支持查询的搭配有:形容词+名词、动词+名词、副词+动词、动词+介词、名词+动词、副词+形容词、形容词+介词。写作教师可以通过查看作文中的各种搭配了解学生作文中较常使用的搭配类型和习惯。

分级词汇:分级词汇目前包括超高频词汇、次高频词汇、学术词汇、非常规词汇、生词对照。用户可以查看作文中出现的各类分级词汇及每种词汇使用的具体实例。生词对照功能则可以很好地将作文中单词的使用情况量化出来。系统的用户可选择相应的词表(系统提供选择的词汇表包括从初一到大学CET-6的不同级别),检索同一作文号下文章未用到的生词。教师可以将单篇作文同全部作文进行对比,抽出作文中未用到的词汇,再推送给学生进行学习。同时教师也可提供自己的词汇表,与系统进行比对。

» 搭配统计比对

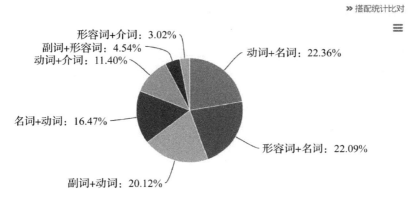

图 6.19　搭配分布对比图（作文 6）

词性搭配	频次	占比(%)
动词+名词	808	22.36
形容词+名词	798	22.09
副词+动词	727	20.12
名词+动词	595	16.47
动词+介词	412	11.40
副词+形容词	164	4.54
形容词+介词	109	3.02

单词	频次	例句
pure	3	we have pure friendships and the only assignment of study .
responsible	3	For example , we are responsible .
advertisement	3	As a advertisement saying that there only is you ca n't imagine , but ...
burden	3	We can live an aboundant life away from heavy burden .
devil	3	Many people would glad to sign with the devil just to be young again ...
emotion	3	After you leave school , we have to learn to manage our emotions and ...
fashion	3	New fashions can be accepted by the young more easily .
formula	3	They buy Grecian Formula and Oil of Olay and do much exercise to delay ...
homework	3	When the teachers requier us to do homework , we always take an effort ...
imagination	3	is that you do n't let the facts get in the way of your imagination " ...

共 540 条结果 10/54 页首页 上一页 [6] [7] [8] [9] **10** [11] [12] [13] [14] [15] 下一页 尾页

图 6.20　生词对照图（作文 6）

数据比对：写作教师可以将任意某个学生的单篇作文与全部作文中的各类数据进行对比。目前系统数据对比支持：单词统计比对、词性分布比对、搭配统计比对、句长分布比对、动词频次比对。数据比对也可以是某两个学生之间进行的比对。通过对比，学生能够直观地了解到自己同别人、同平均水平的差距或者优势,从而对自己的学习进行更有效的规划。

从图 6.21 中两位同学的单词统计可以看出,何同学超高频词汇使用远低于全部学生(69.47% *vs.* 83.94%),学术词汇和非常规词汇都高于其他学生(其中非常规词汇比率是 16.81% *vs.* 4.42%);陈同学正好相反,学术词汇和非常规词汇都低于平均水平,而超高频词汇使用又高于平均水平。写作中的超高频词汇使用越多,意味着词汇量越小,词汇变化不丰富,也难以写出高质量的作文。

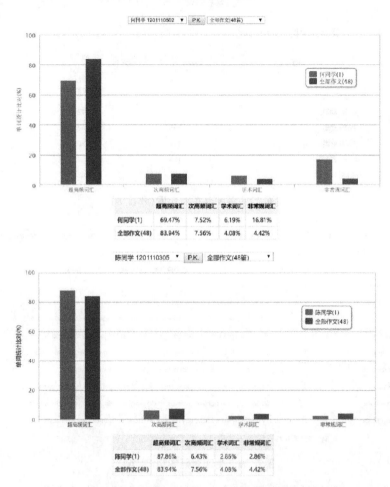

图 6.21　数据比对中的单词统计——何同学和陈同学(作文 6)

图 6.22 是何同学和江同学的句长分布对比。很明显,在超过 20 词以上的长句、复杂句的运用上,何同学远远超出江同学。句子的长度虽然不是判断句子难度和复杂度,也不是判断作文质量高低的唯一标准,但是一篇全文充斥的都是短句、简单句的作文,绝不会是一篇质量上乘的文章。通过图 6.21 和图 6.22 的数据比对,基本上可以得出结论:何同学的写作基础和语言能力,高出数据比对里的陈同学和江同学,也高出平均水平。

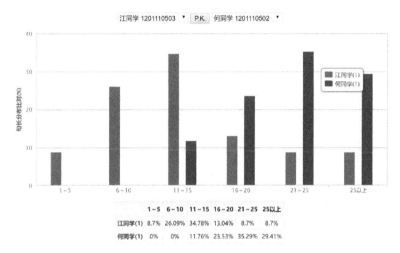

图 6.22　句长分布对比——何同学和江同学(作文 6)

B. 维度分析

批改网从评判学生作文的 192 个测评维度中挑选出几大维度,比如,词汇丰富度、词汇难度、平均句长、从句密度、拼写正确率等,并列出每个学生在各个维度上的测量值。维度概述部分把同一个作文号下所有学生的数据从高到低排列,维度分项提供每一个单维度的曲线分布和走向,为学生和教师分析作文提供直观的数据参考。通过作文数据在各个维度的不同表现,学生可以对比自己与平均值及最高值之间的差距,明确作文的薄弱点所在。教师可以对全班学生在各个维度的表现进行综合考量,对全班学生的写作整体情况进行分析和把控,并分别针对共性化和个性化的问题进行处理。

姓名/学号	词汇丰富度 (6.49)↓	词汇难度 (5.48)	从句密度 (1.05)	平均句长 (17.42)	拼写正确率 (0.993)	分数 (81.70)
何同学 1201110502	8.33	6.42	1.99	25.00	1.0000	93.95
柳同学 1201110313	7.71	5.68	0.00	21.29	1.0000	85.09
殷同学 1201110321	7.69	5.63	0.26	13.24	0.9677	75.21
俞同学 1201110322	7.60	5.98	1.48	17.10	0.9957	85.65
施同学 1201110314	7.48	5.90	1.51	18.24	0.9954	86.58
黄同学 1201110511	7.31	5.63	1.64	16.03	0.9956	83.2
薛同学 1201110319	7.27	5.58	1.58	21.67	1.0000	87.1
康同学 1201110312	7.17	5.67	0.75	12.22	1.0000	82.88
汤同学 1201110316	7.13	5.89	1.33	16.24	1.0000	90.85
范同学 1201110508	7.12	5.81	0.00	13.08	0.9854	76.48
汤同学 1201110315	7.12	5.58	1.25	14.16	1.0000	86.63
黄同学 1201110311	7.10	5.69	0.75	12.27	0.9953	81.08
范同学 1201110306	7.05	5.34	2.15	26.00	0.9903	80.68

图 6.23　维度分析概述(作文 6)

　　这些对学生作文词汇、句子等各方面的数据分析,对各个单项之间、单项与整体之间的比对,既能给学生提供自己作文的具体情况,也能让他们熟悉班级的整体写作水平,找出自己和同学之间的差距,更好地制订学习计划,有针对性地提高某方面的能力。对于教师而言,能更全面地了解全部学生的写作水平和个体状态,在教学中有的放矢,帮助学生查漏补缺,加强强项,提升弱项。这种基于数据库的在线分析反馈,跟教师的手工分析相比,更快速有效,也更为准确,不仅给教师写作教学提供了有力的依据和参考,也给写作教学的研究提供了极大的便利。

　　稍显不足的是,各类的数据分析和比对都只能以一个作文号下(即一个写作任务)的学生为对象,而不能提供同一个学生在系统提交的所有作文的纵向数据分析和比对,以及不同年级、不同班级学生(写作任务和要求一样,但作文号不一样,如作文 6、7、8)之间的横向数据对比。就某一个写作者而言,系统只提供了大概数字,如学生的所有作文分数列表,一共提交了多少篇作文,总计多少词,平均分数多少,等等。这些大而笼统的数字无法帮助教师了解单个学生在一段时间内(如一年内)的写作情况和成长轨迹,或者不同年级学生在同一个水平阶段练习同一篇作文时的情况对比。尤其是单个学生的成长轨迹数据分析,对了解学生的写作能力发展是个重要的参考依据,也是笔者认为在线反馈可以改进的地方。

　　5) 个案分析

　　以上是对基于批改网在线反馈总体情况的综合分析和数据比对。在批改网庞大的数据库里,还涵盖了每一个学生每一篇习作的每一次修改痕迹及每一次修改带来的分数变化。在线反馈的即时性和便捷性、秒改作文的实现使每一次的循环过程(修改→提交→反馈,再修改→提交→再反馈……)极大缩短。分数由低到高的变化,这是学生在使用在线反馈时不停修改作文的动力。笔者的学生绝大部分在提交一稿后,会根据系统的反馈进行修改,少则数次,多则几十次,最多的修改次数达到83次。在不断的修改中,斟词酌句,仔细推敲某一个词、一个句子的用法,对比不同英语表达的微妙区别。虽然这种写作驱动力是来自分数的直接刺激,但语言精炼度和精准度在这个打磨的过程中实实在在地得到了提高。

笔者选取了其中一位学生(下文以 M 同学指代)的习作来做个案分析。M 同学为江南大学英语专业一年级学生,提交作文的时间为一年级第二学期期末。写作的题目和要求请参照前文作文5。打分公式按默认公式,即系统按词汇、句子、篇章结构和内容四个维度进行打分,其中词汇占43%,句子占28%,篇章结构占22%,内容相关占7%。

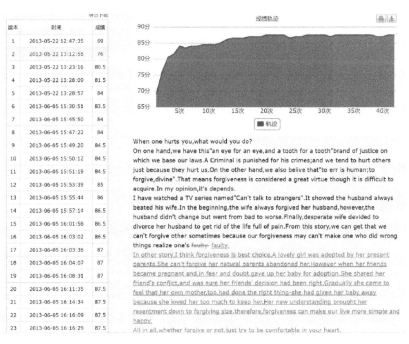

图6.24　M 同学作文修改和成绩轨迹图

M 同学第一次提交作文时间为中午12:47,此后按系统数据显示,一直在对作文进行反复修改、提交。最后一次提交时间为15:57,整个修改过程持续了3小时

10分钟。作文一共修改42次,分数从最初的69分提高到最后的87.5分,从轨迹图可以清晰地看到分数变化的曲线走势。前5次上升趋势明显,约第15次以后分数变化趋于平稳,偶有小幅的下降。笔者结合其他众多同学的成绩轨迹图也发现,并不是每一次修改以后分数必然会上升,下降和上升经常交替出现。

下面是M同学的作文第一稿,系统打分69分。具体在线反馈(按句点评)内容的截图如图6.25。系统给出的综合评价是:作者句法知识扎实,可适当增加从句的使用;作者词汇量积累不错,能较灵活地使用高级词汇;过渡词和衔接词使用的比较不错。

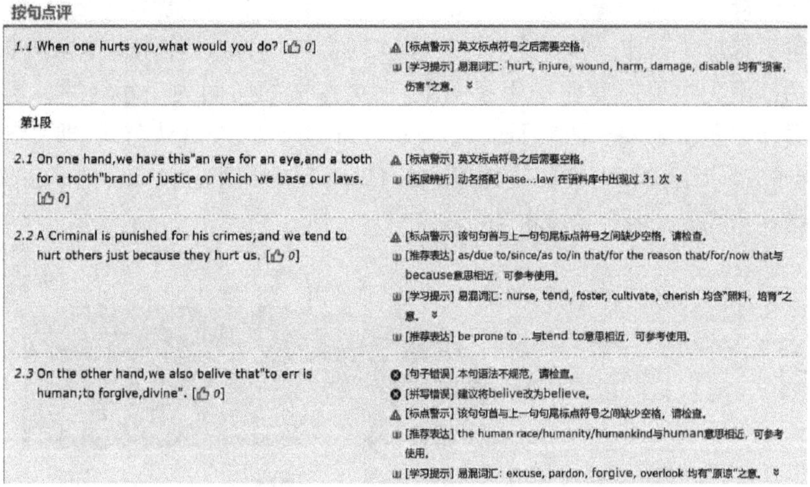

图6.25 批改网的按句点评

第一稿:

When one hurts you, what would you do?

On one hand, we have this "an eye for an eye, and a tooth for a tooth" brand of justice on which we base our laws. A criminal is punished for his crimes; and we tend to hurt others just because they hurt us. On the other hand, we also belive that "to err is human; to forgive, divine". That means forgiveness is considered a great virtue though it is difficult to acquire. In my opinion, it's depends.

I have watched a TV series named "Can't talk to strangers". It showed the husband always beated his wife. In the beginning, the wife always forgived her husband, however, the husband didn't change but went from bad to worse.

Finally, desperate wife devided to divorce her husband to get rid of the life full of pain. From this story, we can get that we can't forgive other sometimes because our forgiveness may can't make one who did wrong things realize one's faulty.

　　细看在线按句点评的每条反馈建议,标点警示9条、拼写错误3条、句子错误2条、动词错误2条、搭配错误1条,其他都是学习提示、推荐表达等纠错性建议,没有关于文章内容、结构、逻辑性或条理性等方面的反馈建议。一个句子的句首和上一句句尾的标点符号之间如果缺少空格,就会给出标点警示。笔者复核这里的每一个纠错性提示,发现标点警示和拼写错误反馈全部正确,句子错误有一处误判("On the other hand, we also belive that 'to err is human; to forgive, divine'"被误判为错误),动词错误有一处误判("… we can get that …")。有趣的是,第一稿的内容和结构是不完整的,明显缺少了一段。作者在第一段引入话题后,第二段阐述了一方观点("on one hand"),第三段用了事例支持,文章没有阐述另一方面的观点(也就是和前面 on one hand 对应的 on the other hand),也没有结尾。

　　M同学随后提交的第二稿,完善了文章的内容和结构,增加了另一方观点和例证,并增加了结尾段。虽然对第一稿的在线反馈没有做任何修正,但结构完整了的第二稿,系统打分提高到76分。

　　第二稿的反馈建议里增加了名词错误、句子错误、词性错误、大小写错误各1个。在第三稿里,M同学修改了第一稿反馈建议里的3个拼写错误及新增加段落的一个词性错误和句子错误,分数提高到80.5分。第四稿继续根据反馈,修改第一稿的拼写错误和句子错误及第三稿里的修改建议。作者自己也把 present parents 改成 adoptive parents,使句意更明确,分数提高到81.5分。第五稿只改了一个拼写错误(devided→decided),分数从81.5比较大幅度地提高到84分。至此,作文经过5次提交修改,已经超过班级平均分(83.5分)。这一段也是6.24图里成绩轨迹曲线上升最大、波动最大的一段。此后的作文分数一直在85分线上下小幅度浮动。

　　从这5次的修改可以看出,在线反馈虽然不对文章内容和结构等做出反馈,但默认的打分公式里篇章结构占22%,内容相关占7%,显然内容和结构的完善会提高作文评分。此外,按照系统反馈提示做出的修改,如果修改正确,也会明显提升评分,如第五稿里只改了一个单词的拼写错误,但是这个单词是系统反馈里的建议,分数从81.5提高到了84分。

表6.8　前5次作文修改内容与评分

作文稿次	修改内容	评分
第1稿	无	69
第2稿	增加两段,使文章内容和结构更完整	76
第3稿	第一稿反馈:belive→believe;beated→beat;faulty→fault ＋句子错误 自己修改:therefore→Therefore 等	80.5
第4稿	forgived→forgave; it's depends→it depends; other→another; present parents→adoptive parents	81.5
第5稿	devided→decided	84

M同学此后的修改,都是对某个单词、词组或者从句进行的小范围修改,作文的评分变化幅度也不大。最后值得关注的是,作者第24次修改后,作文分数不升反降,从87.5分降到86.5分。第24次修改只有一个,前一版本对应的句子中it指代含糊,与前一句缺乏承接和过渡。新的版本增加了承接的内容,让句与句之间的过渡更为自然顺畅。笔者作为教师,在人工批改时会对这个修改做出肯定。但是在在线反馈系统里修改不仅无效,还降低了评分。笔者在别的同学的作文中,也多次发现修改后评分下降的现象。究其原因,可能一方面是因为有些学生确实修改不到位;另一方面,在确定学生修改正确的情况下(如本例中M同学的修改),也证明在线反馈的语料库数据无法对作文的条理性和逻辑性做出判断。

第23稿:That means forgiveness is considered as a great virtue though it is difficult to acquire. In my opinion, it depends.

第24稿:That means forgiveness is considered a great virtue though it is difficult to acquire. Then to forgive or not to forgive, in my opinion, it depends.

从第25次以后到第42次修改停止,作文的分数一直在1分之内变化:从87到87.5分或从87.5分到87分,或连续几次修改后依然保持不变。可以看出,作文评分达到一定的分数段后,要继续往上提升就比较有难度了。这也是与教师反馈的一个很大的不同点。教师反馈,可以根据文章的思想性、逻辑性、流畅性等做总体评价。一篇作文经过作者修改后,即使词汇的变化和句子的难度并没有增加,但思想内容、组织结构等深层语言特征的优化,依然可以很大幅度地提高评分。

本篇作文的最后一稿修改,在线反馈评分 87.5,按句点评判断一个句子错误,其余都是标点警示、学习提示、拓展辨析等。这个句子错误的判断,还是属于误判。句子本身有错误,但系统判断的地方不对。

第 42 稿:What's followed are two attitudes.
点评:[句子错误]请检查 are,确认主谓一致。

在进行在线反馈个案分析的过程中,笔者提取学生的写作资料并进行数据检索和分析。在提取数据时,因为这篇学生作文提交于 2013 年,能浏览跟本篇作文有关的大概信息(如分数、提交次数、修改痕迹、成绩轨迹等),但是点开按句点评,查看具体的反馈建议时,系统显示的是"正在分析,请勿关闭"。片刻之后,分析完毕,显示的分数评语却和原始数据有出入。第一稿原始评分 69 分(见图 6.24),重新分析后评分是 72.5 分(如图 6.26)。

图 6.26　作文重新分析后分数和评阅

笔者无法判断在线反馈于两个不同时间(2013 年和 2018 年)对同一篇文章做出的分数评阅存在差异的具体原因。大胆猜测,可能是因为在大数据时代,信息的更新和自然语言处理技术的进步,在线反馈系统的技术支持或语料库也随之发展更新。对作文的评价打分维度进一步拓展。此外,批改网的反馈点评有"报错"功能。在用户使用过程中,如果对任何反馈或判断有质疑,可以把报错反馈提交到系统(如图 6.27),笔者曾就学生转用教材中的原句被误判而进行报错反馈。用户和在线系统的不断互动、去疑的过程,无疑能进一步丰富系统语料库,提高在线反馈作文评改的可靠性。

图 6.27 用户在线报错反馈

三、小结

何旭良(2013)在对批改网的信度和效度研究中曾指出,批改网的在线反馈作文评分虽然具有比较高的信度和效度,但总体打分偏高。跟教师反馈相比,在线反馈还停留在微观维度的反馈上,宏观维度的反馈有待加强。笔者在进行在线反馈的实践和案例分析中也发现,基于批改网的在线反馈模式具有显著的优点,但也存在明显的不足。在线反馈的优点在于:①"秒批作文",即时反馈——在线批改系统能及时、快速地给出反馈和建议,并如实记录学生提交、修改作文的历史痕迹,生成成绩轨迹曲线图,并保留所有的修改数据,形成个性化的学习者写作数据库。②能促进学生反复修改作文,就单词拼写、大小写、词性、搭配等方面给出修改建议,能够帮助学习者减少语言错误,使写作表达更规范。③能把两个学生之间及单个学生与全班同学之间的写作情况进行数据比对和分析,使学习者能够了解自己和全部同学之间的写作差距或优势,从而制订更加有效的学习计划。④能够让写作教师随时调阅学生作文进行人工批改、布置学生进行同伴互评和群批、读取数据或导出数据、对数据进行整理分析等。在线反馈强大的数据化特点能帮助写作教师更全面地了解学生情况,从而制订更合适的写作教学计划。但是正如研究者们所诟病的,在线反馈由于是基于机器的机械化批改,跟教师的人工反馈相比,存在诸多不足:第一,对表层的语言特征反馈准确度高,而对于深层的语言特征则屡屡出现误判或完全没有反馈。随着句子长度和复杂度的增加,对以句子为单位的反馈的错误率也显著增加。如在笔者作为案例分析的一篇模仿写作的系统反馈里,屡次将来自教材中的原句判为错误。这种误判多少会影响写作者的情绪,并引发质疑。第二,在线评改系统对语篇内容、组织结构、文章逻辑性、连贯性和条理性等没有反馈,而这些都是写作能力发展不可或缺的部分。第三,关于在线反馈系统的数据比对和分析功能,如果能够提供单个学生在使用系统进行写作评改的一段时间(一年或两年)内的成长轨迹数据分析,将能够帮助学生自己和教师了解特定时间内学生写作能力的提升情况。

总而言之,在线反馈作为大数据时代的产物,是对传统的写作反馈模式的一种丰富和有益补充。英语写作能力的提升从来都不是短期内就能达成的。单一的反馈模式,无论是教师反馈还是同伴反馈或在线反馈,都无法给写作者提供最有效率、最优质的指导。在大数据时代的背景下,把各种反馈方式有机结合起来,充分发挥各个反馈方式的优势,才能最大限度地优化写作评改质量,提高学生的写作能力。

第五节 线上线下多稿评改的混合反馈模式

一、多稿评改的混合反馈

不同形式的反馈对学生习作的修改、作文质量的提高和写作能力发展水平起着不可忽视的作用。一般认为,教师反馈能够促成更多的深层语言特征的修改提高,如思想内容、篇章结构、文章整体的流畅性和条理性等;在线反馈能引发较多的表层语言特征修改,如单词拼写校正、词性、搭配等以词及词以下微观特征为单位的局部修改;同伴反馈对语言表层特征和深层内容都有反馈,能有效减轻写作焦虑,激发写作兴趣,培养学生的批判思维能力及分析和解决问题的能力,但是同伴反馈受限于同伴的语言水平和学习动机。三种目前写作教学领域常用的反馈模式各有优劣,如何在写作教学中融合、运用不同的反馈方式,取长补短,最大限度地提高学生文本质量和写作水平,是值得探讨的议题。同时,大数据的时代背景、信息化和技术化的发展特点,给英语写作教学与研究带来系统性的变革,对教师角色、学生角色、学习材料、写作环境及写作的评估和测试等方面产生深远影响(刘润清,2014)。把大数据方法和写作评价与反馈有机结合,形成线上线下多稿评改的混合反馈模式,将是英语写作教学研究与改革的一种有益尝试。

目前尝试将某两种或多种反馈方式加以结合,进行对比的研究并不鲜见。蔡基刚(2011)采用了"在线同伴反馈+线下教师反馈"的模式,经过3个学期的跟踪调查,发现在线同伴反馈能增强学生的读者意识和文章质量意识,能增强学生英语写作的积极性,以及能明显提高学生写作的语言质量。杨丽娟等(2013)对比单一教师反馈、单一同伴反馈、"教师反馈+同伴反馈"3种反馈模式有效性的研究成果证明,两种反馈方式相结合的做法更受学生的欢迎和肯定,效果明显比另外两种单一的反馈模式好。金晓宏(2016)进行了为期一学期的多样性评改反馈教学实验,提出大学英语教师应努力引入包括学生自我评改反馈、同伴评改反馈和教师反馈在内的多稿制评改反馈。李奕华(2015)在对教师反馈、在线反馈、"教师反馈+在线反馈"3种不同反馈方式有效性的研究中发现,"教师反馈+在线反馈"比单一的在线反馈更能提高学生的写作水平。白云和王俊菊(2018)调查教师反馈、自动评改系统在线反馈对学生习作修改过程和文本质量的影响,建议在写作教学中将两种反馈方式加以融合,提升文本质量和写作水平。

刘奕和王小兰(2010)基于blog进行英语写作多元反馈模式尝试,把博客的网络技术引进写作过程,结合教师反馈、同伴反馈、移动平台的同伴互动评改对写作文本进行多元化反馈。黄静和张文霞(2014)通过多种数据收集和分析手段,验证多元反馈对大学生英语写作修改的影响。首先由教师在课堂上讲解任务要求和评价反馈的标准,然后学生完成初稿,提交在线评估软件(句酷批改网)。学生根据在线反馈进行修改后,再发给同组同学互评。互评修改后再接受教师反馈,接受教师反馈后再修改,最后定稿并完成自我反思报告。她们的研究结果证明,这种融合在线反馈、同伴反馈、教师反馈的线上线下多稿评改多元反馈方式,促进了学生多稿写作和不断修改文本的习惯的养成,激发了学生的自主学习能动性,提高了英语写作的能力和教学质量。笔者在实践中也发现,学生对多元反馈模式的参与度和认可度都比较高。

英语学习是教师和学生相互合作,是教师促进学生对事物概念形成和综合能力形成的过程。Lee(2007)提出了写作课堂的六点反馈原则:①反馈有预见性,学生须了解其写作的优缺点以及如何进行修改,比如,在内容、组织结构还是语言方面;②反馈须有针对性,将学习信息准确地传递给学生,并明确教师的"期待表现",帮助学生了解教、学、评的相关性;③学生需要有机会利用教师反馈提高写作水平,缩短"当下表现"和"期待表现"间的差距;④在学习过程中学生能发挥在互评、自评和师生对话中的自主能动性;⑤反馈能够激发学生的写作动力和增强他们的信心;⑥反馈能用来提高教学质量。可见,有效的写作反馈不是单一的,而是双向或多向的信息交互过程;它包含师生互动、生生互动的关系,强调了学习者的核心地位和在反馈过程中的重要角色。

实践证明,单一的写作反馈模式各有自己的效用和劣势,而"教师反馈+在线反馈+同伴反馈"的复合循环反馈活动能最大限度地强化学生英语语言知识及语言运用能力,培养学生写作意识,提高写作文本质量。将教师反馈与同伴反馈、人工反馈与机器(在线)反馈、外部反馈与内在反馈有机融合为一体的混合反馈模式,充分实现了以学习者为中心的多种互动,学习者在不断思考、反复修改、多稿评改的过程中,最大限度地提升写作能力和语言水平。当然,在实施"教师反馈+在线反馈+同伴反馈"的复合循环反馈时也有一些必须要考虑的因素,比如,活动前设计好合理规范、简便易施、有针对性的英语写作任务测量评价表;适当进行同伴互评反馈的培训,增强学生同伴互评反馈意识;采用多人/多次、线上线下的评阅反馈时,要注意对过程的监控和管理;适时对各种反馈方式进行教师监督和上课作业反馈讲评,以查漏补缺,使反馈活动更有的放矢地进行。

二、案例分析

笔者在写作教学实践中,也进行了"教师反馈+同伴反馈""在线反馈+教师反馈"混合模式的尝试。相比单一的教师反馈,混合反馈(多元反馈)方式能节省一部分教师的时间,同时在同伴互评和人机互动的反馈中,学生对自己写作上的薄弱环节有了更清楚的认识。多种反馈方式的互相作用,实现了线上线下的多稿写作。

1. "教师反馈+同伴反馈"的多稿写作

多稿反复写作基于二语习得理论中的输出理论和频次效应。拥有语言知识不等于能使用等量的语言知识,二语习得需要足够的语言输出,在输出过程中才能不断了解自己的不足,及时查漏补缺。多写、多练才能不断提高写作的流利度和准确度。

/ 大数据时代的英语写作教学与研究 /

• 实例1：本篇多稿评改实例为段落写作练习，要求学生使用特定的连接词（教师给出6个，6个里选5个）写成完整的段落。要求段落承转自然，语言流畅，词汇和句子富有变化性。学生写完初稿后即可进行同伴反馈。同伴反馈至少进行两次，也就是两人次的同伴评改。每次反馈后再根据建议进行修改调整，最后定稿。定稿后再接受教师反馈。

第一稿：

> It is universally acknowledged that running can help us lose weight. In fact, most of us have put it into practice as well. We do not only running but also many other things related to it. For instance, we make detailed plans and routines for the miles and the frequency we would move along. Meanwhile, we are pretty sure that we could succeed in slimming as long as our persistence. However, running does not make us lose our weight efficiently according to a scientific research. In other words, as a sport, running is not intense enough to lead to our body's strong reaction. Our body is much witty than we thought. Specifically, contrary to common idea, it first burn up the sugar storing in our muscles and blood and any other areas. We may only achieve part of our weight-loss goal by running several hours continuously, just consuming the sugar, not the fat. Consequently, running could hardly lose our weight technically.

学生的第一稿是关于跑步对于减肥有效与否的写作。段落有层次，词汇和句子有变化性，连接词的使用总体比较恰当。错误也有很多：语法方面，"do not only running"中，do not 后面的动词应该用原形；"as long as our persistence"中，as long as 后面应该接从句而不是名词；"it first burn up"中 burn 应该是第三人称单数等。词汇方面，"lead to""much witty"表达不准确。此外，有些句子之间的承接和过渡不够自然，段落的逻辑性可以进一步加强。

第二稿：斜体部分为第二稿的修改。

> It is universally acknowledged that running can help us lose weight; *in fact, hardly could it technically achieve the goal.* ~~In fact,~~ Most of us have put *running* into practice ~~as well~~. We ~~do~~ not only run but also do many other things related ~~to it~~. For instance, ~~we make~~ detailed plans ~~and routines for~~ *are made as to* the miles and the frequency we

/ 第六章　大数据时代英语写作的评价与反馈 /

would move along. ~~(Meanwhile, we are pretty sure that we could succeed in slimming as long as our persistence.)~~ However, running does not ~~(make us)~~ lose our weight efficiently according to a scientific research. In other words, as a sport, running is not intense enough to ~~(lead to)~~ *trigger off* our body's strong reaction, *for* our body is much ~~(witty)~~ cleverer than we ~~(thought)~~ *assume* to be. Specifically, contrary to *the* common idea, it first burns up the sugar stor*ed* in *the* blood, muscles and any other areas. While it may be true that we ~~(may only)~~ can achieve part of *the* weight-loss goal by running several hours continuously, just consuming the sugar, not the fat; running, *consequently*, couldn't lose our weight ~~(technically.)~~ exactly and precisely.

修改后的第二稿整体比第一稿在逻辑性和条理上都有了提高，主题句比第一稿更明确，更能反映段落的中心思想，句与句之间的承接更自然一些。修改了词汇、语法、表达方面的错误："do not only running but also many other things …"改成"not only run but also do many other things"；"lead to"改成"trigger off"，这个用词改得很精准；"much witty"改成"much cleverer"，如此等等。

第三稿：下划线为第三稿的修改，括号里为第三稿反馈者修改时的补充说明。

It is universally acknowledged that running can help us lose weight. In fact, hardly could it technically achieve the goal. ~~Most of us have put running into practice. We not only run but also do many other things related. For instance, detailed plans are made as to the miles and the frequency we would move along.~~（该句对论证观点不起作用）<u>While it may be true that running helps in burning up the sugar stored in muscles, blood and many other areas, however, according to scientific researches,</u> running does not ~~lose our weight~~ <u>contribute to weight-loss</u> efficiently, ~~according to a scientific research.~~ In other words, as a sport, running is not intense enough to trigger off ~~our body's~~ strong reactions <u>in our bodies</u>, ~~for our bodies are much cleverer than we assume them to be.~~（由于后面并没有体现身体有多聪明，所以删去这句话，而补充说明跑步如何没有引起强烈反应）Specifically, contrary to the common idea, <u>it first burns up the sugar</u>

~~stored in the blood, muscles and any other areas. While it may be true that we can achieve part of the weight-loss goal by running several hours continuously, just consuming the sugar, not the fat,~~ when you run, your heart rate remains relatively stable. Meanwhile, you are not actually burning fat with exercise until your body needs more energy much quicker during high-intensity exercise. ~~running,~~ Consequently, ~~running couldn't lose our weight exactly and precisely.~~ it's not rare to see that some people, though running miles with high frequency, are still gaining weight.（可以换一种说法代替简单的重复的观点，并且与上文构成因果关系）

第三稿修改后与前两稿相比文章的逻辑性和条理性有了更大的提升。删除了对主题句和中心论点不起支持作用的、无关紧要的句子，修补论证逻辑上的漏洞（如第二稿中说"我们的身体比想象的要聪明得多"，但是上下文并没有进行阐释或支持）。同时，词汇更丰富，语言更精炼，表达更精准。

一般经过多次同伴反馈、修改的习作，到了这个阶段，交到教师手里的定稿已经修正了拼写、语法等浅显的语言错误。句子之间的承接、过渡，作文的内容和逻辑等也会有一定的提升。每个学生同伴的语言水平和写作能力的高低，会对提交的定稿质量有不同程度的影响。对于实例1的习作，由于最后一位同伴的反馈质量比较高，因此定稿的文本也不需要进行太多修改。教师反馈对习作进行了肯定性评价，并指出"until your body needs more energy much quicker during high-intensity exercise"这种表达不够清晰（教师反馈：*much quicker than what*？）。学生收到教师反馈后，把这一句修改成"*until your body consumes much more energy than it normally needs during high-intensity exercise*"。

终稿：教师反馈后修改，确定最终稿。教师在班级进行总体反馈、点评。（斜线体为教师反馈后修改的句子）

It is universally acknowledged that running can help us lose weight. In fact, hardly could it technically achieve the goal. While it may be true that running helps in burning up the sugar stored in muscles, blood and many other areas, however, according to scientific researches, running does not contribute to weight-loss efficiently. In other words, as a sport, running is not intense enough to trigger off strong reactions in our bodies. Specifically, contrary to the common idea, when you run, your heart rate remains relatively stable. Meanwhile, you are not actually burning fat with running *until your body consumes much more energy than it normally needs during high-intensity exercise.* Consequently, it's not rare to see that some people, though running miles with high frequency, are still gaining weight.

- 实例2：本篇实例是基于教师给出的写作背景进行叙事文体写作。背景给出了故事的时间设定(夜晚)和人物设定(独自一人在家)。教师强调细节描写的重要性，用细节烘托环境或衬托人物性格。

第一稿：

I had had this feeling for many days, and in the storm evening, I suspected that there must be someone hiding somewhere. The wind was blowing violently with the roar of thunder and lighting. Maybe a rainstorm is coming.

I gazed at the message I had received one hour ago: "See you at 10 pm." But It was already 11 o'clock and I didn't know who sent it. After breaking up with my boyfriend, I had been living alone in this apartment for a long time. Who would it be?

A power failure plunged the whole house into sudden darkness. I felt someone was staring at me. Suddenly, I heard a sound of dripping water. It was clear and continuous, in the same rhythm of the sound of ticking. But it hadn't rained yet. A feeling that there was someone else somewhere arose in my heart. A cold sweat broke out on the back of my neck. I searched every corner in every room, only to find nothing was strange. I realized that the sound of dripping water, was just like the sound of steps.

Without taking a bath, I returned to my bedroom and decide to go to bed. But when I was drawing the curtain, a lightning flashed through the air, lighting up almost everything in my room. Out of the window, a man was staring at me with a nasty grin.

The rain began to fell. With another lighting, the last thing I could see was that the clock on the wall read 10:00. The same as the mysterious message.

第一稿的细节描写应该说已经比较成功地把环境的惊悚和悬念设置了出来：在一个停电的漆黑的夜晚，一个女孩孤身一人在家，陌生人发短信说 10 点见。屋外山雨欲来风满楼，屋内似有似无的脚步声……文中长短句交替，短句如"Maybe a storm is coming""Who would it be?"；长句如"But when I was drawing the curtain, a lightning flashed through the air, lighting up almost everything in my room"；倒装句"Out of the window, a man was staring at me with a nasty grin"等细节都能烘托环境和反映人物的心理活动。语言上还有一些语法（如 decide, want 应为过去式）、大小写方面的小错误。语意的表达有不够清楚的地方，如 "only to find nothing was strange"。有些句子之间的承接不够顺畅。

第二稿：斜线体部分为第二稿的修改。

> *In the evening,* I suspected that there must be someone hiding *somewhere.* I had this feeling for many days. The wind was blowing violently with the roar of thunder and lighting. Maybe a rainstorm is coming.
>
> I gazed at the message I had received one hour ago: "See you at 10 pm." ~~But It was already 11 o'clock and I didn't know who sent it.~~ *But even at* 11 *o'clock, this guy didn't show up and I had no idea of who he/she was. After breaking up with my boyfriend, I had been living alone in this apartment for a long time.* Who would it be?
>
> A power failure plunged the whole house into a ~~sudden~~ *total* darkness. ~~I felt someone was staring at me. Suddenly, I heard a sound of dripping water.~~ *Simultaneously, I heard a sound of dripping water.* It was clear and continuous, in the same rhythm of the sound of ticking. ~~But~~ *However,* it hadn't rained yet. ~~A feeling that there was someone else somewhere arose in my heart.~~ *It suddenly occurred to me that the sound of dripping water may be the sound of steps.* A cold sweat broke out on the back of my neck. *There must be someone else hidden in my house! Trembling, I forced myself to search* ~~I searched~~ every corner in every room, only to find nothing *abnormal* ~~was strange. I realized that the sound of dripping water was just like the sound of steps.~~
>
> Without taking a bath, I returned to my bedroom ~~and decide to go to bed.~~ *The only thing I want to do was to be wrapped with my quilt, pretending*

> nothing happened and got over tonight now. But when I was drawing the curtain, a lightning flashed through the air, lighting up almost everything in my room. Out of the window, a man was staring at me with a nasty grin.
>
> ~~The rain began to fell.~~ *The rain was lashing down.* With another lighting, the last thing I could see was that the clock on the wall read 10:00—*just as that mysterious message indicated.* ~~The same as the mysterious message.~~

第二稿修改的重点是对细节的描写和对环境的进一步渲染。句与句之间的转承更为流畅。第一句话调整了语序，将原来的"I had had this feeling for many days, and in the storm evening, I suspected that there must be someone hiding somewhere"修改成"In the evening, I suspected that there must be someone hiding somewhere. I had had this feeling for many days"，调整后的句意更清楚、简洁，也更符合英文的思维习惯。同样地，后文中把原句"A feeling that there was someone else somewhere arose in my heart"修改成"It suddenly occurred to me that the sound of dripping water may be the sound of steps"。句子调整以后，紧张感骤升！第二段中增加的"this guy didn't show up"，实现了上下文更好地过渡。第三段删除了"I felt someone was staring at me"。因为这句跟结尾设置的一个悬念相似，提前出现在这里淡化了故事结尾的冲突感。写作课上强调过叙事性写作不要"reveal the end too soon"，所以修改时删掉这一句是一个很好的反馈。其他如增加"trembling""forced"，加强了人物的心理状态描写；第四段加破折号，用长句表达人物的心情等，都是对第一稿的润色。

第三稿：下划线部分为第三稿的修改。

> In the evening, I suspected that there must be someone hiding somewhere. To tell you the truth, I had this feeling for many days. ~~The wind was blowing violently with the roar of thunder and lighting.~~ <u>The gales roaring, the thunder growling, the lightning flashing outside</u>, maybe a rainstorm was coming.
>
> <u>Time lapsed. Frightened and puzzled</u>, I gazed at the message I had received one hour ago: "See you at 10 pm." But it was already 11 o'clock now. However, <u>nobody showed up</u>. ~~I didn't know who sent it.~~ After breaking up with my boyfriend, I had been living alone in this apartment for a long time. Who would it be?

A power failure plunged the whole house into total darkness. Simultaneously, I heard a sound of dripping water. It was clear and continuous, in the same rhythm of the ticking clock. <u>Nevertheless</u>, it hadn't <u>begun to</u> rain outside. It suddenly occurred to me that the sound of dripping water ~~may~~ could be the sound of steps. A cold sweat broke out on the back of my neck. There must be someone else hidden in my house! Trembling, <u>I took a deep breath</u>, ~~forced myself~~ struggled to search every corner in every room only to find ~~nothing abnormal~~ <u>no one was here</u>.

~~Without taking a bath~~ <u>Not in the mood to take a bath</u>, I returned to my bedroom—the only thing I wante<u>d</u> to do was to <u>wrap myself with quilt</u> ~~be wrapped with my quilt,~~ pretending nothing happened and got over tonight now.

"God bless me," I prayed as I walked towards the windows to draw the curtain. ~~But when I was drawing the curtain~~ <u>The moment I touched the curtain</u>, a lightning flashed through the air, ~~lighting up almost everything in my room~~ <u>and lit up the room as bright as day</u>. Out of the window, a man was staring at me with a <u>creepy</u> ~~nasty~~ grin.

<u>The rain started to lash down.</u> ~~The rain was lashing down.~~ With another lighting, ~~the last thing I could see was that the clock on the wall read 10:00—just as that mysterious message indicated~~ <u>I caught a glimpse of the clock. It read 10:00</u>.

  第三稿的修改幅度不大,主要还是完善细节上的描写,让句子意思更清楚。增加了一些短句和动词的用法,如用了三个动词和排比句式来描述屋外暴风雨欲来的场景"The gales roaring, the thunder growling, the lightning flashing";看匿名短信时增加了动词描述"frightened and puzzled";描述颤抖着去查看房间角落时增加了"I took a deep breath""struggled";把"be wrapped with my quilt"换成主动语态"to wrap myself with quilt";以及最后结尾处换成两个短句"I caught a glimpse of the clock""It read 10:00";等等。在叙事性文体中长短句交替使用,使长句之后的短句更有力量和冲击感。第四段增加"Not in the mood to take a bath",更好地承接上下文。此外,第一稿中"only to find nothing was strange"表达的问题,后面的二稿、三稿反馈者显然都看到了,第二稿改成"only to find nothing abnormal",第三稿改成"only to find no one was here"。这里第三稿的意思传达得最清楚。

定稿:提交给教师,听取教师反馈(略)。

教师进行了反馈和总体性评价,肯定文章的成功之处并提出了几点修改建议。

①"I had this feeling"和第一稿里的"I had had this feeling",哪个更准确?②前文说已经 11 点了,没人出现,后文中的钟(哪里的钟?墙上?位置应该说清楚)显示又是 10 点,怎么回事呢?③停电了,屋里一片漆黑,女主去查看房间时怎么看得见的?

终稿:教师反馈后修改,确定最终稿。教师与其他终稿一起,在班级进行总体反馈、点评。(斜体为接收教师反馈后修改的句子,第一段为直接纠错,其他部分学生修改)

In the evening, I suspected that there must be someone hiding somewhere. To tell you the truth, I *had* had this feeling for many days. *Outside* the gales were roaring, the thunder growling, the lightning flashing. ~~Maybe~~ A rainstorm was ~~coming~~ *on its way*.

Time lapsed. Frightened and puzzled, I gazed at the message I had received one hour ago: "See you at 10 pm." It was already 11 o'clock now. However, nobody showed up. After breaking up with my boyfriend, I had been living alone in this apartment for a long time. Who would it be?

A power failure plunged the whole house into total darkness. Simultaneously, I heard a sound of dripping water. It was clear and continuous, in the same rhythm of the ticking clock. Nevertheless, it hadn't begun to rain outside. It suddenly occurred to me that the sound of dripping water could be the sound of steps. A cold sweat broke out on the back of my neck. There must be someone else hidden in my house! ~~Trembling~~, I took a deep breath, *with a flashlight in my shaking hands*, struggled to search every corner in every room, only to find no one was here.

Not in the mood to take a bath, I returned to my bedroom—the only thing I wanted to do was to wrap myself with quilt, pretending nothing happened and got over tonight.

> "God bless me," I prayed as I walked towards the windows to draw the curtain. The moment I touched the curtain, a lightning flashed through the air and lit up the room as bright as day. Out of the window, a man was staring at me with a creepy grin.
>
> The rain started to lash down. With another lighting, I caught a glimpse of the clock *on the wall*. It read 10:00.

关于钟的时间,学生解释后,教师认同,因此没有修改。因为故事是带有悬疑惊悚性质的,之前时间已经 11 点,结尾时墙上的钟显示 10 点,跟匿名短信"10 点见"呼应,为什么墙上的钟的时间停在 10 点,这其中的原因,可以留给读者更多的思考空间。

2. 在线反馈 + 教师反馈

在线反馈以句酷批改网为平台,教师发布写作任务和要求,学生在截止日期前提交作文。教师在系统进行反馈后,进行人工批改,再反馈给学生。因为实施在线反馈和教师反馈的时候,自动写作评改系统的互评和群批功能还不是十分完善,比如,不能设置在截止日期后修改,因此同伴反馈的方式没有融合进来。

因为在线反馈的即时性,学生提交作文以后系统在数秒之内就能打分并给出反馈建议,所以学生把作文提交到批改网后,会根据修改建议进行"修改—提交—反馈—再修改—再提交—再反馈—再修改"这样的数次循环,少则数次,多则几十次甚至上百次。即时批改,促使学习者反复修改也是在线反馈系统的最大优势之一。下面以一位同学(以下简称 F 同学)的在线反馈和教师反馈为例。因为前文中就在线反馈已做过详细阐述,所以本部分只是简要概述"在线反馈 + 教师反馈"相结合的多稿评改混合反馈。

- 多稿混合评改实例 1:

作文题目为 What is happiness?(作文③)。从图 6.28 可以看出,F 同学一共在线提交了 20 稿,从第一稿的 72 分一直到最后一稿的 83.5 分,教师反馈后再修改,最终教师评分 87 分。我们这里选取其中 3 个版本,从细节上来分析根据在线反馈进行多稿修改的特点。

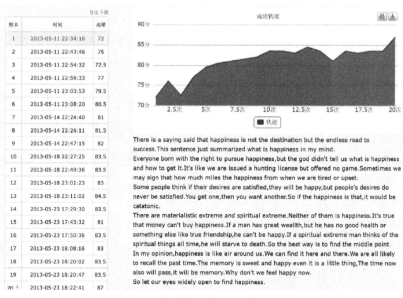

图 6.28　F 同学作文修改和成绩轨迹图

第一稿：系统打分 72 分。

　　There is a saying said that happiness is not the destination but the endless road to success. This sentence just summarized what is happiness in my mind.

　　Everyone born with the right to pursue happiness, but the god didn't tell us what is happiness and how to get it. It's like we are issued a hunting license but offered no game. Sometimes we may sign that how much miles the happiness from when we are tired or upset.

　　Some people think if their desires are satisfied, they will be happy, but people's desires do never be satisfied. You get one, then you want another. So if the happiness is that, it would be catatonic.

　　There are materialistic extreme and spiritual extreme. Neither of them is happiness. It's true that money can't buy happiness. If a man has great weallth, but he has no good health or something else like true friendship, he can't be happy. If a spiritual extreme man thinks of the spiritual things all time, he will starve to death. So the best way is to find the middle point.

> In my opinion, happiness is like air around us. We can find it here and there. We are all likely to recall the past time. The memory is sweet and happy even it is a little thing. The time now also will pass, it will be memory. Why don't we feel happy now?
> So let our eyes widely open to find happiness.

在线反馈系统给出的评语:文章词汇表达多样,请继续保持,也能较准确地使用高级词汇,采用了简单的衔接手法,行文流畅;从句数量偏少,且文中有几处句子错误。

系统的"按句点评"功能给出了具体的修改建议和提示,以第一段为例(学习提示等不包括在内)。

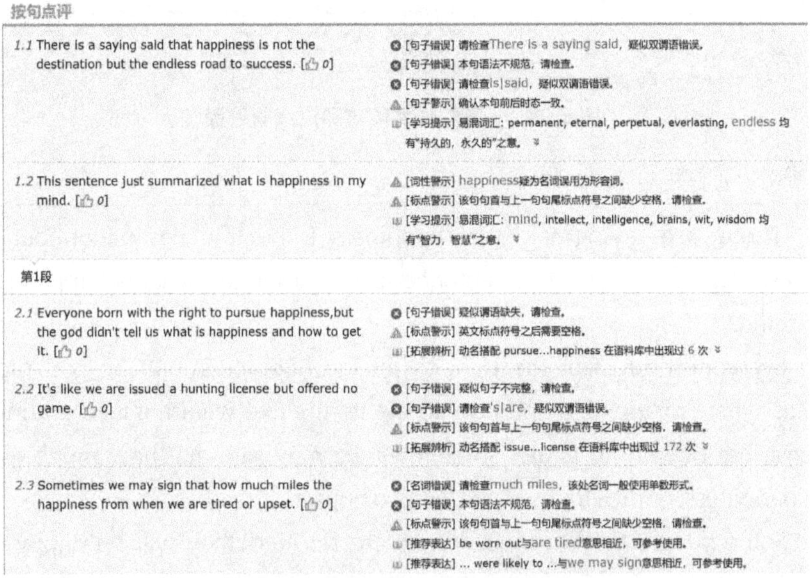

图 6.39　在线系统第一、二段批改反馈示意图

第一段系统共提示 6 处错误:3 处句子错误、1 处句子警示(语法)、1 次词性警示、1 次标点警示。除了词性警示属于误判,其他几处均属有效的修改提示。第二段提示句子错误 4 处、标点警示 3 处、名词错误 1 处。其中有 2 处的句子错误属于误判:"It's like we are issued a hunting license but offered no game"一句来自课文内容转写,系统判为"疑似句子不完整,请检查","请检查's|are,疑似双谓语错误"。值得注意的是,笔者在实践中发现,几乎所有学生都会被警示标点用法有误。可能因为不习惯电脑写作,标点符号后不留空格。

而且在修改时大部分学生关注点在其他错误上,如拼写、语法等。

第十三稿:系统打分 84.5,也是打分最高的一稿,文中下划线为写作者新增。

> As a saying goes that happiness is not the destination but the long road to success, which just summarizes the happiness in my mind.
>
> Everyone wants to be happy and everyone was born with the right to pursue happiness, but such was the social condition that we weren't told what is happiness and how to get it. It's just like we are issued the hunting license but offered ~~no game. To make things worse, sometimes~~ game. <u>So much so that sometimes</u> we may complain that how far the happiness is from us when we are tired or upset.
>
> In some people's ~~point of view, they~~ opinion, <u>they</u> will be happy ~~with~~ <u>when</u> their desires are well satisfied, but as we all know that people's desires do never be satisfied thoroughly. What's more, if the desires just are for their own, even they get the ~~so-called~~ happiness, yet it is catatonic and not real.
>
> There are materialistic extreme and spiritual extreme, neither of which is happiness, and it's universally acknowledged that money can't purchase everything. For example, if a man possesses great wealth but without health or true friendship or something else, he can't be happy. ~~On the other hand~~ <u>In addition</u>, if a man ~~doesn't care~~ cares about materials <u>not</u> at all, he would starve to death. Consequently, the best way to find the happiness, to some degree, is to find the middle point.
>
> From my ~~opinion, happiness~~ point of view, happiness is so much like the air around ~~us that~~ us, <u>which</u> can be felt here and there. As human beings, we are all likely to find happiness <u>when we</u> recall the past ~~sweet~~ time. However, don't forget that the present time is bond to be a memory. ~~So~~ Why don't we be happy now?
>
> In conclusion, let our eyes wide open to find out real happiness.

第十三稿的在线反馈评语:语句间的衔接成分用得不错,同时文章中的过程性词汇很丰富;作者在句法层面做得很棒;作者词汇基本功很好,高级词汇表达也比较恰当。

这一版系统的"按句点评"具体建议,主要是标点警示(15 处),另外 1 处句子错误提示,1 处词性警示。除了标点符号警示正确,句子错误和词性警示两处反馈都属于误判。如下:

From my point of view, happiness is so much like the air around us, which can be felt here and there. [句子错误] 动词 felt 一般不用作被动式。

However, don't forget that the present time is bond to be a memory.

[词性警示] bond 疑为名词误用为形容词。

第二十稿:作者最后一版修改稿,系统打分 83.5 分,比第十三稿还要低一分。

> As a saying goes that we have no right to pursue happiness without producing it than we have no right to consume wealth without producing it, which just summarizes what is happiness in my mind.
>
> All people want to be happy and everyone was born with the right to pursue happiness. However, we were not told what is happiness and how to get it. It's just like we are issued the hunting license but offered no game. So much so that sometimes we may grumble complain that happiness is out of touch.
>
> In some people's opinions, they will be happy when their desires are well satisfied, but as we all know that people's desires do never be satisfied thoroughly. What's more, if the desires just are for their own, even they get the happiness, yet it is catatonic and not real.
>
> From my point of view, happiness depends on ourselves. When we feel tired, we can choose to listen to music for relaxation; when someone need to be helped, we can give our favor; when we go back home, we can buy some gifts with our pocket money, then the happiness belongs to us. That is to say, happiness needs to be created by ourselves.
>
> All in all, happiness is so much like the air around us, which can be felt here and there. Besides, whether happy or not depends on ourselves. Happiness is also like the beautiful butterfly. When you try to chase it, it may fly farther and farther away, while when you stop to enjoy the life, it may stop in your shoulder quietly.
>
> In conclusion, let our eyes wide open to find out real happiness and smile to yourself.

这一稿跟上一稿比,修改的地方很少,只有一个单词的修改,把"grumble"改成"complain"。"按句点评"里,系统给出的建议有词性警示 1 条、句子错误 3 条、标点警示 9 条(看来所有的标点提示错误都被学生无视了)。词性警示为误判,句子错误 3 条里有 1 条为误判。

教师反馈基于最后一稿进行,大部分都是纠错性反馈。教师人工批改后评分 87 分,教师评语如下:In spite of some mistakes, you have produced some beautiful sentences here! Please pay more attention to the use of punctuation marks, and use space key wherever necessary。

表6.9　第20稿教师反馈(F同学)

原　句	教师反馈
As a saying goes that we have no right to pursue happiness without producing it than we have no right to consume wealth without producing it, which just summarizes what is happiness in my mind.	than?
However, we were not told what is happiness and how to get it.	about the idea of happiness
… but as we all know that people's desires do never be satisfied thoroughly.	are
What's more, if the desires just are for their own, even they get the happiness, yet it is catatonic and not real.	the happiness is catatonic and not real even though they get it
just are for their own	are just for their own
when someone need to be helped …	needs
give our favor	do them a favor
That is to say happiness need to be created by ourselves.	needs
When you try to chase it, it may fly farther and farther away, while when you stop to enjoy the life, it may stop in your shoulder quietly.	Beautiful!
In conclusion, let our eyes wide open to find out real happiness and smile to yourself.	let's keep our eyes wide open

在多次系统"在线反馈+1次性教师反馈"的模式中,学生通过每一次作文"提交—在线反馈—修改—提交—在线反馈"的循环,能最大限度地修改语言上的错误,提升语言表达精准度。在系统多达 20 次的反馈建议和修改后,教师人

工批改时基本上已经不需要修改表层的语言错误(如拼写、简单的语法错误等),可以把精力集中在思想内容、句法、语篇结构等宏观维度上。同时,因为在线反馈的一些局限性,教师的人工反馈可以纠正系统误判,更全面地评判作文,弥补在线反馈的不足。

- 多稿混合评改实例2:本篇作文写作题目是"My opinion on intellectual dishonesty"(作文③),作者 H 同学(H 同学的语言水平和写作能力在班级名列前茅),共修改、提交了14次。第1次提交系统打分82分,修改到第7次打分86分。第8次教师人工批改后改为90分。此后作者根据教师反馈继续6次修改,但系统的打分始终低于90分。有趣的是,在笔者选取该篇作文作为实例,提取数据进行分析时(2018年),系统重新打分后的分数大大高出该作文提交时候的分数(2011年11月),其他作文也有类似现象。

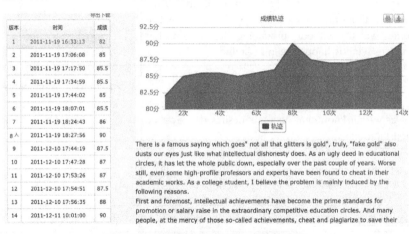

图6.30 H 同学作文修改和成绩轨迹图

表6.10 批改网在线反馈同一篇作文两次打分

修改版本	时间	成绩	时间	成绩
1	2011-11-19 16:33:13	82	2018-08-02	90.5
2	2011-11-19 17:06:08	85	2018-08-02	92.5
3	2011-11-19 17:17:50	85.5	2018-08-02	92.5
4	2011-11-19 17:34:59	85.5	2018-08-02	92
5	2011-11-19 17:44:02	85	2018-08-02	92
6	2011-11-19 18:07:01	85.5	2018-08-02	92
7	2011-11-19 18:24:43	86	2018-08-02	92

（续表）

修改版本	时间	成绩	时间	成绩
8（人工）	2011-11-19 18：27：56	90	2018-08-02	92
9	2011-12-10 17：44：19	87.5	2018-08-02	92.5
10	2011-12-10 17：47：28	87	2018-08-02	92.5
11	2011-12-10 17：53：26	87	2018-08-02	92.5
12	2011-12-10 17：54：51	87.5	2018-08-02	92.5
13	2011-12-10 17：56：35	88	2018-08-02	92
14（人工）	2011-12-11 10：01：00	90	2018-08-02	/*

*注：系统在最后一次人工批阅后，成绩以人工批阅成绩为准，不做变动。

图 6.31 在线反馈评语：语句间的衔接成分用得不错，同时文章中的过程性词汇很丰富；作者句法基本功不错，可适当增加从句的使用；作者词汇基础扎实，拼写也很棒。

图 6.31 H 同学第 9 次修改版——在线反馈打分（2018 年 8 月）

作为一篇高质量的学生习作，在第一次提交系统后，在线反馈的"按句点评"给出的修改建议不多：1 个名词错误、1 个词性警示、1 个搭配警示、1 个名词警示、1 个动词错误、1 个冠词警示。而除了 1 个词性警示，其他都属于误判。

第八稿：教师对此版做出人工批阅。

There is a famous saying which goes "not all that glitters is gold", "fake gold" also ~~hoodwinks~~ bamboozles people just like what intellectual dishonesty does. As a scandal in educational circles, not only has it impaired the original author's right, but also disappointed the whole public, especially over the past couple of years. Worse still, even some high-profile professors and experts have been found to cheat in their academic papers. As a college student, I contend that the problem is mainly induced by the following reasons.

First and foremost, intellectual achievements have become the fundamental standards for promotion or salary raise in the increasingly fierce intellectual competition. Meanwhile, many people, at the mercy of the so-called fame, cheat and plagiarize to pursue a higher title of a technical post, and on account of which, a dilemma between bettering lives or losing all the reputation they've painstakingly earned has been brought about. From another perspective, the current penalties are still too tolerant. And as a consequence, the high return and the low risk have been an invitation to intellectual dishonesty and with masses of people following suit, the phenomenon has become much more severe.

In summary, this has reflected the decline of our traditional virtue "calling a spade a spade". Therefore, public awareness of the detriment of such behavior should be raised and inspections over intellectual dishonesty should be enforced. Particularly, corresponding punishments must be undertaken to prevent cheating from happening. Anyway, we should always be down-to-earth and remember that honesty is a must, and without it, we may end up paying much more.

教师反馈: You understand the title perfectly and there is a great variety in both vocabulary and sentence structure. The linking devices are mostly well used. Except for a few minor mistakes, this is a beautiful work.

表 6.11　第八稿教师反馈（H 同学）

原　句	教师反馈
Worse still, even some high-profile professors and experts have been found to cheat in their academic papers.	时态：to have cheated …
From another perspective, the current penalties are still too tolerant.	搭配：penalties … tolerant?
In summary, this has reflected the decline of our traditional virtue "calling a spade a spade".	calling a spade a spade：此处用法不妥，可删。

教师反馈后，H 同学又根据教师反馈做进一步修改（6 次），继续丰富词汇和句子结构，完善文章逻辑和条理。最后一稿在线反馈只有一个修改提示：[名词错误] glitters 为不可数名词，一般无复数形式。跟第一稿的提示一样，属于误判。

第十四稿：最终版，教师将此最终版作为范文推荐给全班同学。

> There is a thought-provoking saying which goes "not all that glitters is gold". "Fake gold" also bamboozles people just like what intellectual dishonesty does. As a scandal in educational circles, not only has it impaired the original author's right, but also disappointed the whole public, especially over the past couple of years. Worse still, even some high-profile professors and experts have been disclosed to have cheated in their academic papers. As a college student, I contend that the problem is mainly induced by the following reasons.
>
> First and foremost, intellectual achievements have become the fundamental standards for promotion or salary raise in the increasingly fierce intellectual competition. Meanwhile, many people, at the mercy of the so-called ~~fame~~, prestige, cheat and plagiarize to pursue a higher title of a technical post, and on account of which, a dilemma between bettering lives or losing all the reputation they've painstakingly earned has been brought about. From another perspective, the lax enforcement and light penalties are incredibly predominant in the current society. And as a consequence, the high return and the low risk have been an invitation to intellectual dishonesty and with masses of people following suit, the phenomenon has become much more severe.

> In summary, this has comprehensively reflected the decline of our traditional virtue. Hence, public awareness of the detriment of such behavior should be raised and inspections over intellectual dishonesty should be enforced. Particularly, corresponding punishments must be undertaken to prevent cheating from happening. Anyway, we should always be down-to-earth and remember that honesty is a must, and without it, we may end up paying much more.

大数据时代赋予了写作教师和写作者更为丰富的内涵,也使得多稿评改混合反馈模式成为可能。教师和学生都被赋予了多元角色,教师从传统评价反馈的权威角色转变为多元反馈环节的一环,成为活动指导者、读者、协助者、评议者和反馈者;学生也不再只是单一的写作者,同时也是读者、评议者、反馈者和互动合作者。学生处在教学和学习活动的中心,可以更充分地了解自己的写作过程,发挥主观能动性,在反馈基础上思考并提高书面表达的思想性、准确度和流利度。"在线反馈+同伴反馈+教师反馈"的混合多元评价体系,融合师生互动、生生互动,结合线上线下、内部反馈和外部反馈,促使多个阶段协同合作,全方面促进学习者英语写作能力的提升和语言能力的发展。

第七章 大数据时代英语写作的课程设计

科技的进步、互联网的发展使人类进入了一个信息化的大数据时代。课堂教学与信息科技的结合成为一种不可回避的趋势。英语写作教学也经历了从传统课堂的一本书、一支粉笔,到多媒体教学,再到科技化、信息化的翻转课堂。课堂不再是以教师为中心的"一言堂",学生也不再只是知识的被动接收者。教师角色和学生角色都发生了变化。《大学英语教学指南》在英语写作能力培养、学生自主学习能力培养等方面也提出了较高的要求,指出把现代信息技术运用到大学英语写作教学中具有重要的意义。新型的英语写作课程设计,能够为如何解决传统课堂教学中出现的问题、优化大学英语写作教学提供参考。课程设计的终极目标,还是为了培养学生的思辨能力,切实提升他们的写作能力。

第一节 写作课程设计理论基础

一、建构主义学习理论(Constructivism)

建构主义学习理论是 Piaget 于 19 世纪 60 年代提出的,随着多媒体和网络技术的飞速发展,建构主义学习理论也显示出其越来越强大的生命力。建构主义关于学习的观点有以下几个方面:①建构主义认为人的学习是学习者自我构建知识体系的过程。学习不是由教师向学生传递知识,而是学习者通过自己的知识背景和体验,将外部环境的信息纳入自己已有的知识结构当中,不断丰富、适应、主动建构知识的过程。建构主义学习理论突出了人在学习中的主体位置,为自主学习方式的实行提供了理论依据。②建构主义学习理论强调环境的重要性。也就是说,学习是具有社会性和情境性的,学习者的主观世界是和社会环境相互联系和作用的。学习的目的是为了达到与外部环境的平衡。当知识的建构发生在课堂中时,教师和学生即构成外部学习环境,学习者的认知结构需要在教师和同学的帮助下才能得以完成重构(黄慧、王海,2007),学习过程是一个双向建构的过程。建构一方面是对新信息的意义建构,将外部环境新的信息纳入已有的知识体系并完成超越;另一方面是对原来知识体系的改造和重组。

二、输入理论与输出假说(Input Hypothesis & Output Hypothesis)

Krashen 提出的输入理论认为语言习得可以通过接触可理解性输入(comprehensible input)来实现。他用"i+1"的公式来定义输入理论,学习者当前已有的语言知识或能力水平为"i","i+1"代表学习者通过接触适合自己能力水平的语言输入来达到的更高层次。这个"1"包括学习者听到或看到的能够理解的语言材料。这些语言材料的难度要略高于学习者已有的知识体系,但是又不会超出他们的理解范围。Krashen 的输入理论强调语言的习得是学习者接触到足够的语言材料后自然发生的,而不是通过教师讲解获得,语言输出只表明语言习得已经发生但是不能促进语言习得(Krashen,1989)。输入理论带给英语教学的启示就是教学应该以学生为中心,为学生创造学习语言的环境,让学生自己发现语言的规则。

Swain(1993)基于"沉浸式教学"的实验发现,仅仅有可理解性输入还不足以保证二语学习的成功,还需要"可理解性输出",并提出了输出假说(Output Hypothesis),强调语言输出在二语习得过程中的重要作用。在 Swain 的实验中,学生经过几年浸入式的语言学习,获得了足够的语言输入,却没有获得本族语者类似的语言产出能力。原因就在于语言输出活动不足,学生没有足够的机会输出语言。而英语写作作为一项重要的语言输出方式,学生在用语言表达自己的想法时,通过内部、外部反馈的共同作用,会意识到自身的语言不足以精准、有效地传达自己的观点,从而提高学习者自我反思能力和语言学习的主动性(Schwind & Siegel,1994)。

三、互动假说理论(Interaciton Hypothesis)

Long 在 20 世纪 80 年代初提出了互动假说理论,并在 90 年代中后期进行了更新。Long(1996)吸收了 Swain 的输出假说,认为意义协商是指通过可理解性输入,连接学习者大脑机能,尤其是选择性注意及输出来促进语言习得。以意义协商为形式的这种言语互动能够修正并调整互动结构,使语言输入可理解,从而促进语言发展。更新后的互动假说更好地体现了对语言学习认知复杂性的认识,为语言课堂中的结对和小组活动提供了依据和支持。

四、英语写作教学法

国外英语写作教学法经历了半个多世纪的发展,比较有代表性的有20世纪60年代前后的"结果教学法"、20世纪70年代的"过程教学法"、20世纪80年代的"体裁教学法"和"任务教学法",以及20世纪80年代中期开始的"内容教学法"。

结果教学法(又译作成果教学法)强调语言习得是"刺激—反应—巩固加强"的过程。结果教学法的典型模式:教师课堂讲解写作理论—分析范文—学生模仿写作—教师批改习作—讲评习作。写作教师在课堂上处于主导地位,学生被动吸收;写作教师关注学生的写作成果,通过评改、反馈、纠错来提升学生写作能力。结果教学法的英语写作教与学是单向的。

与此相反,过程教学法把语言学习看作复杂的心理认知和语言交际活动,以学生为主体,强调多稿多改的写作过程和师生互动、生生互动。过程教学法把写作过程分为四个阶段:写前准备、草稿、修改、编辑。每一个阶段都可以回到上一个阶段或第一个阶段。写作是一个循环的多稿写作、同伴互评和教师反馈的多向过程。

体裁教学法的重点是分析文本和模仿范文的体裁特征,引导学生掌握不同体裁的语篇所具有的不同交际目的和篇章结构,帮助学生完成某一体裁的撰写(秦秀白,2000)。体裁教学法比较适合学术论文写作或应用型的写作教学。

内容教学法通常以不同专题内容来组织教学,帮助学生在写作过程中拓展和深入了解专门的知识领域。内容教学法认为教学目标具有双重性,学习者既要掌握专业内容知识,又要尽力提高语言能力(常俊跃、赵永青,2010)。内容教学法对教师的知识体系要求较高。

任务教学法让学生参与以意义为中心的语言使用活动,强调语言学习的社会性和交互性。任务教学法分为任务前阶段、任务循环阶段、语言聚焦阶段。教学步骤包括集思广益、收集素材、写出报告、分析反馈语言等。任务教学法得以成功实施的条件是创造师生互动、生生互动及学生与社会之间的互动交流环境。

国内外学者们对不同教学法各自存在的不足也进行了研究和对比,达成共识:结果教学法评估方法单一,反馈结构滞后,学生只关心结果(写作的分数),同类错误频发;过程教学法对写作的流程和时间长度需求较高;体裁法的范文分析容易使写作课堂枯燥乏味,学生缺乏兴趣,写作同质化严重;内容教学法对语言水平低、已有的知识体系不完善的学生挑战大,对写作教师的知识结构要求高;任务教学法对于教师来说难以把握写作技能训练的系统性等(徐昉,2012)。

显然,没有哪一种写作教学法可以不加融合或改变就直接拿来用。国内学者们结合多年的英语写作教学和理论实践,从自己教学对象和教学环境的实际情况出发,提出了适用于自身的英语写作教学法。比如,清华大学杨永林教授所带领的体验英语教学团队,以 TRP 为依托,进行体验英语写作教学。同样基于该系统进行写作改革的,还有北京科技大学的数字化英语写作实验课程。团队充分利用 TRP 的特点,把信息技术和英语写作课程进行深层次融合,构建数字化英语写作教学模式(陈娟文、王娜,2016)。广州外语外贸大学的王初明教授提出和实践的"以写促学"的"写长法",旨在改变传统的英语写作教授方式,通过加大英语的书面运用量,有效地释放学习潜力,让学生写长作文带动其写作能力和英语水平的全面提高。2002 年,团队又对"写长法"教学进行改进和完善,给学生提供写前阅读输入,布置与阅读相关的写作任务,实践"以读促写""以写促学""由长到精"的英语写作理念。

第二节 写作课程教学目标的重新定位

英语写作课程作为英语专业的一门主干课程,对学生的英语学习能力具有十分重要的作用和影响。大数据时代的写作课程目标,也应该兼顾专业基础知识和实用写作技能,并与数字化、信息化的时代特点紧密结合,促进学生综合素养的提升。新型的英语写作课程设计,建立在建构主义学习理论、输入理论、输出假说和互动假说理论基础上,强调以学习者为中心,教学和写作过程中师生互动、生生互动。立足大数据背景,写作课程的教学目标从内容到形式都需要重新定位。

一、新型读写能力

写作是一项基本的语言技能,是语言输出的一种重要形式。但事实上,读写常常是一起出现的。特别是在大数据时代，人们每天都在日常生活中接触到海量信息，无论是传统的纸质阅读，还是新型的电子阅读；无论是文字、图像、音频还是视频。读写能力已经跳出了印刷媒介时代，它的涵义不仅只是理解语言文字的能力，更是对文字以外的声音、图像、色彩、空间等多模态信息的查找、甄别、选择、阅读、理解、加工、编辑的综合能力（陈庆斌，2016）。新型读写能力是传统读写能力的"i+1"，包含但又超越传统读写能力，具有多重性和变化性。也就是说，传统的写作课程教学目标是帮助学生掌握英语写作的基础知识和技巧，提高英语写作能力。而新型读写能力在此基础上，还包括熟练使用计算机进行文字输入和排版、利用搜索引擎查找所需信息、分析并整合信息资源、使用各种移动客户端和平台进行思想交流等能力。

二、写作评价与反馈的能力

一方面，传统的写作课程，评价和反馈都是以教师为中心进行的单向行为。学生作为被动的接收方，面对教师费时费力批改出来的作文却并不领情，只关注分数，把作文束之高阁的学生也为数不少。另一方面，教师是传统意义上的知识传授者和权威，学生不认为自己具有评价作文的能力。新型的写作课程设计以学生为中心，借助自动写作评改系统的在线反馈，把学生互评、在线反馈与教师反馈结合起来，学生不仅仅只是写作者，更是读者、评价者和反馈者。教师引导的互评反馈，在促进学生写作能力提升的同时，培养学生对文本的鉴赏能力、分析和解决问题的能力、如何进行有效评价反馈的能力，从而最终促成学生批判思维能力的养成。

三、自主学习的能力

大数据时代，英语写作的教学和学习内容不再局限于课堂，还延伸到了课堂外的网络空间和外部学习环境。海量网络资源和庞大的数据库、自动写作评改系统、在线学习网站、优质的数字化课程视频等为写作提供了新的方法和途径。打破区域界限的协作写作、随时随地学习的移动写作也为实现个性化自主学习提供了多种选择。通过在线写作课程的学习和网络技术，能够有效开展基于网络的读、写活动，并在写作智能平台实现师生、生生互动，使学生获得必要的写作指导和帮助。在新的教学环境下，教师指导学生通过自主学习获得数据和进行分析，寻求最符合自身需求的写作方法和手段。而这种以学习者为中心的教学和学习模式，也使得教师可以利用大数据分析，了解学生对网络课程的学习和在线反馈使用等情况,进而明确学生多样化的学习需求,并以此为根据"量身定做",设计更适合学习者需要的教学活动,为个性化的自主学习提供指导和帮助,从而提升学习者的写作能力,最终达成自主学习能力的最优化。

第三节 英语写作课程设计示例

笔者从个人的写作教学实践和经验出发,结合各种写作教学理论研究,尝试性进行新型写作课程的设计,以期为写作教学同人和研究者提供一些参考和启示。

无论是基于怎样的理论基础,采取何种英语写作教学法,写作课堂教学的步骤并不神秘,脱离不了写前、写作、评价与反馈几个基本阶段。每阶段强调的重点可以有不同,过程可以循环反复。

本课程的设计总体分为写前、写作教学和写作过程、写后三个大的阶段。

本课的写作教学内容是篇章写作,体裁是说明文,教学时间是写作课程的第二学期。教学课时和具体内容如下:

教学内容:Exposition development by process analysis。

教学课时:2课时(90分钟)。

教学方式:网络资源运用+多媒体授课+师生互动+过程写作+同伴反馈+教师反馈。

教学目标:

(1) 掌握 process analysis 类说明文的写作方式和技巧;

(2) 把 process analysis 写作技巧熟练运用于各种步骤、方法、流程类说明文体;

(3) 完成一篇说明文(developed by process analysis);

(4) 对同伴作文的评改和反馈;

(5) 了解折叠纸鹤的步骤,以及成功完成折纸。

教学重点:process analysis 类说明文的写作方法和技巧。

一、写前

教师在本次写作课前,提前2天通过班级 QQ 群发给学生如何折叠纸鹤的视频(图7.1,视频只有音乐背景,无中文或英文讲解)。要求学生观看视频后,把折纸的大概步骤用英语写出来,对词数和语言准确度等不做要求。观看视频后,鼓励以小组形式进行讨论和分析,确定步骤。最后以小组为单位写一份纸鹤折叠的大致流程。对预写过程中不熟悉的专业词汇或表达,鼓励学生查询网络或使用语料库。

教师同时按学生人数准备用于折纸的彩色纸张,写作课堂备用。

图7.1　写前视频——*How to Make an Origami Crane*(视频来源:网络)

二、写作教学和写作过程

写作课堂中,教师用一个课时(45分钟)的时间讲解 process analysis 类说明文的定义、写作方法、写作技巧、范文示例、注意事项等。教学内容大纲如下(图7.2)。

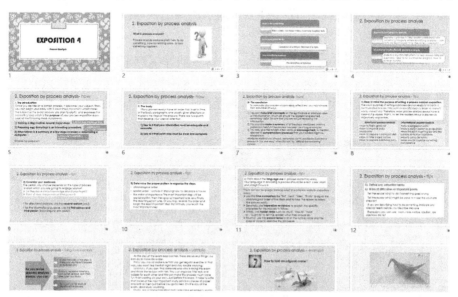

图7.2　写作教学内容 PPT 截图(部分)

（1）What is process analysis?

（2）How to develop an exposition by process analysis?

（3）Exposition by process analysis—tips.

（4）Exposition by process analysis—things to remember.

（5）Exposition by process analysis—example.

（6）Exposition by process analysis—practice.

（7）Exposition by process analysis—assignment.

第二个课时进入写作过程。在这个过程里师生、生生进行充分互动,通过课堂讨论、问答等交互方式,共同完成写作。

教师先请学生拿出课前观看视频后写出的纸鹤折叠过程英文稿。问学生问题:Is this a directional process analysis, or an informational process analysis? 请几位学生回答。如果有不同意见,让学生进行讨论后,教师给出答案:A directional process analysis。

教师选择几组学生的预写作文在班级分享,问:Can we make an origami crane following this/that process? 因为只要求学生写出大概的而不是详细的纸鹤折叠步骤,学生大多只给出 5~6 个步骤。所以除了原来会叠的同学,按照这个写出的步骤是很难完成纸鹤折叠的。

教师此时拿出彩色折纸(学生惊喜、欢呼),放视频(视频长 3 分 47 秒),要求学生跟随视频折叠纸鹤。为了让全班同学能跟上视频里的折叠速度,教师控制视频播放进度。

在大部分同学在完成纸鹤折叠后(有极少部分没跟上视频速度,或没明白某些关键步骤的叠法,在课上没能及时完成),关闭视频。少部分动作快的同学还利用边角料折叠了其他作品。图 7.3 是部分学生送给教师的千纸鹤和其他折纸作品。

图 7.3 process analysis 写作课学生作品——千纸鹤和其他折纸作品

学生开始 process analysis 的说明文写作。动笔前,教师最后两次信息输入:

(1)因为考虑到写作中折纸对应的英文有难度,教师给出关键英文词汇,或者鼓励学生分享他们在网络上找到的专业词汇,如下:

square 正方形;origami paper 折纸;rectangular 长方形;triangle 三角形;

crease 折痕;press the crease 压出折痕;flip over(折纸)翻过来;

fold horizontally 水平折叠;fold diagonally 对角线折叠;align 对齐;

edge 边;center line 中线。

(2)再次提醒学生关注第一节课里讲过的说明文写作的注意事项:

① Check the order of the steps to make sure you haven't skipped or repeated any.

② Consider your audience—use the second person for directional process analysis.

③ The pattern to organize?—Choronological order.

④ Add any necessary transitions, such as first, second, next, then, after, later, and finally, etc.

⑤ Warn of difficulties or important points.

⑥ Try to sum up the results or benefits of the process in the end.

大部分学生在课堂上完成了说明文写作的基本步骤。纸鹤的折叠步骤很细,要写清楚是有难度的。但是课前学生观看视频的时候已经讨论并预写过,而且教师鼓励他们利用网络搜索词汇和写作素材,加上课上的词汇提示和流程复习,所以学生基本都能完成写作练习。课程结束前,教师布置本课课后作业。

Write an exposition to describe precisely how one of the following things is done:

① How to make dumpling.

② How to cook _____.

③ How to get ready for a trip abroad.

④ How to prepare a surprise party.

要求:小组写作,词数不限,可以选用其他主题,只要是对 process 进行说明解释的就可以。写完后同伴互评与反馈,提交最后版本的电子稿。

三、写后

课堂上学生完成"How to Make an Origami Crane"的说明文写作以后,教师给出两个版本的范文对照,并在课后通过班级QQ群发给学生。教师提示学生注意两个版本的用词有何不一样,让学生分析哪个版本更好,更能帮助他们的目标对象成功完成这个过程(折纸)。提示学生注意连接词的使用,如何在某些重要步骤做出警示或强调等。两个版本文本请参照书后附录。

小组合作进行的process analysis写作,要求分配好每个人的角色,并注明。写作前小组brainstorm,构思讨论完毕后,由一人写第一稿,小组成员进行同伴互评反馈,并标注每一稿的反馈人,反馈要留痕迹。经过小组互评反馈后,完成终稿,提交电子版给教师。

最后教师评改反馈后,班级点评、分享。

第四节 写作课程评价与反馈

一、本次课课后习作实例与点评

学生实例:

How to Make Dumplings—Step by Step
INGREDIENTS

Wrappers:面皮
- 500g flour
- 300ml water
- 1/3 tsp. salt

Sauce:蘸料
- Soy sauce
- Vinegar
- Minced garlic
- Horseradish sauce 山葵酱
- Chili powder
- Chili oil

Fillings:馅料
- 500g ground pork
- 450g chopped Chinese cabbage
- 250ml water
- 2 tbsp. soy sauce
- 2 tbsp. cooking wine
- 1 tbsp. green onion
- 1 tbsp. sesame oil
- 1 tbsp. vegetable oil
- 1 tsp. ginger
- 1 tsp. salt

- 1/3 tsp. MSG 味精

STEPS

  • **Make dumpling wrappers.** Mix enough flour and water as needed in a large bowl. Mix them fully until you get a smooth dough. Cover the bowl with a preservative film for 10 minutes. Then put the dough on a clean chopping board. Cut it into small pieces after you have kneaded it well. Use a rolling pin to roll them into circular wrappers at last.

  • **Make fillings for dumplings.** Mix enough chopped Chinese cabbage with the ground pork. Then add a teaspoon of salt and 1/3 teaspoon of MSG and wait for 5 minutes. Add some finely chopped ginger and green onion, 2 teaspoon of cooking wine, 2 teaspoons of soy sauce, a tablespoon of sesame oil and a tablespoon of vegetable oil. Stir until they're well-blended.

  • **Wrap fillings.** Take a wrapper and place a spoon of filling in its center. Fold the wrapper and pinch the edges together tightly until you get a dumpling.

  • **Boil dumplings.** Bring a pot of water to boil. Then add the dumplings to the water. Wait for the water to boil again and add some cold water. Repeat it three times. And when dumplings float to the surface, they should be good enough to go. Fish them out and place them in a plate using a colander.

  • **Enjoy your dumplings with your favorite dipping sauces.** Dipping with vinegar is the best choice in China!

ATTENTION PLEASE

Wrappers:

  • Use strong flour or special flour for dumplings, because they could make dumplings chewier, and plain flour can't be boiled for a long time.

Fillings:

  • Better mix the fresh meat and vegetables up in proportion. Vegetables can make meat more palatable and promote digestion.

  • Stir the fillings in one direction. It can make the fillings tight and tasty.

  • When adding salt, don't add too much. If you add a little, it's no problem, because you can dip sauce to make up for the light taste.

Sauce:

  • No matter what sauce you like, always dip some vinegar, because it helps with your digestion.

教师点评:学生的这篇习作,从内容到形式都比较符合 process analysis 的说明文写作。习作令人惊喜地从 ingredients 开始,到细节化的步骤描述,到最后的注意事项提示,很完整。为什么说开头的调料和成分部分的介绍让人惊喜?因为相比西方的烹饪,中国人烹饪的方式比较自成一套,不太注意用 tablespoon 这样的量词来精确描述盐、酱油、醋等的比例。大部分同学在类似的文体写作中,用的就是"some""a little"等不精确的说法。此外,步骤的描述虽然还不够完善(没有细化到菜谱的程度),但用词简洁,步骤清晰,语言整体准确。最后一部分注意事项提示也分别与前面的步骤对应,层次清楚,颇具实用价值。

二、写作课程评价与反馈

1. 给两个写作班级建立的写作 QQ 群。在为期一年的写作课程结束后、群解散前,学生的评价(部分)(图7.4)。

图7.4　写作 QQ 群对课程的评价截图

2. 江南大学本科教学质量检测系统评教。

江南大学目前的教学质量评价分为两次:期中一次主观性评价,期末一次打分。总体来说,笔者开设的写作课程获得了同学们的认可,对写作教学方式和内容、评价与反馈等都给予了肯定。图7.5 显示的是学生对写作课程的部分主观评价。

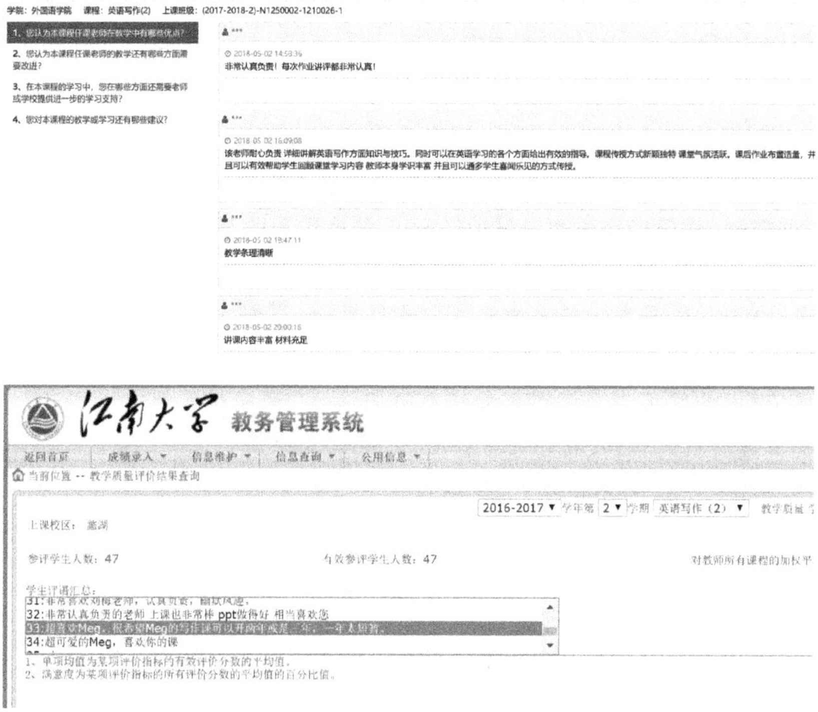

图 7.5　江南大学评教系统对写作课程的评价截图

（上图：2017—2018 学年；下图：2016—2017 学年）

评价摘录：

1. 超喜欢 Meg（学生对笔者的称呼），很希望 Meg 的写作课可以开两年或是三年，一年太短暂。

2. 认真负责，讲解全面仔细，教会我们很多。

3. 教学内容充实，教学生动，能够调动学生参与到课堂当中。上课该严谨的时候严谨，该轻松的时候轻松，收放自如，认真负责，关心学生。

4. 对于写作方法的教学清晰，对于学生作文给予指导。

5. 内容很有针对性，老师很认真。

6. 十分认真负责，上课准备充分，有水平。

7. 内容丰富有趣，老师讲解生动。

8. 该老师耐心负责，详细讲解英语写作方面知识与技巧。同时可以在英语学习的各个方面给出有效的指导。课程传授方式新颖独特，课堂气氛活跃。课后作业布置适量，并且可以有效帮助学生回顾课堂学习内容，教师本身学识丰富，并且可以通过学生喜闻乐见的方式传授。

9. 非常认真负责！每次作业讲评都非常认真！

10. 老师上课很认真、很幽默,也很投入,课堂氛围挺好的。

11. 超级棒的老师,布置的活动很有趣,作业也适中,讲课很有启发性。

12. 教学方法有趣,教学内容有条理,每节课都干货满满,有深度！有内容！

13. 老师上课的逻辑非常清晰,课件内容很有条理,一目了然。老师人格魅力强,很有趣,总能带给学生新鲜的话题。课后作业的量适中,老师的批改也非常认真。

14. 首先,老师本人性格非常好,很有耐心,很细心,对待工作非常认真,PPT非常有条理。每次作业都会认真批改,并且摘抄优秀和相对需要改进的作文做成PPT,非常用心。课间会放视频调节气氛,同时增加我们的见识。与我们的交流没有很大代沟,相处非常开心,上课很轻松。

15. 准备充分,讲解清晰,上课幽默。

16. 态度认真负责,教学方式幽默有趣,专业指导性强,积极对学生的作业进行反馈指导。

17. 认真负责,有许多写作案例和练习。

18. 上课生动、有趣、认真,与学生互动强。

19. 老师课前、课间会给学生放有趣的英语学习视频,吸引学生注意力。课上老师也积极跟学生进行互动,很有意思。

20. 很喜欢这个老师的上课方式,能有比较大的收获。课后也会和同学进行交流,解决同学的问题。

21. 一如既往的专业、细致、风趣幽默,和学生打成一片,是收获最大的课程。

22. Meg让原本枯燥的作文课很有趣,课后很耐心地回答同学们的问题。很友好。

23. 超级喜欢你,一位很懂我们的老师。

24. 每次写作作业都很享受,很可爱的老师,教学风格活泼。

在写作课程的评价里,学生最主要的反馈是老师上课认真负责,讲课幽默生动,方法多样。写作话题有趣,课堂互动多,写作作业有意思,等等。"老师很懂我们"这样的评价,是笔者作为教师很喜闻乐见的。因为现在的学生都是90后或00后,在大数据时代,教师如果还因循守旧,固守在传统的课堂教学里,不更新知识,不用与时代接轨的教学方式,不去努力适应新的信息化和数字化的教学环境,面对浸泡在网络技术与信息革命中长大的新一代,就真要被网络课程和人工智能取代了。

第八章 学生习作与评析

第一节 学生习作常见错误与分析

即使是英语专业的学生,在英语写作中犯的各类错误也是屡现不止的。本章的共性错误分析,意在总结笔者从教 20 年来搜集的学生写作中常出现的错误类型,分析错误原因,结合习作实例,为学习者提供参考和借鉴,加强写作文本的纠错意识。很多时候,作为读者或同伴或老师看来很明显的错误,写作者自己却发现不了。一方面是语法知识不牢固;另一方面是没有意识到这是一种错误。有趣的是,笔者在同伴反馈的实践中,也发现有相当一部分学生在检查自己的作文时发现不了错误,在评改同伴的作文时却能更准确地找到同伴的错误,虽然随后做出的修改不一定正确。这里分析的学生错误主要是词法和句法层面,文章思想内容和结构等宏观方面的问题更与写作主题、写作个体相关,在本节最后稍做探讨。

从词法、句法来看,学生语言质量不过关,语法错误多,用词随意,句子不规范。语法错误在词语层面体现得最多的就是拼写错误、用词错误和搭配不当。在句子层面上出现的问题包括人称代词指代不明,主语缺失,主谓不一致,句子结构不完整,悬垂句、主从句时态不一致或者全文时态不一致,从句引导词误用,等等。此外,写作不讲究形式和格式,标点符号中英文不分,中式英语频现。具体表现如下(所有例句均来自学生习作)。

一、词语层面

1. 拼写、大小写

在批改网在线反馈的错误分析里,拼写错误一直"遥遥领先",占第一位。当然这和用电脑打字、键盘输入时操作不熟练有关。但是在平时学生提交的纸质版作文中,拼写错误也时时出现。原因可能是对单词本身不熟悉,误拼,或写作时粗心,写完后没仔细检查修改。

例1:Moreover, the greatest benifit of being twenty is we have the courage to do whatever we want.(应为 benefit)

例2:On the other hand, if parents sometimes are too busy to company with the child, she or he will feel more solitary than the one who has silbings.(应为 siblings)

例3:As far as I'm concerned, there are advantages and disadvatages in this issue.(应为 disadvantages)

例4:Even we may argue with each oher, but we have a lot of happyness.(应为 happiness)

例5:When getting old, you use various cosmeties to hide the wrinkles round your eyes, and you use Grecian Formular to hide the gray in your hair.(应为 cosmestics)

例6:Wether to have only one child depends on the parents' confidence after considering their situation.(应为 Whether,这个词还经常被误拼为 weather)

例7:On the contrary, there are some poor people who live a happy life, and they don't persue a large amount of money.(应为 pursue,误拼率非常高)

例8:Maybe some people would say young people are troubled by all the unknowns in their future; However, we benefit from our growth, and we make critical decisions for ourselves and pursue what we want.(应为 however,小写)

最后一个例句里 however 的用法,学生误用的非常多。however 前面是分号或者逗号时,however 首字母应该小写,后面用逗号。

2. 用词错误

(1) maybe 和 may be。

这两个词前者是副词,后者是两个词:may 是情态动词,be 是系动词。学生混用的情况非常多。

例 1：... however, the older don't have the enthusiasm to do it just like a teenager, as a result the older maybe a out man.

这一个句子里的错误很多,这里只看 maybe 的用法错误:as a result 后面的句子缺少谓语,应该用 may be 而不是副词 maybe。

例 2：The only child stay at home and no sisters or brothers to play with him or her, at this time, an only child maybe a lonely child.

例 3：Everything is the best, then the child maybe the best.

(2) various 和 varied。

这两个词一个用来作定语,一个常用作表语,意思相近,用法却不一样,也容易被学生误用。

例 1：Every morning when I wake up, I will start to expect my next life. Every day will be various.（应为 varied）

例 2：Broadly speaking, the reasons that people advocate having an only child are various.（应为 varied）

(3) company 和 accompany。

例 1：On the other hand, if parents sometimes are too busy to company with the child, she or he will feel more solitary than the one who has silbings.（应为 accompany,而且是及物动词,后面不用接 with）

例 2：But why my friend admired me, maybe he can get accompany from parents and friends, he is willing to have a sibling who is the cloest person except parents.（应为 company）

(4) alone 和 lonely。

例：These are what prevent the parents from having another child. For the children, they may feel it good to get their parents' full love and heart, and they don't feel alone or there's need to have a sibling. (应为 lonely)

（5）另外还有-ing 形容词和-ed 形容词不分，如 interesting 和 interested, tiring 和 tired, boring 和 bored, exhausting 和 exhausted, 等等。

例：It will not be very tired to do so because we are young, we are energetic! (应为 tiring)

3. 词性错误

词性错误也比比皆是，把形容词误用作动词、把副词误用作形容词，把形容词误用作副词，把名词误用作形容词，等等。

例1：So I think an only child is more possible to be a lonely child. (人作主语应该用 likely 而不是用 possible)

例2：It is known that our country is becoming stronger and stronger in the integrated power; however, our society becomes more and more commercialism and formalism at the same time. (名词误用为形容词，应为 commercialized)

例3：We may feel happy if we have a health body, some of us may think happiness is related to money and some of us can feel happiness around us when we are with our family. (名词误用为形容词，应为 healthy)

例4：From my point of view, happiness can be expressed in many ways: you have made true friends, and live in a harmony family. People who you love are all in good health and etc. (应为形容词形式 harmonious)

例5：You can try everything you are interested in because you are full of energetic and enthusiasm. (名词误用为形容词，应为 energy)

例6：Don't forget that honest is our Chinese traditional virtue whenever at any time and wherever in any areas. (形容词误用为 honesty)

例7：Some think it does really harm to the social ethics and the author's benefit. (harm 和 harmful 没分清楚，要么用形容词 it is really harmful, 要么名词 does real harm)

例8：One person who is honest may not be very successful, but if he lack of honesty, he certainly can do nothing. (应为 lacks honesty, 用动词形式，后面直接接名词)

lack 可以作动词，后面直接接宾语，也可以作名词，后面常接 of，还可以用于 be lacking in 的结构中。学生通常混用动词和名词的用法。

例 9：To forgive other people is to relief ourselves.（名词误用为动词，应为 relieve）

4. 词组/搭配错误

例 1：For an example, the parents will take their baby to some formal or informal occasions so that their child will learn much new things.（搭配错误，应为 for example；many new things）

例 2：A heating topic in recent weeks is about a little girl named "Xiao Yueyue".（a hot topic）

例 3：Dream is the source of happiness. Use the dream to start a light future, and be a happy guy.（a bright future）

例 4：Now, I can try different fresh things.（new things）

例 5：They don't ever feel lonely because they're always ready to participate in activities or make friends, during which they take effort to show the best of themselves so that they can be accepted and then be loved as a wonderful person.（make efforts）

例 6：Once you gave up your characteristic for becoming a smooth person with popularity, you became ever more timid to secrete the true ideas in your mind.（a popular person）

例 7：Such as the parents will pay more attention to the child, they can give most of things which their child want, and the child can receive all of them.（应为 most things 或 most of the things）

most + 名词，有 of 的时候一定也有 the（most of the + 名词）。看似非常简单，但是仍然有不少学生犯这样的错误。

例 8：… we will achieve a sense of language …

achieve 不跟 language 搭配使用，可以 acquire language，achieve a goal，但不用 achieve language。

二、句法/句子层面

1. 谓语动词用法错误

谓语动词用法错误多受汉语句法影响。汉语里动词能连用,通过"连动结构"来组成句子很常见。而在英语中,一个句子只能有一个谓语。汉语的负迁移使学生习作中常出现双谓语用法错误。

(1) there be 句型中已经有动词 be,后面不能再跟谓语动词。如果有动词的话要用"there be … doing 句型"。这种错误出现率非常高。

例1:Just like there are not two leaves which own the same veins, <u>there are not two people share</u> the same thoughts. (应为 there are no two people sharing the same thoughts,句子意思的表达显然也有问题)

例2:On the contrary, <u>there are some poor people live</u> a happy life, and they don't persue a large amount of money. (应为 there are some people living)

例3:Though intellectual dishonesty is in short supply today and getting scarcer, <u>there are still something and someone make</u> us feel gratified. (应为 there are still something and someone making)

(2) like 和 be like 的区别。

like 可以作动词,也可以作介词。学生常常把 be like 和 like 混用。作动词用时意思是"喜欢"。"像……一样"时要用 be like。

例1:Our hearts <u>like</u> fields full of flowers.
修改:Our hearts are like fields full of flowers.

(3) think 后面动词的用法。

think 后面的动词应该用动名词结构。

例:Other people <u>think have</u> the right to control others can make them feel happy.
修改:Other people think having the right to control others can make them feel happy.

（4）情态动词或助动词后的谓语动词用法错误。

例 1：If everything surrounding us <u>can satisfied</u> us, we will be very happy. (can satisfy，情态动词后用动词原形)

例 2：Oppositely, if he knew it, maybe he <u>would felt sad and succumbed</u> to the disease. (would feel sad and succumb)

例 3：Meanwhile, overwhelmed by these problems, they <u>might constantly invoked</u> death for relief and deliverance. Although depression leads to such a high probability of suicide, it doesn't receive the corresponding attention. (might constantly invoke)

（5）谓语动词是被动语态，误用主动语态，导致双谓语用法错误。

例：What's more, from cheating on exam we can easily know that you <u>are not take seriously</u> about yourself. (用被动语态 are not taken seriously)

（6）谓语动词后应该接动名词作动词的宾语，而不是动词原形。

例：So in the daily life, I <u>advocate fight</u> back the people who hurt us if necessary. (应为 advocate fighting)

（7）谓语动词后面应该接不定式，而不是动词原形。

例 1：It is the intellectual dishonesty among people that <u>push them lie</u> to themselves. (应为 push them to lie)

例 2：Unlike children with siblings, an only child can't always <u>have someone keep</u> his or her company, so it's more likely that an only child <u>get</u> lonely. (应为 have someone to keep；句子里还有一个主谓一致用法错误：get 应为 gets)

2. 主谓一致用法错误

主谓一致可以说是句法错误里最常见的错误之一，包括性、数的不一致。

例 1：Any person under thirty <u>want</u> to accelerate the speed of being old. 主语是 any person，谓语动词用单数。

例2：Being young <u>give</u> you a good cause to be crazy, to be yourself.

动名词结构 being young 为主语，谓语动词用单数。

例3：From what has been discussed above, we can safely <u>drew</u> the conclusion that there <u>is</u> at least three sorts of virtues of being young.

there be 句型修饰的是 three virtues，be 动词应该用复数。同时 drew 在情态动词后，应该用动词原形。

例4：For most of the people, getting older means we <u>becomes</u> more mature and have a deeper understanding of our lives.

从句中主语是 we，从句的谓语动词应该用复数。

例5：Firstly, <u>many young couple</u> think there are no other children in the family to associate with, an only child <u>don't</u> know how to associate with others.

many young couple 表示复数概念，couple 应该用复数形式。后面句子的主语是 an only child，谓语动词应该用单数。

例6：However, an only child <u>are</u> sure to be spoiled to some degree, and then <u>they</u> become self-centered and dependent when they enter society, and inevitably cause problems to the public.

句子主语是 an only child，谓语动词应该用单数。同时，并列结构后面的主语又是复数，前后人称不一致。

3. 语序问题

句子中出现的语序问题，有的是某一个词的位置前置，如学生受中文的影响，经常把诸如 also, could 等情态动词放在谓语动词之前。有的是句子内在的逻辑顺序问题，很多句子表达的意思在逻辑上或者重要性上是有先后之分的，而这往往也是容易被忽略的一点：学生写作时通常只注意意思表述是否准确，没有去考虑句子的逻辑性和语序问题。

（1）also 的位置。

受汉语负迁移的影响，学生经常会把 also 的位置前置。

例1：He <u>also could</u> turn to parents or teachers or cousins or classmates and so on.（应为 could also）

例2：They <u>also are</u> given too much love while payback isn't acquired by their parents. No doubt they turn mean and selfish.（应为 are also）

例3：As members of our society, we also should hold the view to object the intellectual dishonesty to build a peaceful and fair world.（应为 should also）

（2）疑问句里谓语动词的位置。

例：Why they are desperated to become younger and younger?

（3）同一个句子里动词的排序。

例1：... when turning to the right, the lake is sparkling under the sunshine and surrounded by shrubs and trees.
这个句子在语法上并没有什么问题，但是从句子结构和意义上来说，描述的是同一个对象时，应该是先用静态的动词 surrounded，然后是动态的 sparkling。
修改：... when turning to the right, the lake, surrounded by shrubs and trees, is sparkling under the sunshine.

例2：What was common to all these heroes was that they did not fear death, danger, and hardship.
本句中 death, danger 和 hardship 3 个词在让人 fear 的程度上是有先后之分的，就可怕性（从低到高）而言，它们的排列顺序应该是 hardship, danger, death。
修改：What was common to all these heroes was that they did not fear hardship, danger and death.

例3：He said he had lost interest in life, fame, position and money after that tragedy.
与上例同理，对 life, fame, position, money 都失去兴趣，这几个对于人的重要性，很明显也是有先后顺序的（钱、地位、名望、生命）。
修改：He said he had lost interest in money, position, fame and life after that tragedy.

4. 人称指代不一致或指代含糊

在同一个句子内部或者同一个段落中间，经常会出现指称代词不一致或者指示代词指代不明。

例1：Marvin told Jim he was getting too old.

人称代词 he 指代不明，读者不知道。

例2：If we have a young attitude towards yourself and your life, regardless of your age, we will always be young.

一个句子里的人称代词一会是第一人称，一会是第二人称，很混乱。这也是写作的大忌。

例3：In other words, these bad habits are killing you. Next, these bad habits have a negative influence on students' academic performance. Consequently, we should pay due attention to young people's daily habits so that we won't waste our life.

第一句用第二人称 you，第三句用的人称换成了 we，应该保持一致。

5. 句子不完整

一个完整的句子至少包括主语和谓语两部分（祈使句除外）。句子缺少主语或谓语或将句子的一部分（通常是连接词引导的那部分或从句）分离出来独立成句，都是属于此类错误。

（1）断句。

例1：As for me, a child with no siblings to live together.

无主语从句。

例2：Because I think the process is more important than the result.

例3：Because parents must be the most concerned about our people in the word.

because 引导的原因从句被当作完整的句子。

例4：In summary, eat healthy food and exercise more to strengthen our physical health. Keep a positive attitude towards life to make our mentality healthy. But I want to say the virtues of being young.

say 后面从句谓语缺失。

例5：Thanks for companion, for the danger but a sweet experience.

无主语从句。

（2）主语或谓语缺失。

例1：However, we not only should responsible for ourselves, but also consider the feelings of others.

谓语应该是 be responsible，be 动词缺失。

例 2：When old, your body condition <u>will not as good as before</u>.

缺少 be 动词作谓语，应为 will not be as good as before.

例 3：I strongly believe that <u>happiness a feeling</u> that make us smile or laugh from heart.

宾语从句中谓语缺失，应为 happiness is a feeling.

例 4：<u>Keeping a positive attitude</u> towards life to make our mentality healthy.

主语是 keeping a positive attitude，句子中缺少谓语。

例 5：For instance, there is no trace of wind all day long；<u>willows sadly beside the river，</u> without a little angry；cicadas desperately shouted "Hot！Hot！"

谓语缺失。

例 6：Frankly, I am in favor of <u>Microblog a blessing</u>.

从句后谓语缺失。

例 7：While sitting in class, she realized she had lost a ring. But happily <u>found</u> it in the women's room after class.

but 从句中主语缺失。

6. 悬垂结构

悬垂结构指在逻辑上不修饰任何句子成分的介词短语（包括动名词作宾语的介词短语）、不定式短语、分词短语或省略形式的状语从句。悬垂结构最明显的特点就是短语/从句的逻辑主语和句子主语不一致。

例 1：<u>Sparing</u> no efforts to think of how to defeat her, all of a sudden, <u>an idea</u> jumps up to my mind.

句子主语是 an idea，分词 sparing no efforts 的逻辑主语是作者（人），句子主语和 spare 的逻辑主语不一致。修改方法就是使两个主语一致。

修改：Sparing no efforts to think of how to defeat her, all of a sudden, I had an idea.

例 2：<u>To improve</u> one's writing skill, <u>regular practice</u> is necessary.

句子主语是 regular practice，to improve 的逻辑主语是 one。

修改：To improve one's writing skill, one must practice more often.

例 3：When on the top floor of the moutain, the cars looked like tiny fish in a stream.

句子主语是 the cars，从句的逻辑主语是人。

修改：When we stand on the top of the mountain, the cars looked like tiny fish in a stream.

7. 时态不一致

学生作文中经常将现在时和过去时混用，同一个句子里主句是过去时，从句里又变成了现在时，或者前一句/前几句是过去时，下一句变成了现在时。

例 1：What's more, the luxurious library collects an unbelievable number of books, which benefited me a lot.

例 2：A tangled warfare began, and with the addition of someone who fish in troubled water to raid others, the fighting became even more chaotic.

例 3：I nodded without hesitation since she was an experienced traveller while I always lost my way and make things out of control.

例 4：I look around and engraved the time and the place in my heart.

例 5：For example, Xiao Chuanguo cheated in his academic papers and ask others to hit Fang Zhouzi.

例 6：The magnificent changes in our body overwhelmed us and strike us as puzzled, but excess hormones contribute to extra enthusiasm as well, contributing that teenagers are energetic and even restless all day long.

8. 语态错误

语态错误主要指主动语态和被动语态混用，这种错误相对不那么常见。英语里有一些词是不能用于被动语态的。熟悉这些词的用法，可以减少语态方面的错误。

例 1："I can't surrender! Just defeat yourself!" These words repeat constantly in my mind.

应为 are repeated，用被动语态。

例 2：Nowadays we find more and more dishonest things were happened in our daily life, especially in the intellectual property.

happened 没有被动语态,这里应该去掉 were。

例 3：Happiness can be got easily.

动词 got 一般不用作被动语态。

9. 结构不对称,包括比较结构、排比句式、并列结构等

例 1：People <u>ride bikes</u> on the driveway, <u>jaywalking on the streets</u>, and sometimes may <u>run</u> the red light …

句子中动作是并列的,呈排比句式,应该用一样的结构,这里都用动词词组形式。

修改：People ride bikes on the driveway, jaywalk on the streets, and sometimes may run the red light.

例 2：… have some people <u>leading</u> you and <u>push</u> you in your study.

and 连接的前后词语或短语并列,这里应都为 v.-ing 或动词原形。

修改：… have some people lead you and push you in your study.

或者：… have some people leading you and pushing you in your study.

例 3：They will do great help to <u>develop</u> children's habits and <u>teaching</u> them to be polite and kind.

and 前后的动词词组是并列结构。

修改：They will do great help to develop children's habits and teach them to be polite and kind.

例 4：The use of the Internet is more <u>common and widely</u>.

and 前后结构并列,都应该用形容词形式。

例 5：We would meet the style we appreciate through <u>numerous choices</u> <u>and imitate it</u> at the beginning.

and 前后应该是并列结构,这里应该都用名词或名词词组。

10. 语义含混、重复

这种句子虽然没有很明显的语法或句法错误,但是表达含糊或语义重复。

例 1：… which <u>makes me find it hard to</u> move at all …

修改：Which makes it hard to move at all …

例 2：You can talk to <u>people those who may</u> come from all over the country …

修改：You can talk to people from all over the country …

例 3：All of a sudden, I heard some <u>strange</u> noises <u>which were unexpected</u> in the quiet dark room.

奇怪的噪音之所以奇怪,就是因为没听过类似的,或者不同于熟悉的噪音,后面的 which were unexpected 就显得多余了。

修改：All of a sudden, I heard some strange noises in the quiet dark room.

例 4：Some swindlers who may <u>put their QR-code on the bikes to scan the</u> consumers.

修改：Some swindlers may put the wrong QR-code on the bikes for users to scan.

例 5：Rambling along the path westward, you will enjoy the most beautiful view, in my opinion, on campus：a small brook, just beginning to <u>meander</u>, is <u>winding</u> slowly round our library.

这个句子本身写得不错,但最后两个用词语义重复了,都表示流水的蜿蜒,可以删除一个。

例 6：And <u>in terms of ideal education</u>, different people have different <u>views</u>. Now, I'll show my opinions. When <u>it comes to the ideal education</u>, I think ….

这个句子几乎都是在重复同一个意思,啰嗦了半天还不见观点出现。

修改：In terms of ideal education, I think …

例 7：I <u>rolled the envelope into a mess</u> by <u>kneading without opening it</u>, <u>littering</u> it up to the garbage can.

这里就是表达"把信揉成一团扔进垃圾桶"的概念。

修改：I rolled the envelope into a mess, littering it up to the garbage can.

11. 中式英语

最后以中式英语作为学生句法层面常见错误结尾。中式英语可以说是中国学生英语写作中比较普遍的问题之一。受母语负迁移的影响,学生英语习作中的句式结构和词汇经常出现不符合英语表达习惯的情况。中式英语出现的原因,有的是因对相关词语、搭配等的不熟悉,有的是因为中西方文化背景的差异,最根本的原因是中文和英语两种思维方式的不同。要避免中式英语的出现,除了积累基础的语言知识和加强对文化背景的了解外,更重要的是学会用英语思维和写作。

例1:They put the interests of the people in the first position, as long as people need, they give everything they have.

中式英语的表达"只要人们需要,他们就会付出所有",应为 they are ready to give everything they have when necessary。

例2:Last but not least, when we are young, our fresh mind can remember a lot of things so that we can absorb new knowledge easier.

fresh mind 这种表达让人摸不着头脑,学生想要表达的就是年轻记忆力好,句子后面已经表达出相关意思,这个中式英语词可以直接删除。

例3:Once you gave up your characteristic for becoming a smooth person with popularity, you became ever more timid to secrete the true ideas in your mind.

"give up your characteristic"和"a smooth person"都是中式表达,学生想表达的意思其实后文已经说了,就是 a popular person without personality。

例4:The patriotic spirits of Qu Yuan inspire people deeply and they will pass on from generation to generation.

"the patriotic spirits of Qu Yuan"——屈原的爱国主义精神,典型的中式思维。用英语表达的话,可以直接说"Qu Yuan inspired people to be …",后面把具体的特点表达出来。

三、谋篇布局层面

在写作的篇章内容、组织结构的宏观方面,学生常出现的问题是没有明确的主题句,表达没有层次,句与句之间、段与段之间不讲究逻辑关联和承接过渡。最突出也最明显的问题,就是英语作文中主题句(topic sentence)的使用,以及句与句之间关联词和衔接手段的运用。

英语段落的构成大致可分两类:一类是典型的"主题句—阐述句—总结句"结构;另一类则有点像汉语的以某一中心思想统领的形散神聚结构,但注重形合的英语常常使用许多衔接和连贯手段,以便从形式上显现各种组合关系。第一种类型的文章占了英语类文章的大多数。

汉语段落通常都围绕一个较为含蓄的中心思想,其表述方式多为迂回式和流散式的,句与句之间的意义关联可以是隐约的、似断非断的。当然,也有不少十分注重逻辑推演的段落,句际之间环环相扣,但有相当数量的汉语段落都是形分意合的,没有英语中常见的那些连接词。

这两种迥然不同的写作特点,当然是由中西方思维方式的不同所决定的。西方是直线型的思维方式,中国人是曲线型(环形)的思维方式(图8.1)。反映在写作上就是:英语的直线型的思维方式喜欢开门见山,开宗明义,先直接把观点和目的亮明,然后再通过列证据、摆事实、讲道理等来支持观点。中文的曲线型的思维方式,表达的时候不习惯一开始直接挑明目的,喜欢迂回环

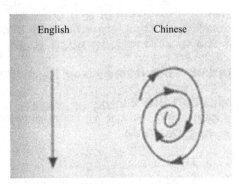

图8.1　中西方思维方式差异图

绕,俗称"拐弯抹角",含蓄地、隐约地,最后引出目的。受汉语思维方式的影响,我们的学生在写英语作文时也没有养成用"主题句—支持句—总结句"谋篇布局的意识。在句与句之间、段与段之间也不习惯用关联词来加强文章的逻辑性和层次性。

在写作教学和实践的过程中,笔者都会反复强调英语写作在篇章结构上与中文最大的不同,并进行了多次练习巩固。遗憾的是,即使经过一年的英语写作练习和训练,没有了写作老师的强调和提示,学生到了生活中需要用英语写作的时候(如申请签证或留学),还是会出现这方面的问题,这些学生包括传统意义上的好学生。下面以一封学生申请留学的推荐信为例,第一版是学生拟的草稿,第二版是经教师详细指导后的修改版。出于举例需要,仅选取了正文中间部分的三段。

> 第一版

As her English teacher in her freshman year, I have to admit that she is one of the most talented students I've ever met. Her diligence and enthusiastic devotion left a deep impression upon all of us. I can always see her listen to me carefully with simply nodding or taking some notes, which shows that she also ponders in the course of absorbing what I taught. As the most active student in class, she would put her hand up high at almost each question I raised. She could always come up with many impressive ideas from a rather unique perspective to solve some demanding problems.

XX is the monitor of study in our class, contributing much to the academic atmosphere with her high GPA (3.98/4.0), impressive IELTS test score (8.0) and her responsible attitude towards her work in class. With great passion for public speaking and BP debate, she has won many awards in these fields. In this October, she went to Nanjing for the FLTRP Public Speaking Contest on behalf Jiangnan University with the result of Second Prize in Jiangsu Province. She is the deputy leader of the school Public Speaking and Debate Team and this whole team is said to have become a great motivation for those English-lovers in school, inspiring many students to think deeper and use imagination to seek for the uniqueness in everything.

She is industrious as well as engaged in all kinds of activities. Since this summer vocation, she told me, she has participated in 5 workshops all together, including XXX Summit which only enrolled 20 persons in China. During her educational trip to Singapore, her active engagement in class also won her a recommendation letter from NUS. I was told by many of her other teachers who had sung high praise for her on the grounds of her creativity, curiosity and critical thinking. She loves asking questions so much that every teacher had a very deep impression of her.

第一版在进行推荐信里常规的"自我推销"模式时,陈述的优点分散,没有层次性。第一段是关于专业学习方面,第二段又是学习和英语比赛方面。每一段都没有明显的主题句,给人的感觉就是一堆优点的罗列,难以让人留下深刻的印象。

第二版最大的改变就在于每一段都有一个明确的主题("主题句+支持细节")。每个主题概括一个方面的优点,同时这些优点又是层层递进的。第一段谈课堂内个人的学习方面(achieve excellence in her own study);第二段上升到对集体和更大的 community 做出的努力和贡献;第三段再推进一步,关于自我完善(self-improvement)和对优秀的永无止境的追求。每一段都辅以支撑的细节。

第二版

XX impressed me first at my Comprehensive English class when she introduced herself to us. Different from her nervous and intimated freshman classmates, she was fluent in English and confident about herself. In fact, I later came to realize that it was such a delightful thing to have a student like XX in the class, who is always attentive, active and responsive, ready to come up with original ideas and interesting answers. I've never met a student who has such a great passion for and devotion to English study. Her efforts were paid off: she achieved high GPA (3.98/4.0) in the first year and scored 8.0 in the IELTS test. This October, she was chosen to represent Jiangnan University for the FLTRP Public Speaking Contest (a high-level national speaking contest), and won a second prize in the provincial selection.

As the class representative and the deputy leader of the school Public Speaking and Debate Team, XX not only endeavors to achieve excellence in her own study, but also tries, in every possible way, to contribute to improving the academic performance of her class, and the school as well. She gives talks to share her experience in English learning, organizes workshops to motivate students who are interested in English public speaking & debating, and volunteers to be a teaching assistant to encourage and inspire other English lovers to be better every day.

What impresses me most about XX is her power for self-improvement. She is constantly pushing herself forward for further progress. She has participated in 5 workshops during the past year, including XXX Summit which only enrolls 20 persons in China. She took an educational trip to Singapore this summer and was highly recognized by professors from NUS because of her active engagement in class and her positive attitude in learning. Teachers who have taught her easily remember her, a girl who smiles a lot, asks questions a lot, and challenges a lot.

第二节 学生习作与评析

在英语写作中,教师对学生习作共性错误的总结和分析,可以帮助学生发现问题,在修改自己习作和同伴反馈的过程中积累经验,增强对常见错误的敏感性。同样,分析解读优秀范文,指导学生多读、多背美文佳作,多记、多用好词和好句,教师的这些行为可以帮助学生写出尽可能接近目标语的文章来。而优秀范文,一方面来自英语文学作品,另一方面则来自学生们自己的创作。教师可以在课堂上对学生的优秀习作进行表彰,分享一篇习作的出色之处,如恰到好处的用词、优美的句子、独到的谋篇布局等。只要文章有闪光之处,教师都可以进行全班共享。看着自己笔头的文字变成 PPT 上的美文被全班同学欣赏,写作者可以增强自信心和提高写作兴趣,激励自己下次写出更精彩的作品。同班同学意识到这些出色的文字并非那么高不可攀,也会在自己的写作练习中斟词酌句,反复打磨,争取让自己的名字也能出现在下次被表扬的行列里。那些被老师赏析过的精彩词汇、优美句型、巧妙构思等,会成为一种良性循环,引导学生养成精益求精的良好写作习惯。

本书因此特意选择了数篇学生的优秀习作,与读者一起共赏。笔者读到这些文章时,或惊呼或赞叹,或感怀或哀伤,或忍俊不禁乐不可支,更有震撼莫名,情绪久久难平。笔者为学生们的进步感到欣喜,更喜欢与他们一起,流连在优美的语句和精彩的构思里,享受写作!

优秀习作1

A Call to My Dad

16 级　左铭瑶

That was the year of the economic crisis. Thousands of people lost their jobs, my father being one of them.

I stepped out of the library and immediately a strong heat smote up into my face. Nevertheless, the blazing sun never drove away the gloom hanging over the city. Few people were in the street. I came here only to return some books as it seemed to me, in this particular time, it was better to borrow books than buying new ones.

When I raised my head, I saw a small shadow on the roof of the shopping mall across the road, sliced by the blinding sunlight, like a flimsy sheet of paper. A few seconds later, I realized that it couldn't be a piece of paper because no paper fell at that speed.

I must have stood there petrified for about ten minutes as the screams, the screech of brakes, and the shrilling of the cicadas became louder and louder, eventually depriving me of my hearing, until the ambulance sirens afar pulled me back. Then my hand, acting faster than my brain, reaching for the phone and dialed my father's number.

"Dad?"

"Yes?"

"…."

"What's wrong?"

"Nothing, I just finished and I'm coming home for lunch."

"Oh, okay. We'll be waiting for you."

I was being silly. I knew he wouldn't.

I knew. Yesterday, around the midnight, I was awakened by some hazy sounds of the turning pages and nib scratching on the papers. Tiptoeing to the door, by the dim light piercing into the crack, I saw father sitting on the sofa, with various papers and want ads spreading before him. Under the furrowed brows were his eyes glinting with an eager ray of hope.

He was stubborn, sometimes obstinate. For many years I had hated him for that, but this time, I was assured by his stubbornness.

评析： 本篇习作简洁、精炼，构思精巧，语言优美，无任何多余表达。看似平淡的语气，却把在经济萧条背景下父亲失业后艰难求职，同时又尽量不让女儿担忧，将努力维持女儿世界安稳的这份深情表现得淋漓尽致。

从文章开头平铺直叙的背景交代，到第二段对环境中隐隐不安的暗示和悬念的设置，细节处处铺垫到位而没有任何多余，如 strong heat, blazing sun, gloom, few people, borrow books instead of buying books,等等。第三段的情节逐渐展开，悬念层层堆积，细节描写更到位，a small shadow, sliced, blinding sunlight, a flimsy sheet of paper, no paper fell at that speed。像纸张一样飘下来的，原来是差点酿成事故的高空坠落的尖锐玻璃。

第四段描写差点被玻璃砸中的惊险。女儿清醒过来第一反应是去打电话给父亲。这段细节描写同样非常精彩：petrified, screams, the screech of brakes, the shrilling of the cicadas, depriving me of my hearing, ambulance sirens, my hand acting faster than my brain …用词精确到位，句式变化多样，情节推到最高潮，但情绪还没到最高点，作文题目在此处得到呼应。

接下来的简短对话，让心绪得到安抚。文章慢慢走向真相和揭示叙事的核心：父亲身负重压的不放弃(Under the furrowed brows were his eyes glinting with an eager ray of hope)和平时让女儿讨厌的固执(stubborness)，此刻却是一家人的精神支柱。文章至此将情绪推至最高点，点题，结束。全篇简洁明了，又意味深长,实在是一篇不可多得的佳作。

优秀习作2

Poet

15 级　付一甲

"Let us just hard pretend, ignoring the eyes full of stars in the rainstorm." Finally I wrote this verse as his epitaph.

The last time I went to the hospital to see him, he was still sleeping. He had been sleeping for a long time, peacefully and unconsciously. Pouring in through the rusty window, sunshine warmed his face and hair gently. Bees outside the window were trying to get in.

Several years ago, I was not a poet yet, but a friend of a poet. At that time, I was caught in a dilemma of life. I struggled and suffered, only to realize that for me, it was too hard to live, as well as to die. Sitting by the river in a little mountain village, we talked about suicide. He told me, "You should never choose to die because of the tough life, and you should never struggle to live because of the fear of death. Both of these two choices mean you are a coward." Dusk was coming, like a transparent amber. Sunlight sank into the river and disappeared. He turned his face to the setting sun, as if he was talking to me from a long distance, with a lonely shadow behind him.

I survived the hardest time. Last year we went to the same place. He was still an outstanding poet, an amazing genius. Geniuses are always hard to understand. Taking a deep breath, he turned his back to me, and closing his eyes in the morning breeze, he opened his arms as if to hug the rising sun. He said, "Nietzsche called himself a madman, but I can't. I just feel a madman lives in my heart, constantly reminding me that the world I saw is a huge illusion." He jumped into the river, and I knew he could not swim.

The doctor suggested stopping his treatment and removing his life support. Although his heart was still beating, the hope of his revival was slim. His brain, with too much thought there, had been oxygen-starved for too long. A bee flew in and landed on his pale hand, and did not move until his mother began to sob. She signed on the consent.

When his breathing machine was stopped, I thought that after all he could breathe freely now. I had never known a man as brave as he was, as great as he was, and as lonely as he was. He was dying. I saw a madman get out from his body, and give off strong light like a summer sun. The bee flew away, with its wings sparking brightly.

  Recently I called his mother. "What are you doing lately?" she asked me amiably. Looking at Van Gogh's self-portrait on the wall, I answered with a smile, "Writing poems." There was a silence for a while. Then she said, "I'm really lucky. I'm still a mother of a poet. God bless you, boy."

  So let us just hard pretend, ignoring the eyes full of stars in the rainstorm.

  评析：当时在全班读完这篇习作的时候，全班先是沉默，继而爆发出热烈的掌声。文章和上一篇一样，貌似语气平淡，缓缓道来，却有种震撼人心的力量，让人不觉置身其中，与作者感同身受。

  文章题目取名"Poet"（诗人）。作者是个诗人，更重要的是，作者曾经的挚友也是个诗人。文章以一句诗开头，而这句诗，是作者写下的墓志铭。发生了什么呢？读者这时好奇心已起。故事随后采取倒叙手法，中间穿插闪回，追述了作者的好友——一名诗人短暂却壮烈的一生。故事开头的情景是在医院，好友已经卧床不起，安静地躺在病床上。这里作者没有直接讲述自己或好友的心情，而是通过对医院环境的描述，来表达对命运的无可奈何和不甘：Pouring in through the rusty window, sunshine warmed his face and hair gently. Bees outside the window were trying to get in. 注意这里试图从窗外飞进来的蜜蜂，也是一种隐喻。

  随后作者追忆几年前，当他陷入困境时，好友如何帮助他渡过最艰难的时刻。这一段的场景是在黄昏的河边，两人讨论到自杀、生与死的选择。注意这个时候的 suicide 是作者的想法，而好友说，"you should never choose to die because of the tough life, and you should never struggle to live because of the fear of death. Both of these two choices mean you are a coward"（不能因为生活太艰难而去选择死亡，也不能因为害怕死亡而选择苟且偷生，只有懦夫才会这样做）。这里已经为后文做了铺垫和暗示：作者不能因为害怕生活艰辛而去求死，而后文好友正是因为不害怕死亡而选择了结自己的生命。小村的河边，黄昏，落日最后一丝光线，落日下好友的声音仿佛很遥远，特别是好友的孤单身影"with a lonely shadow behind him …"，对心理感受未提一字，但心境已经跃然纸上。

  叙事的高潮在下一段：同样是河边，却是早晨，朝阳初升。这样的对比也很巧妙，黄昏暗示一天将要结束，人生的黄昏则是生命即将走到尽头。而朝阳喻指生机和希望,好友却是在这样一个早晨结束自己的生命。但真的就只是生命结束了吗?作者描述好友结束生命前一刻的动作:opened his arms as if to hug the rising sun。一段生命的结束也许是另一段生命的开始。医生抢救无果,呼吸机停止的那一刻,具有象征意义的蜜蜂又一次出现:A bee flew in and landed on his pale hand。而好友也终于解脱了"after all he could breathe freely now",病魔终于不能再桎梏他的身体"madman get out from his body",死亡何尝不是一种重生,bee再次出现"The bee flew away, with its wings sparking brightly"。

文章结尾,作者也成了一名诗人,好友的母亲说:"我很幸运,我仍然是一个诗人的母亲。"文章在这里升华,也点题。作者以前不是诗人,受了好友的影响,成为诗人。而对于逝者母亲,人虽然不在了,留下的那么多诗歌,儿子何尝不是以另外一种形式存在呢?文章最后一句和开头第一句墓志铭呼应,对生命的感悟、人生的态度,不言自明。

一篇好的习作,离不开精彩的用词、优美的句子,却也绝对少不了巧妙的构思和情节的铺垫,本文就是这样的一篇代表作。

优秀习作3

Gardenia
16 级　史一凡

1

Trivial trees cast shadows, leaping across the cicadas.

Those several days, a little girl began to appear from time to time in my dreams. Invariably she walked into a two-story architecture from the comparatively dim porch, wearing a chiffon dress. I could hardly recognize who she was because of the darkness. The sight of her back really impressed me and the odd thing was that the porch was still dark, even though it was daytime. Her constant visit actually disturbed me a little bit, while curiosity and appetite for truth overwhelmed me, meanwhile, pushing me to adventure in the dream.

Who was she? Moreover, why did she exist in my dream? Maybe the porch had phenomenal magic, thus seducing little kids entering. And what's the grisliest might be the house itself, it may be the nest of a spooky serpent … Well, well, it's amazing …

With my eyes open and my feet peeking out of the end of the blanket, refreshing fragrance mixed with the wind gladdened my heart; I ceased my imagination about the girl.

2

Last summer vacation, I stayed with my grandma in the village. She was extremely lonely and missed me so much. With time going by, my grandma's memory was gradually obscure. My father, her beloved little son, was in a great passion to pick her up to the urban area to live with us. However, you know, the aged always had some sentimental attachment to the cropland and the rustic serenity.

That was true.

The lush leafy camphor trees along the roadside swung their branches and leaves and released a fragrant smell, seeming like an invitation to the passers-by. Masses of gardenia grew with energy, so innocent and beautiful. The smell of gardenia gave me a feeling of ecstasy, on top of this, it seemed that the smell opened my mind and compensated what I had lost for so long a stage. Piquant. In such quiet space, I always contemplated alone, drawing conclusions about life, such as, "life sometimes is like froth flowing in the sky, hard to touch and master."

"Evan, lunch time!" My grandma yelled from the dining room.

I stopped to be woolgathering and ran to her.

Just for entertaining her, I told my grandma about the girl in my dream. "Grandma, is there a little girl who's always in a white dress? About 7 or 8 years old?" I asked her, with an eager bite of the Double Fried Pork Slices, hoping that she could think of someone in white dress once appeared in her life and exercising her aging brain. "Ah! And she often has a gardenia hung on one side of her chest." Added me. My grandma looked at me kindly and laughed.

"She must be the girl who lives in the opposite bank," my grandma said with her eyes narrowing into slits. Perhaps she was forming a picture of the girl in her mind. She grinned a wide grin.

"Excellent!" My grandma's response threw me into ecstasy. So great that she could still remember something!

3

Everybody loves little lovely girl, I must say. What? Envy? A little ...

ha-ha ...

As a freshman, I adored those lovely little girls too. Past twenty years witnessed my industriousness and happiness to chase my ideal college, and of course, I made it.

However, I myself was an out-and-out tomboy.

My wardrobe was filled with T-shirt and blue jeans. In the parlance, I seldom tried on a dress. In the deep space of my memory, it seemed an institutionalized concept that I was not expected to wear a dress. To my curiosity, I did not need a dress either in the past several years. Even though that I dressed and behaved like a boy, a love letter appeared on my desk weeks ago when I was on campus, enclosed with the letter, there was a purely white gardenia with beads on it, giving out an intoxicating fragrance. It belonged to one of my classmates, specifically, a boy who was both tall and smart. I was wide-eyed after reading the words, simple but overwhelmingly strong, governed my mind. —"I like you."

Maybe it is a trick. First, I could hardly believe it in that I was such a common girl, with no splendid capacities and features.

Then I stole a glance at him. His face reddened with great shyness. The moment our eyes met, both of us evaded each other in bewilderment. Afterwards, however, we could not help allowing our sights to meet again. Goodness. When I look back on the scene, it brought me a kind of indispensable warmth. Who knows that? It may be the best symbol of innocent youth. The gardenia. The shyness. The secret. Above all, the girlish heart.

4

Meandering with my grandma in the path behind our house, and complimenting the rapid development in the hometown, my heart was full of excitement and keen wish. Faintly I heard my name reverberating in the air, Evan, Evan ... It was a man's voice, raucous and rough.

What? My name?

I turned around, only to find a girl. Of course, she was the girl "who lived in the opposite bank" as my grandma explained before.

She turned to me with a small handful of dried flowers in her little hands. They were gardenias. Exactly, she herself was walking towards me. With her appearance clearer, I was getting more and more nervous. However, all the scenery vanished the moment she was about to show up in front of my eyes. Next second, I found myself sleeping in my bed, with my grandma sleeping beside me. At the same time, I found a line of tears was running down my face.

What's the matter? ... Well, I can certainly say I must have some elusive relation with the girl because of a new character's shout.

I needed some time to get rid of the nightmare.

On the other hand, my grandma was inclined to forget what has happened several days before. Thinking of her kindness and painstaking life, I was very sad. What a poor woman! All right, maybe one day, I should suffer from amnesia myself in my old age. With unfailing childlike appetite for the joy of game, she suddenly would like to tell me more about the girl living in the opposite bank.

Okay, I could not refuse her sincerity while I have no interests in what she was going to tell me.

She told me that the little girl living in the opposite bank once owned a nickname, Gardenia, due to her extreme love for the flower. She was the apple of her family's eyes. One day, it was in the afternoon, a middle-aged man sexually insulted her. The heinous man told her that her father was staying at his home, and invites her to come back home with him so that she could find her father.

What a poor little girl! What a disgusting guy!

5

I knew that I was again in a dream, a nightmare, which meant my half-sober state of mind. This time, I saw the two-story architecture and the comparatively dim porch, the girl in a chiffon dress, her impressive back and a man's back. The two were walking into the house. In order to resolve the mystery, I followed them inside.

"Uncle, where's my dad?" the girl was asking in a sweet voice.

I hid myself behind the door so that I would not be found and driven away, or maybe I just knew that I was in the dream controlled by myself. While staying in the space, I was not afraid at all.

"Your father told me that he would go to buy you some toys and bring you some fresh gardenias," the man said in smile. "Let's play a game and wait for your dad?"

"Yes!" replied the girl happily.

The man, with his eyes squinting, stripped his trousers ...

Anger and shock pushed me to stop his shameless behavior. I was going to beat him with a vase on the table; however, my passion was curbed when the girl who lived in the opposite bank turned back suddenly, her eyes, her nose, and birthmark in her back ... The girl was ... me ... me myself.

All of a sudden, my world collapsed without any reservation.

6

After the incident, nothing seemed to change in the village. The man who owned a two-story house was wealthy enough to drive us away from the region. His daughter bought me some snacks as compensation. Undoubtedly, she knew her father well and was habituated to dealing with his trouble and nuisance. Together with his daughter, his wife came to our home in a rage.

"His wife shouted at the little girl who lived in the opposite bank that she should not wear dress because it was like a deliberate seduction." I went to my grandma for some more so-called details which was unknown to me.

Once upon a time, my family called me gardenia. Once upon a time, I loved to wear a white dress, singing and dancing in the farmland. Once upon a time, the village seemed to be so peaceful but also, dark.

None of the family would be willing to turn to the police for help, or go to the court to reveal the evil. Engaging in a lawsuit can not only cost a lot, but also result in others' backbiting the girl. You know, it was a stigma in one's life, and, the family's shame.

Maybe my body preferred to forget the memory. Or maybe I was too young to keep them in mind. However, I actually remembered everything bad.

Additionally, no previous photos before my attending elementary school were kept in my house, thus failing to show such thorough differences in my nature and appetite. In fact, I would like to express my sheer gratitude towards my family for their consideration and thoughtfulness. I chose to forget, and I did. The following 10-plus years, I lived in a world of optimism and freedom and was surrounded by love and care.

7

In the dream, it occurred to me again the boy, the clean words and the pure gardenias. I smiled a big smile, as if I had never been hurt, walking into the police station.

评析：读完本篇习作,笔者当时就起了一身鸡皮疙瘩:震撼! 意料之外又似乎有迹可循……笔者读完习作,第一个念头就是希望这不是真实经历,而是虚构的。精彩的情节设计、精妙的构思、细腻的文笔,看似漫不经心的叙事其实环环相扣、节奏紧张,让读者沉浸其中欲罢不能。故事里有两条线:一条是明线,主角是作者"我";另一条线是"我"视野里的故事主角——小女孩。明线暗线各自发展却又相辅相成,直到最后融为一体,故事的紧张感达到顶点。

第一节,故事的起因:"我"梦境里经常出现的小女孩,走进一栋两层小楼。阴暗的门廊及楼里的漆黑一片却让作者觉得小女孩的背影异常清晰。作者这里的用词已经处处在为情节做铺垫:dark porch (even in daytime), little girl in a white dress, the porch seducing little kids entering,等等。作为旁观者的作者,仿佛被某种力量吸引,想去探寻真相,作者这里的用词很到位:curiosity and appetite for truth overwhelmed me。因为是旁观者,作者的心情是轻松的,对屋子的想象是:it may be the nest of a spooky serpent。

第二节,故事闪回到现实生活中祖母居住的小山村。用细腻的笔触描述小山村的平静和美好:道路两旁摇曳着的樟树像是在盛情地邀请客人来访"invitation to the passers-by"；栀子花开的芳香美好"gardenia … so innocent and beautiful"；"the smell of gardenia … a feeling of ecstasy … opened my mind",记忆的大门徐徐开启。祖母会知道梦境里喜欢穿白裙、口袋里装着栀子花的七八岁小女孩吗? "a little girl in white dress" "has a gardenia hung on her chest …"记忆逐渐衰退的祖母仿佛还记得:must be the girl who lives in the opposite bank。"我"的探索真相之路似乎很快能找到答案。

第三节,故事回到作者这条明线,交代作者自己的情况:大学新生,衣柜里全是T恤和牛仔裤,对不穿裙子习以为常的假小子似的女孩,在收到班上男生带着栀子花清香的表白信(intoxicating fragrance)后,作者用一种看似漫不经心的口吻,把平凡女孩(a common girl, with no splendid capacities and features)对初恋的懵懂和欢欣雀跃写得栩栩如生——"stole a glance at him" "our eyes met … evaded each other in bewilderment" "could not help allowing our sights meet again" "a kind of indispensable warmth"。同时,作者在这里也用洁白的栀子花,指代美好无瑕的初恋时光。

第四节,故事回到小山村——和小女孩可能交会的地方,情节缓缓推进。平静的小山村似乎并不平静,"我"仿佛听到一个沙哑、刺耳的(raucous and rough)男人声音在唤自己的名字;祖母嘴里"住对面银行的小女孩",手里捧着干枯的栀子花向"我"走来,"我"却看不清面容。随着女孩越走越近(appearance clearer),"我"却越来越紧张(more and more nervous)。然而还没看清面容,下一刻已从梦里惊醒,脸上却带着泪痕(tears running down)。到底怎么回事?小女孩发生了什么?相信读者读到这里心里也产生了疑问。作者在这里并没有把答案和悬疑保留太久。记忆衰退的祖母突然兴致勃勃地告诉"我"对面小女孩的事情:这个特别喜欢栀子花因而被人称为"栀子花"的孩子被父母视若珍宝。然而某天下午,被一个中年男人哄骗去找爸爸,然后中年人 sexually insulted her。

故事至此,似乎真相大白,让人心疼的孩子,让人诅咒的中年男人。然而作者的这条明线和故事里的小女孩的另一条暗线,她们之间的唯一交集,只是祖母嘴里探寻到真相后就结束了吗?"我"能做些什么呢?

第五节,故事并没结束。作者通过前文里非常成功的叙事节奏,把真正的真相通过梦境叙述出来,悬疑和紧张感在这一节被推到了极点。正因为这种巧妙的构思和设计,读者在接触到真相的一刻,内心才会受到巨大震撼!作者依然是用梦境在推进情节发展,梦里的"我"看到了小女孩和中年男人走进屋子,我悄悄地跟着,伺机而动帮助小女孩。作者通过对话描写交代人物,告诉读者,罪恶将要发生。"我"忍无可忍(anger and shock pushed me to stop),准备将桌子上的花瓶砸向罪恶的人(beat him with a vase on the table),这个时候,小女孩转过身来,"我"顿时僵住(这里的用词是"my passions was curbed",精彩)。真相呼之欲出:"her eyes, her nose, and birthmark in her back … The girl was … me … me myself!"读到这里,读者被作者的叙述牢牢吸引住,对文中"我"的震撼和难以置信完全感同身受。作者设置的两条线:明线"我"和暗线"爱栀子花的小女孩"融合成一条线。多日里若隐若现的记忆,梦里一直出现的小女孩,全部清晰起来,读者的心随之也变得沉重(my world collapsed)。

第六节,对真相的细节补充。曾经刻意遗忘的十几年前的往事一一浮现。作者用平静的语气,简洁却有力地控诉了山村的愚昧、落后:受害人竟然是"stigma in one's life""the family's shame"。施暴者妻子助纣为虐,居然认为七八岁孩子穿裙子是"a deliberate seduction"。看似荒唐可笑的借口,作者何尝不是借此在控诉社会中对女性的歧视和偏见呢！因为施暴者在当地势力大，受害者求助无门只能远走他乡。作者在文中用了一系列的排比句，来描述回忆起所有真相的心酸和无奈："Once upon a time, my family called me gardenia. Once upon a time, I loved to wear a white dress, singing and dancing ... Once upon a time, the village seemed to be so peaceful but also, dark." 家里人尽量抹平相关的一切印记来保护她 "no previous photos" "their consideration and thoughtfulness" "I chose to forget, and I did" "live in a world of optimism and freedom" "surrounded by love and care"。故事到这里似乎可以结束了，受害者走出阴影，岁月从此静好。但是正义和真理呢？结局给了读者一个答案。最好的解脱，不是逃避，而是勇敢地正视它，这才是社会良好的秩序得以维持的根本。

文章很长，但行文流畅，从头到尾一气呵成。叙事节奏和层层递进的情节，颇显作者的功底。语言虽有瑕疵，但瑕不掩瑜，精准的用词、多变的句式结构、细节的运用等，都是一个成功故事不可缺少的部分。

优秀习作 4

The Night Before College

16 级　冯虹阳

If there's any night I would never forget now and in the future, the night before college must be one.

Thinking back then, the trees stood still like a tower, no matter how the wind blew. I just had dinner and was lying on a deck chair, watching the white clouds wandering ahead. Nothing could be better than the nice dinner and the cool drinks after a long burning day.

That day looked like another normal day of my summer vacation before my college life until my mother asked me when the school would begin.

A casual glance at the phone changed everything. Then the drinks was tipped over and spilt everywhere, winds came from nowhere shook the tree violently. The white clouds ahead was gone, replaced by some malicious dark clouds. Everything are just messed up within one second.

An anxious feeling flushed up, making me stunned. I had no idea what I felt at that moment. Was I excited or worried? Was I thrilled or frightened? I didn't know. All I could remember was how uncomfortable, how unsettling I was, felt no right thing to do, just pacing impatiently around the house, looking for something to hold on to.

Then came my mother. She said one sentence and only one. The one I still bear in my heart. "You are a grown man. Face it yourself." Somehow my mind was cleared up at that very moment for that very sentence.

It was a night to remember. Maybe it's the cool drink. Maybe it's mom's words.

评析：普通人的生活中或许并没有那么多生与死的考验，或者惊心动魄的瞬间。如何把一个平平无奇的故事写出不平常的味道来？本篇习作给出了一个很好的答案。

文章的题目是上大学的前一晚。上大学的前一天晚上有什么好写的呢，不很平常吗？这是读者可能会有的疑问。作者的叙述也是从这样一个寻常的晚上开始的。作者很善于通过环境的细节描写衬托心情：风吹树不动(trees stood still like a tower, no matter how the wind blew)，夏天一天的酷热过后，作者酒足饭饱，喝着冰冰凉的饮料(nice dinner, cool drinks)，躺着看天空白云飘(watching the white clouds)，多么惬意啊！

转折来了，妈妈的一句话打破了这种惬意，"哪天开学？"原来明天就是！毫无准备呀，于是心情不美了，各种慌乱：饮料打翻了(drinks tipped over)；风狂树摇(wind … shook the tree violently)；白云不见了(white clouds gone)，取而代之的是"malicious dark clouds"；心情五味杂陈(excited or worried, thrilled or frightened, uncomfortable, unsettling)，手足无措，只知道在屋子里乱走一气，想抓住点什么东西才好(pace impatiently around, look for something to hold on to)。

最后还是妈妈的话平复了作者的情绪。平常一晚的不平常，全是心情在作怪呀！

优秀习作 5

The Old Locust Tree

15 级 刘瑶瑶

People say that "smell carries memory". The smell of gunpowder might revive the formidable hardship a soldier pulled through, resounded by yelling and crying; the smell of ink might remind a retired professor of the days when he was lecturing vigorously and paving exuberantly in the classroom, weighed by those avid and inquisitive gazes; the smell of the sea might awake a sailor's experience of steering the boat and carving out his way in the storm, threatened by monster waves and colossal fear as well as loneliness. There is a kind of smell lingering deep in my memory, occasionally flooding into my heart, evoking enormous rosy nostalgia and retrospection inside me. That is the delicate fragrance of the old locust tree, a tree that colored my childhood with peace and happiness.

I used to stand under the tree, looking up through its lush leaves and intricate branches and smiling. I saw the sunlight pouring in the tree and flowing on those leaves. The lovely light spots are like lively sprites jumping up and down, left and right, tickling the green leaves into giggling laughter. I observed the gentle and caring touch of the wind, caressing the head of the tree and whispering to it in a mothering tongue. I stood there, hair flying, arms spreading, head raising, content with just being indulged in such peace and pleasure. "The tree must be happy," I thought, "observing the world without disturbance, thinking to infinity without constraint, speaking to the world without reservation." After a while, when I was idle and drowsy, I would sit against the tree and close my eyes, with the refreshing wind bringing the sweet fragrance to me, as if there were flowers blossoming in my mind.

Almost every time I would be wakened up by mum just before falling asleep, sometimes for meals, at others for schoolwork or other trivial matters. Mum would look at the grand tree and said cheerfully, "I will find some day to pick up some locust flowers to make locust pastry!" Looking at mum, looking at the tree, I felt I was smelling the newly made locust pastry.

On summer noons, mum would bring me to the tree, sit in the shadow and teach me to recite poems and practice writing calligraphy. Mum was strict with me on study. Sometimes we would talk of something entertaining and we both burst into laughter. Sometimes I would feel unable to follow mum's instructions and throw the pencil away, choking and sobbing. Our voices merged into the rustling of locust tree leaves. Our faces shone by the sunlight leaked through the branches. The tree embraced us and watched us in silence.

I have always thought the tree was loving me. When I was leaving it, I could always feel the wind was holding me up and pushing me back, as if the tree has asked it to keep me. "Stay," I heard the tree saying, "stay with me."

"I will stay. I have never left. You are in my heart. As always."

评析： 本篇习作与其说是一篇叙事文，不如说是一篇散文。作者有很强的语言功底和比较大的词汇量。作为一个二年级学生，能够把低频的高级词汇准确、得体地用在写作中，实属难能可贵。因为很多学生往往在追求词汇的高级和低频时，写出来的句子却略显尴尬。本文的词汇极其丰富，而且用得都恰到好处，精彩的示范非常多。

作者用如散文一般的笔触开始刻画 "smell carries memories" 的概念，在读者面前展开一幅幅生动的画面：关于战士，火药的气味会让战士忆起刚熬过的艰苦生活（the formidable hardship a soldier pulled through）；关于退休老教授，墨水的气味会让他想起课堂里热情授课的情景（lecturing vigorously and paving exuberantly）；关于水手（awake a sailor's experience of steering the boat and carving out his way in the storm）。由此引出主题，也就是作者记忆深处对老槐树的美好回忆。这一段的用词非常精彩：排比句式里的 "revive" "formidable hardship" "resounded" "weighed" "avid and inquisitive gazes"；自己流连的记忆 "lingering" "flooding into" "evoking enormous rosy nostalgia and retrospection" "delicate fragrance" 等。

随后是老槐树下的记忆回溯和美好瞬间，作者强大的词汇量和良好的语言功底把作文变成了美文鉴赏："looking up through its lush leaves and intricate branches and smiling" "sunlight pouring in the tree and flowing on those leaves" "lovely light spots are like lively sprites jumping up and down, left and right, tickling the green leaves into giggling laughter"。绿叶 "tickling ... into giggling laughter" 的描写简直令人拍案叫绝。后文中的 "gentle and caring touch of the wind ... caressing ... whispering to it in a mothering tongue" 又十分形象生动，温柔的风抚摸着树梢，像母亲一般喃喃低语，多么美好的画面！而后引出 "indulged in such peace and pleasure" 里的作者对老槐树的印象 "The tree must be happy"，因为可以 "observing the world without disturbance, thinking to infinity without constraint, speaking to the world without reservation"。因此，在树下和树共度的时光也是快乐的。老槐树下有那么多美好的回忆：饭菜里的槐花香，和妈妈一起的学习时光，读书，画画，写字，因为开心而大笑，因为伤心而啜泣……作者笔下的老槐树下的光阴如此美好，让读者也不禁心生向往。

值得注意的是，对于英语中高级词汇和低频词汇的使用，把握好度是非常重要的。用得太多就有堆砌辞藻之嫌，语言徒有华丽的外表而没有真情实感是写作大忌。情感的真挚和丰沛，永远都是叙事性写作的重点。值得肯定的是，本文的作者在这两点上都把握得不错。

优秀习作6

Footsteps

15级　戴巳婧

For my entire childhood, I lived with my mother in a fairly nice but extremely rural place. My parents' marriage broke down and they separated since I was 7 years old. What is more, my father never paid maintenance for my mother and me. So my mother, a poor woman, had no choice but to work even harder than before to support me. Every summer and winter vacation throughout elementary school, she locked me at home and went out for work. My mother didn't allow me to go out alone in order to keep me safe. Therefore, I always spent my whole day with homework and boring TV programs in an empty house.

But something horrible happened when I was 9 years old, which I still remembered it was in an August evening. That is a zinger of a day and it was raining cats and dogs. Due to the bad weather, I thought my mother would come back home much later than usual. Out of sheer boredom I lay on the bed and watched TV in the bedroom. The Movie Channel was showing a horror film, which was a Japanese movie in the 1990s. In fact, I rarely watched a horror film alone, even until now. But just as a saying goes, "Curiosity killed the cat." So, for the first time, I began to watch it. The movie was extremely terrifying for a 9-year-old little girl and several times I was almost leaping out of my bed. As the dusk was growing darker and the rain was slowing down, I looked outside the window and thought my mother would come back soon. As I looked back at the television, the fearsome ghost in the movie was staring at me fiercely and gloomily. Suddenly, there was a blackout and darkness pouring into the house. At that time I heard a beep from the air condition before it switched off. Staring at the black television screen and holding my breath, I sat on the bed motionlessly. Then, I realized it was the power that was gone.

By that time it was completely dark outside and the rain had already stopped. Everything fell into silence. In a quiet room, if you press your ear against a pillow, you can hear your heartbeat. In the darkness, I could hear my heartbeat clearly because of fear and helplessness. Just after a few minutes, it came to me that I should find a candle so as to see the light again.

When I was ready to get out of bed, a strange voice occurred—"tah tah". It was like the sound of the heel of leather shoes. I was so scared that I went back to bed again, promptly covering my head with the quilt.

"Is that a thief breaking into my house?" I thought. "So what on earth can I do?"

Closer and closer came the sound, getting louder as it came; my heart was in my mouth. I predicted that the thief would break in the bedroom and discovered me in the next second. However, I waited for several minutes in despair. Consequently, no one entered my room. It seemed that nothing had happened. The strange sound also disappeared.

"Maybe not a thief," I thought.

As I calmed down a little, the strange sound was on again. This time, another horrible thought came into my mind. I remembered the plot of the horror movie I just saw—the female ghost killed every human cruelly each time she heard the sound of his or her breath. Still hiding under the quilt, I became more and more convinced of this possibility.

"The ghost must be next to me! Just out of the quilt!" I panicked.

I squeezed my eyes tightly shut, also holding my breath.

"This can't be happening!" my mind roared. "Mom! Please help me! Please, Mom!" I screamed as loudly as I could, of course just in mind, for I dared not emit any sound in case of being caught by the ghost. It filled me with a kind of dread that is, even after all these years, indescribable.

Just when I affirmed that I was going to be killed by the ghost, I heard the door opening. And the next second, every light in the house was on.

"Honey, where are you?" I heard my mother's voice! She pushed back the quilt and looked at me stunningly.

"What happened to you, honey?" she asked urgently.

"I ... I don't know ... I don't know what happened." My fear of the whole event being ineffable was coming true.

"What do you mean that you don't know what happened? Oh, look at you. How can you be so sweaty?" she asked again.

"I don't know ... I was afraid. Mom, I miss you." I burst into tears.

She held onto me tightly and comforted me without saying another word.

Even until now, I don't know what that sound was and where it came from. After that horrible experience, I have never watched horror films alone.

Maybe, I really met a ghost that day.

评析：本文的主角是一个9岁小女孩，雨夜她独自在家，因为禁不住好奇心驱使，看了电影频道的一个恐怖片，随后家里突然停电。

作者对环境的刻画和心理描写很成功："the fearsome ghost in the movie was staring at me fiercely and gloomily" "a blackout" "darkness poured into the house" "a beep from the air condition before it switched off" "holding my breath" "sat on the bed motionlessly"。沉浸在恐怖的电影情节中时，面对突如其来的停电，女孩吓得大气不敢出，一动不敢动。这是一种如临其境的真实描写。对于环境特别是安静的细节刻画："In a quiet room, if you press your ear against a pillow, you can hear your heartbeat" "When I was ready to get out of bed, a strange voice occurred—'tah tah'. It was like the sound of the heel of leather shoes."

作者的心理通过与自己的对话来映衬："Is that a thief breaking into my house?" "So what on earth can I do?" "Maybe not a thief."脚步声靠近时，紧张得心都跳到嗓子眼了，"my heart was in my mouth"的表达非常到位。当声音消失，作者逐渐平静下来后，异常的声音又来了。这时候恐怖电影中的类似情节加深了作者的恐惧，"The ghost must be next to me! Just out of the quilt!" "panick" "eyes tightly shut" "holding breath"，细节描写成功地反映了作者的心理。

随后一段文中作者的恐惧达到极点。通过细腻的心理活动和动作的刻画，作者成功地传达了当时的心理感受，本能地向不在场的妈妈呼救："This can't be happening!" "Mom! Please help me! Please, Mom!"使用了一系列表达词（"my mind roared" "screamed as loudly as I could" "filled me with a kind of dread"）。然而怕到极致却不敢喊不出来，"dared not emit any sound" "scream ... of course in my mind"，这种巨大的让人几乎窒息的恐惧，作者用了一个词来总结——indescribable，这种恐惧感多年以后作者仍然清楚记得。后文中妈妈回来了，也有sweaty这样的细节补充当时的感受。这件事的后遗症，就是作者再也不敢一个人看恐怖片了。

文中结尾很简单，但是留给读者满满的想象空间，"maybe I really met a

ghost that day"。真是这样吗,这个 ghost,恐怕更多来自内心吧!

优秀习作 7

The Teaching Building

16 级　赵旭阳

I had never lost my way before that day.

I still paid extra attention to the way I came into the teaching building. I always try to remember that when I go somewhere for the first time.

The bell rang, which indicates the end of my first day in junior high school. I went downstairs, slowly, just as if I was 70 years old with all the worry and hesitation in the world dwelling in my mind.

"Hey, what's wrong with you?" she caught up with me and said.

"I forget the way out," I said in depression.

She ran in front of me and went straight down. After a freeze within one second, I followed in.

It was until I stepped out of the door that I realized we were still not on the right way. It was a back door leading to the back garden. I walked around. We were surrounded by all kinds of plants with so large leaves that I felt as if we were travelling in the tropics. Amazingly, I saw a scarlet rose blooming lonely among the greens.

I stretched my hands and tried to pick it. I could feel the thorns penetrateing my fingers clearly as bleeding, but strange enough, they didn't hurt me as expected.

And something stranger happened. The moment I picked the rose in my hand, it began to wither.

"Come here, I have something for you," I called her in a hurry as I was also running towards her.

She turned back, only to see a bald stem, with all petals falling on the ground.

I had never seen her face so clearly that I even couldn't believe it was true. The sunset was shining, softly enlightening her face, skirt and skin. Her pin was shining in orange. Her tassels beside legs were swaying in breeze. Stars were glimmering in the dark blue sky east.

And she smiled, with all the petals came dancing in the melody of the wind.

Suddenly, she grasped my hand, and ran back to the building, as if she finally recalled the way after racking her brains. I followed with ecstasy. Feelings were that I had never been so filled with safety, for I was definitely sure she would lead me out.

She went upstairs and upstairs, until there were no stairs at all—we came to the roof. The darkness in the sky was engulfing the last lights in the west, slowly, but irresistibly.

I suddenly realized that, there was no way out at all, for the building itself is a maze. Ironically enough, it was a long time until I realized life is a maze as well.

Then she ran toward the sun, faster and faster. I followed her, with no hesitation this time.

She jumped down, so did I.

It hurt a lot. I opened my eye, and found myself falling out of my bed.

评析：你跳，我也跳。这是电影《泰坦尼克号》里的一句台词。本篇中也出现了类似的情节，当然类似的也仅此一点。

文章题目为"教学楼"，内容似乎跟教学楼没有太多关系。教学楼只是一个引子，或者是某一种环境的代表。这也是本篇习作的特色，并没有明显地代表某一类型的故事叙述，没有陈规旧俗的框定，也就显得有趣。

开头部分读者很容易以为是校园青春剧，迷失在像迷宫一样的教学楼里的男孩和女孩，寻找出去的路。作者强调了自己路盲的特质："pay special attention to the way""try to remember""went downstairs slowly as if I were 70 years old with all the worry and hesitation in the world dwelling in my mind"。最后还是迷路了，遇到了陌生女孩，犹豫了一秒跟上。注意这里是犹豫后才跟上，跟后文形成对照。作者善于通过人物动作表达思想感情。女孩"ran in front of me""went straight down"，作者"followed in""stepped out""walked around""travelled into"，一系列的动作描述后，来到了楼后的花园里。作者看到了花园里一朵殷红的玫瑰，摘下来想送给女孩。奇怪的是，玫瑰刺扎进手指，流血了却感觉不到疼；还有玫瑰花一摘下来瞬间枯萎，这一切似乎都在暗示着某种不同寻常。寻找出口的短暂旅途带了些冒险和奇幻的色彩。读者读到这里想必也好奇接下来要发生什么。

来到顶楼了,天色渐晚,已经无路可寻(The darkness in the sky was engulfing the last lights in the west, slowly, but irresistibly),engulfing 用得精妙无比。作者这时意识到教学楼就是一个迷宫,而人生也正如迷宫一样。女孩朝太阳跑去,这一次,我没有犹豫立刻跟着跑去。女孩跳下了楼,我也跳了。

很疼。是悲剧发生了吗。哦不,梦醒了。所以玫瑰刺扎手不疼,一摘玫瑰花瓣即枯萎……在梦里一切奇幻都顺理成章。

全文构思精巧,奇妙又有趣。以梦为大场景,代指人生像迷宫一样,处处面临抉择。行文流畅、明晰,善用细节烘托环境和人物,有些地方的场景和人物的外貌形态描写堪称经典:"The sunset was shining, softly enlightening her face, skirt and skin. Her pin was shining in orange. Her tassels beside legs were swaying in breeze. Stars were glimmering in the dark blue sky east."还有把女孩的微笑和风中飞舞的花瓣比作"she smiled, with all the petals came dancing in the melody of the wind",非常优美。

优秀习作 8

Blue

16 级　郑淑娴

"Daddy, where are we going?"

"Heading to the beach, sweetie." Hands on wheel, I heard my own voice.

In the rear-view mirror, Bonnie's limpid blue eyes twinkled with merriment. What incomparable, inspiring eyes, like a singing dolphin wandering in the depths of the sea—the same feature shared by every heroine of my novels. No wonder angels are always depicted as girls of 7 or 8; such charmingly innocent eyes can only be possessed by them.

"Bert, have your eyes on the highway. Be careful," said Elsa beside.

"Oh darling you know I can only have eyes for you, don't you? How can I ever shift a moment to the cars …"

"Oh, save it! You were just looking at Bonnie." Elsa's lips pouted invitingly, gilded by the flowing sunshine, so soft and delicate the curve. Sweet air.

"Stop it! S …" Beep! Beep! Screams were piercing the air. "Daddy!"

… "Daddy!"

Eyes popped wide.

"Whew, a nightmare." Bert sat up slowly, his head feeling a dull pain. Elsa wasn't here. A twinge of insecurity hit upon Bert—so much so that he shouted, "Elsa!" No response. Before he could take a deep breath for another shout, Bonnie came running in.

"What's up, Dad?"

"Sweetie, call your mom in. I'd like her to read my new episode in Chapter 6. I finished it last night."

Bonnie's mouth quivered in the suspicion of a smile. "Mom's gone on a vacation, don't you remember?"

Bert was about to say something, when he noticed a little girl appear in the doorway, whose blue eyes resembled Bonnie's to such an extent that one single sight of them already dazzled him. "Anyway, who's that girl? Seems to be the same age of you."

Bonnie turned back. It took her several seconds to reply, "She's my daughter, Dad."

Bert laughed, "Naughty. Another game of make-believe, isn't it? You know how much I wish your mom had brought forth twins 8 years ago, then you'd had a sister as a lifelong playmate."—instead of some unknown neighbor living in the block—Bert darted an impatient look at the little girl, who was leaning against the wall and peering at him.

Bonnie sat down on the edge of the bed, saying nothing.

"By the way, what's the date today?"

"28 April," Bonnie answered.

A faint smile flashed across his face. "Um, that's right. The year?"

"Dad, you must have had a bad sleep last night," she complained. "It's 2009. Everybody knows."

He frowned, paused for a moment, and continued, "Think it over, sweetie. Is it 2009 or something else?"

Silence.

"Do you remember the beach we went to yesterday? With your MOM," Bert hinted. "What's the date stamped on those entrance tickets?"

Bonnie lowered her head, her face unclear to see.

"No worries. If you're unable to figure it out right now," he patted her hand consolingly. "Let's leave it tomorrow. Now, could you help me by calling in auntie Mary?"

Bonnie nodded in relief, stood up and ran out, as if set free from a cell.

Bert sighed. He cast a glance at his desk opposite—where the table lamp was still on—strewn with piles of paper of neat handwriting. Crushed spitballs filled the wicker basket at the foot of the desk—and some rolling down on the ground, in which lied a mass of scribbles. He raised from the bed and sat at the desk. Holding the pencil, he began to conceive the plots where he stopped last night.

"Bert?" Mary came in, with a glass of water in hand.

He rose his head. "Morning Mary. Did Bonnie take the pills today? She started talking nonsense again just now."

Mary put the glass on the desk, "Not yet."

Bert nodded. "The daughter thing, mom's out on vacation, wrong date, all things like that. You know … it's 1989 … how could she have said 20 years ahead in the future? Anyway, do you know where Elsa's been? It's abnormal of her to get up so early."

"I'll go and see."

"Thanks."

Mary went out and closed the door. Waiting there, with a trace of bitterness, Bonnie asked, "Have you dissolved his pills in that glass of water?"

Bert sat there, contemplating the photograph on the desk—on the beach lied Elsa. He wrote down once again, "I can only have eyes for you, darling."—the same, repeated, only line occupying throughout all the mounting piles.

评析：一篇好的文章，文笔、想象、构思、叙事一个都不能少。本篇习作这几方面都结合得很好。还有一个很大的特点，就是对话的描写。有效的对话能给文章增添不少色彩。但是对话描写不那么容易，什么该写，什么该省，该怎么写，不是单独运用技巧就可以水到渠成的。作者不仅需要对笔下人物的性格揣摩透彻，还要能敏锐地察觉、体会对话后面人物的性格张力。对话的功能一般有三个：一是提供背景知识；二是揭示人物关系；三是推动情节发展。本篇习作一共有4段不同人物之间的对话，三个功能都有体现。

第一段对话是主人公一家三口去海边，对话在父女、夫妻之间展开。对话很简短，然而背景和人物介绍得很清楚，核心句子第一次出现，丈夫对妻子说："Oh darling you know I can only have eyes for you"。最后女儿失声高呼"Daddy"，随后车祸发生。

第二段长对话发生在父女之间。这段对话最长，对情节的推动和发展，对人物性格、心情的描述都起到关键的作用。一开始是从噩梦中醒来的父亲，一开口就喊妻子的名字"Elsa"，答应的却是女儿，"What's up, Dad?" "Sweetie, call your mom in. I'd like her to read my new episode in Chapter 6. I finished it last night"。女儿嘴唇微颤，回答"Mom's gone on a vacation, don't you remember?"妻子因车祸丧生，转眼20年过去，而失去那一段记忆的丈夫却懵然不知。在此段对话里，女儿Bonnie已经长大成人，又生了和当年的Bonnie一样大的女儿。Bonnie两次试图让父亲回到现实中，一次是当父亲问起Bonnie的女儿是谁，"who's that girl? Seems to be the same age of you"，"she's my daughter, Dad"。这里对Bonnie的动作又有细微的刻画：Bonnie turned back. It took her several seconds to reply. 然而父亲却把她当成8岁的女儿在淘气："Naughty. Another game of make-believe, isn't it? You know how much I wish your mom had brought forth twins 8 years ago, then you'd had a sister as a lifelong playmate."第二次，当父亲问起日期，Bonnie再次如实相告（"By the way, what's the date today?"，"28 April"，"Um, that's right. The year?"，"Dad, you must have had a bad sleep last night," she complained. "It's 2009. Everybody knows"）。然而父亲依然停留在20年前："think it over, sweetie"。Bonnie沉默，父亲继续问道："Do you remember the beach we went to yesterday? With your MOM"。对话明确地告诉读者，父亲的时间停留在20年前去海滩后的第二天。"What's the date stamped on those entrance tickets?"这里的细节描写非常到位，对于Bonnie来说也是无比扎心，"lowered her head, her face unclear to see"。

究竟是父亲失忆还是女儿生病？第三段对话在Mary和父亲之间进行，进一步推动了情节发展。"Morning Mary. Did Bonnie take the pills today? She started talking nonsense again just now"原来父亲以为生病的是女儿。"not yet"。在父亲随后的对话里，女儿试图唤醒父亲，却被父亲认为是她生病的依据："The daughter thing, mom's out on vacation, wrong date, all things like that. You know ... it's 1989 ... how could she have said 20 years ahead in the future? Anyway, do you know where Elsa's been? It's abnormal of her to get up so early"。到底是谁生病？这里作者设置了悬念。父亲又问起妻子的下落，Mary的回答

很正常:"I'll go and see"。

最后一段对话是女儿和 Mary 之间的,只有一句问话:"Have you dissolved his pills in that glass of water?"至此,四段对话描写完毕,答案揭晓。父亲在20年前的车祸中失去了妻子,从此父亲记忆一直停留在20年前。父亲对妻子深沉的爱,女儿知道真相却为了父亲的感受不忍告知的痛苦和无奈,Mary 作为保姆或者亲戚(文中没有具体交代)的同情和配合,都一一展示了出来。

在文章结尾,父亲看着桌上妻子的照片,嘴里自言自语"I can only have eyes for you, darling"。这句深情的告白,也是堆满桌子的文稿上唯一的一个句子。作者并没有明确说明为什么会写满这么厚的一叠纸,这里面想象的空间都留给了读者。也许父亲内心是知道真相的,但是仍拒绝去面对。因为承认女儿没错,承认今年是20年以后,意味着挚爱的妻子已经永远地离开了。

本篇习作还稍显稚嫩,但是全篇的对话描写、环境的烘托、人物性格的塑造、文字的运用技巧等都是值得肯定的,不失为一篇优秀的叙事文。

优秀习作9

The Dragon Boat Festival

11 级 何磊静

When it comes to the Dragon Boat Festival, presumably the first idea occurring in our minds is that we are going to jump at a statutory holiday. Nevertheless, by no means can we afford to lose sight of the splendid history and long-cherished tradition of the festival. The Dragon Boat Festival is believed to derive from the Warring States Period during which there existed an upright, loyal and highly-esteemed poet Qu Yuan, who was so patriotic that after being disgraced and dismissed by the evil and corrupt officials, he resolutely leapt into the Miluo River. And thereafter, people began to commemorate him on the 5th day of the 5th month of the lunar calendar—and that may be the widely accepted origin of this festival.

As a consequence, plenty of traditions have been carried forward, not only to commemorate Ou Yuan, but also to celebrate this festival. For instance, an increasing number of people partake in the celebration by eating zongzi which is a glutinous rice pudding, wrapped to form a pyramid using bamboo or reed leave. And the festival is highlighted by the dragon boat races, in which competing teams drive their boats forward rowing to the rhythm of pounding drums. And when some men positioned at the bow set off firecrackers, tossing rice into the water, the toasty warm day is filled to overflowing with uplifting gaiety and excitement. Simultaneously, the festival's significance as a time for warding off ill-fortune and disease is symbolized by a number of customary practices such as hanging calamus and moxa on the front door, and pasting up pictures of Chung Kuei (a nemesis of evil spirits). Adults drink hsiung huang wine and children are given fragrant sachets, both of which are said to possess qualities for preventing evil and bringing peace.

Whereas, the crystallization of our history and culture is on the verge of giving way to the modern culture, which urges us to preserve the cultural relics. The Dragon Boat Festival, as one of the most cherished festivals in China, has undoubtedly nourished our nation and taken root in our culture. Thereby we need to carry forward the tradition so that we can impel the construction of spiritual civilization and develop cultural diversity, which eventually fosters our national identity and value. Because on account of the vicissitudes of the Chinese festivals and traditions, it is definitely outrageous to see other countries snatching our own cultural heritage.

评析：同样是大学一年级学生的一篇习作,本文作者也展现出平时良好的学习习惯和语言功底,词汇量和写作能力跟同年级学生(甚至高年级学生)比,都较为突出。

本篇习作是关于端午节的说明文,命题作文,要求第一段介绍端午节由来,第二段介绍庆祝活动和传统,第三段总结。看似没有太多发挥空间,但是作者凭借其丰富的词汇量和反复修改(先在线反馈,然后教师反馈),把文章改成了精品。开篇指出端午节作为法定节日并无特别之处,紧接着就用倒装句强调"by no means can we afford to lose sight of the splendid history and long-cherished tradition of the festival",并提出自己的观点。对端午节起源的介绍,用到的词汇有"derive from""widely accepted origin";关于屈原,用到的词汇有"upright, loyal and highly-esteemed poet Qu Yuan""being disgraced and dismissed",这里两个动词的用法采用了押头韵的修辞手法。

第二段端午的习俗和庆祝活动,难的地方在于怎样用英语表达有中国特色的词汇,很多同学的这一部分会出现大量的中式英语,这一点作者做得很好,语言有特色,词汇和句型富有变化,如吃粽子的习俗"For instance, an increasing number of people partake in the celebration by eating zongzi which is a glutinous rice pudding, wrapped to form a pyramid using bamboo or reed leave"; 庆祝节日的传统活动, 如划龙舟 "and the festival is highlighted by the dragon boat races, in which competing teams drive their boats forward rowing to the rhythm of pounding drums"。两个习俗都是用一句话说明,句式复杂却表达得清晰明了,hightlight 可以说是点睛之词。其他的表达还有与驱邪相关的表达 "warding off ill-fortune and disease" "preventing evil and bringing peace"。"be filled to overflowing with uplifting gaiety and excitement" 等用得也很精妙,足可以作为佳句供其他同学借鉴。

最后一段继续保持这种较浓的书面语韵味,保持复杂的句型和丰富多变的词汇: the crystallization of our history and culture, on the verge of, giving way to, preserve cultural relics, nourished, taken root, carry forward the tradition, cultural diversity, fostering national identity and value, vicissitudes, 等等,恰如其分地把平时的积累运用了进来。

优秀习作 10

Mr. Light

15 级　陈钰冰

Chapter One

He did not show up in the corner of the corridor, at 6:55.

Hiding disappointment in mind, she shuffled to the canteen for the sake offood, bearing in mind his favorite choice of breakfast—a bowl of sweet potato congee, with a boiled egg.

Due to his absence, she took the seat randomly.

Weirdly, in the near distance, she felt that she could still see his handsome profile appear as well as his gleaming hair, in the rays of morning light, "How could that be?" She rubbed her sleepy eyes, eliminating the possibility of dreaming and stared at that direction again.

None, only a few specks of dusts were dancing joyfully in the light.

"What's wrong with him? He never misses the time. Is he ill? Oh my god, is it serious? Shall I send a caring message to him or ask him to bring some medicine? I have quite a lot …" Ridiculous thoughts continuously flooded from her imaginary.

Pretending having meals elegantly was a waste of time since he was not here today. Stuffing her mouth swiftly , she finished her brief meal ahead of usual time.

Chapter Two

He was in her neighbor class. Two big and bright windows of every classroom, as clear as crystal, existed in the side of corridor. She doubted it was designed for head teachers' convenience to supervise the behavior of students. Anyway, it was quite at her convenience to pry on his daily lives with the help of them. Every time she passed by the windows, she could not help but turn her head unconsciously to see him. It seemed so odd from other people's points of view that you stand still, letting your sight penetrate the windows. Therefore, for the sake of avoiding possible misunderstanding, she racked her brains for hundreds of times, trying to make up a perfect excuse. Eventually, going to the washroom became a veil to cover her deepest secret, considering the fact the washroom stood at the end of the corridor, a place which you have to pass by his class if you want to go. She took every precious chance to glimpse him.

Funnily, she has never realized that going to the washroom hundreds and thousands of time in a short period itself was odd enough.

Wherever he sat, she could locate his seat in class effortlessly but accurately.

This time was no exception. "There he is." Her heart was pounding with wild joy the moment she discovered him. He seemed fine, chatting with someone and wearing a big smile.

She loved to see his smile, indeed, with a small unnoticeable dimple showing in his left cheek. Nevertheless, she found his smile was too dazzling this time for she could clearly see that he was talking with a girl intimately. She knew that girl, so cute and so amiable, who could easily overshadow her in the crowd.

An envious rage, burnt as blaming fire, tortured her inner side.

What else could she do? Nothing! She could do nothing but eye them jealously.

Chapter Three

She could not remember exactly why she fell in love with him. She could only remember it was a mid-summer night, accompanying with the chirping of cicadas. On the stage, he sang a lovely song, together with guitar playing. His long and slender fingers crossing the strings were so nimble that they caught her eyes. His deep velvet voice echoed off the plaster walls, hovering around her mind from then on.

She never revealed the truth in front of her friends. Pretending to be inadvertent and appearing scornful whenever they mentioned about him, her blush face blurted out her secret.

After classes, the library was her first choice. While she was dealing with her homework, she found herself hit by sudden emptiness. She could not help but wonder meaningless thoughts:

What he is doing? No, no, I should focus on my own business. All right, let's see if I could find him. I will just give one glimpse; otherwise I can not concentrate.

It did not take a long time for her to decide to find him for she again justified for her absent minds.

Where is he? He prefers the first floor to the second floor, prefers the squirrel table to round tables, and prefers sitting alone to sitting with others. Bearing that thought in mind, she rushed downstairs, searching for every corner of the library.

It was easy for her to pick him up. He was immersed in his own business: he shook his head continuously, frowning for a while. Then, seemingly struck by a fresh idea, he scribbled furiously on his draft paper.

Ballooned with overwhelming happiness, she watched so absorbedly as if the time was frozen, totally forgetting about her one-glimpse promise.

Sometimes, she felt like a professional detective, sometimes a magical witch, for she could predict his time schedule precisely. She would summon the courage to create the chance of coincident greetings. He would never have imagined that how many times she calculated in order to meet him exactly at the point.

She knew everything was meaningless. Love without response was inevitably meaningless.

Feeling that her heart was tangled by intertwined cirrus of love, so tightly there is no escape.

Chapter Four

As the time flowed, another starry night arrived. She finally emancipated from tedious night self-study. As soon as the bell rang, she packed her bag immediately. The first thing she wanted to do was to check whether he was still at his classroom.

The time he went back to dormitory was never regular. There were some clues but they were still hard to catch. Gradually, she had already formed a habit of checking his classroom regularly in order to figure out his certain time to leave.

Minutely inching towards the back door of the neighbor class, she, as a timid squirrel, looked around cautiously to make sure that there was no one noticing her, and raising her head with a quick glimpse. As expected, a familiar figure came into her view.

"Yes, he is in." She calmed her sudden satisfaction down, preparing for the second-time check.

This period of time was the most embarrassing because she had to keep watching him in case he left without her realization. She was eager to follow his steps back to her dormitory. However, it was not only inappropriate to stare still at others' classroom from the corridor, but also quite hard to explain to her classmates if they curiously raised up questions like why she lingered here or whether she was waiting for someone. She must find reasonable reasons, or do something else. But the question was, if she pretended to go to the washroom or somewhere else, he was very likely to leave without her realization, only leaving an empty seat. She made the same mistake today. He had gone before she came back.

A sense of disappointment overwhelmed her chest. She swiftly tiptoed from the corridor, hoping to view his silhouette from behind.

There were times that she was lucky enough to catch up with the pace of his steps. She would intentionally keep the distance from him, avoiding his awareness of her existence.

Following, following him until at the corner of corridor, where it begins, where it ends.

Tomorrow is another day. Or, it is another turn.

The End

Deep in the night, she wrote down several lines of Funeral Blues, which she thought in accordance with her inner feelings.

He is my North, my South, my East and West

My working week and my Sunday rest

My noon, my midnight, my talk, my song

"He is my light. " She finished the last line herself, silently.

评析:本篇习作作者业余时间也喜欢写作,还是某中文文学网的签约作家。作者根据情节发展驾驭语言结构和词汇的能力较强,文笔细腻丰富,尤其擅长心理刻画和细节描写,将情窦初开的女孩那种惴惴不安又无时无刻不在挂念着对方的小心思描写得淋漓尽致。

文章开篇直入主题:定点去食堂吃饭的女孩没有发现经常关注的人,从疑惑到失望到各种担心揣测。从人物动作、神态到心理描写都非常细腻:暗恋的人不在,就"took seat randomly",怕看错了"rubbed her eyes",最后确认确实不在,于是不再保持优雅的吃饭仪态,而是匆匆"stuffing her mouth swiftly"等。心里活动:"What's wrong with him? He never misses the time. Is he ill? Oh my god, is it serious? Shall I send a caring message to him or ask him to bring some medicine? I have quite a lot …"。种种女孩的小心思、小动作,活灵活现。环境描写也相得益彰,如"None, only a few specks of dusts were dancing joyfully in the light",想见的人不在,只有晨光中的灰尘飞舞,非常符合失望的心情。

第二部分交代故事背景,暗恋隔壁班的男生,每次路过时都会偷偷瞥一眼。这一段用了非常多的细节来刻画女孩暗恋的小心思:为了使自己的"路过偷瞥"不那么明显,每次都是假装去卫生间,因为他的教室是必经之路,却没曾想"going to the washroom hundreds and thousands of time in a short period itself was odd enough";无论他在教室哪个角落,都能"locate his seat effortlessly but accurately";又一次看到他,女孩欢喜雀跃(her heart was pounding with wild joy);但是这次发现男孩跟另一个女孩相谈正欢,"An envious rage, burnt as blaming fire, tortured her inner side",这些细节刻画成功地把人物形象和性格立体化起来。

第三部分开头闪回到女孩暗恋上男孩的瞬间,用更多的笔墨刻画这种"love without response"。作者形容女孩就像一个"professional detective, sometimes a magical witch",因为总是能准确预测到男孩的时间表,什么时候在图书馆的哪个角落,什么时候回宿舍等。寻找男孩的描述非常有代表性,用一系列的排比句揭示了寻人时的心理状态,也形象地把女孩的迫切心理刻画了出来,"He prefers the first floor to the second floor, prefers the squirrel table to round tables, and prefers sitting alone to sitting with others"。找到男孩后,细腻的神态和细节描写:"He was immersed in his own business: he shook his head continuously, frowning for a while. Then, seemingly struck by a fresh idea, he scribbled furiously on his draft paper"。女孩那刻的心情瞬间由阴转晴,心花怒放,时间似乎都停止了(Ballooned with overwhelming happiness, she watched so absorbedly as if the time was frozen)。女孩暗恋时心理的细微变化和情绪的大起大落,被作者刻画得生动传神。

第四部分继续心理和动作描写,推动情节发展。女孩的行动发展到从教室里偷偷地看,到回宿舍路上偷偷地跟,跟得近怕发现,跟得远又看不见。字里行间都是这种患得患失、易忧易喜的心情变化。然而,什么时候会有转折呢,会有回报吗?作者在本节最后说到"Following, following him until at the corner of corridor, where it begins, where it ends",一语双关,答案没说破,但读者读到这里想必已了然。

结尾部分,女孩(或者说作者)用几行诗总结了这段无果的暗恋,点题。对于暗中默默关注、爱慕着男孩的女孩来说,他的确就是一道光,照亮她的世界,尽管他从不曾知道。诗韵律优美,对仗工整,情感真挚,也是全文的精华:"He is my North, my South, my East and West; My working week and my Sunday rest; My noon, my midnight, my talk, my song."

当然,本篇习作也存在一些语言上的小错误和可以改进的地方,比如,"whether he was still at his classroom",此处介词应用"in his classroom";从句"which she thought in accordance with her inner feelings"中缺少谓语等。相信如果作者有更多时间打磨语言,会写出更优秀的习作。

结 语

　　大数据时代，是人们利用数据技术更好地解决当前生活和工作中存在的问题的时代。大数据带来信息处理技术的革新，带来思维和行为方式的变化，也带来全新的时间和空间概念。教育大数据汇聚存储了教育领域的信息资产，能够提升教育环境与教学活动的感知性，提高教育管理水平、决策与评价的智慧性。简而言之，大数据是智慧教育系统建设的"支柱"，而数据挖掘和分析技术是连接教育大数据与智慧教育的桥梁（柯清超，2013；杨现民等，2014）。江南大学已经全面铺开"智慧教室"的建设，教师的上课录像、上课课件、上课资料、学生上课的反应等都能在校园网络上实现点播和数据分析；"雨课堂"（师生互动的教育应用）的开发和实施，使教师即使面对人数众多的班级，也可以实现课堂内与学生的零距离互动。

　　大数据使得在线学习、碎片化学习、移动学习、泛在学习成为日常。大数据技术和外语教育的深度融合，对教师的教学内容、教学方式、教学环境、教学评价及学生的学习内容、学习方法、认知方式等产生方方面面的影响。从大数据的细节里，人们可以分析出学习者的性格、学习风格、认知倾向、动机类型等，也可以分析出教师的教学理念、认知方式、习惯性教学行为、与学生的互动倾向、反馈时的风格、知识面的宽窄、教师的魅力、学生的评价等。总之，任何教授、学习、使用数据的行为都会在网上留下数据指纹。以大数据时代背景下的外语教育为分析蓝本，可以管窥英语教育在新生态环境下的发展方向和途径。

　　相比英语语言其他技能的学习和发展，英语写作与大数据的结合更加紧密。大数据时代使得资源的分享和使用前所未有的丰富多样。对于学习者而言,各种网络资源、语料库、英语学习网站等,都给写作提供了取之不尽的素材和话题来源。自动写作和在线反馈等数字化写作平台,进一步让英语写作变得智能化和自动化。除了掌握整合资源和运用资源的能力,学生的自主学习能力、交互学习、合作能力,对作品的鉴赏和反馈能力等都得到进一步加强。同时,如何有效地利用数据技术,如何科学、合理地掌控自主学习进度和内容,等等,也将对学习效果产生深刻影响。对于写作教师而言,能否融合大数据技术与传统写作课堂,如何进行数据整理和分析,如何进行新型的评价与反馈,如何激发学生的写作兴趣和提升习作能力,等等,都是大数据时代带来的挑战和机遇。

　　大数据赋予教师和学生新的身份。教师从唯一的资源来源和提供者,转变为资源的整合者和管理者;从知识传授的权威者转变为知识的协商者;从写作的单一评价反馈者转变为写作过程的指导者和交互评估者。相应地,大数据也赋予了学习者多重身份,从知识的被动接收到成为学习的中心,从写作者到读者,从接受评价者到互动反馈者。尤其是写作评价与反馈方式的变革,把教师反馈、同伴反馈、在线反馈有机结合的多元反馈方式,能缓解写作教师批改大量写作作业时"费时低效"的压力,增加师生互动和生生互动,减轻学生的写作焦虑,切实提升学生的写作能力。另一方面,教师基于大数据技术与学生的互动、生生互动等都能形成数据。对数据的挖掘和分析,能进一步帮助教师了解学生在英语写作过程中常常会出现的共性问题、遇到的困难或存在的误区,把握班级学生的总体情况及个性化特征,从而在英语写作教学过程中因材施教,优化教学内容和教学计划。

　　长期以来,英语写作教学面临着教师不愿教、学生不愿学的尴尬局面。写作是一种孤立的个体行为,写作教师更是孤军奋战,但是大数据时代可以使这一切发生根本性的改变。整合教师资源,推进专业团队建设,最大限度地减少重复性劳动,最大可能地提升学生自主学习能力和写作能力,建立新型的师生关系和学习伙伴关系,这些都是大数据技术带来的机遇。在享受新技术红利的同时,也不能忽略大数据时代可能带来的新问题。比如,一些自动纠错软件可能会导致学生拼写和语法能力的下降;唾手可得的网络资源也为学生的抄袭提供了方便;一些流行的、有趣的应用可能提供便利时也浪费了学生更多的时间

(王海啸,2014)。这些都需要教师正确认识并在学生学习过程中采取适当的措施加以监管,及时干预和纠正。此外,虽然新时代的学生普遍具有更强的信息技术运用能力,但不排除有不太擅长甚至完全不懂的学生,在这种情况下教师的指导和协助也是必要的。

总而言之,在大学英语教学"提高质量、缩减课时"的改革大环境下,大数据时代的到来,就像教育界的一场及时雨,使英语教学的实效性、工具性和数字化的实现成为可能。大数据时代的英语写作教与学,借力于数字化和信息化的技术,未来人机互动常态化、数据分析科学化、教学方式多元化、评估方式即时化等都将有无限可能的发展空间。

附录

Process Analysis 说明文写作范文 1

版本 1：本文使用第二人称 you。文中对某一个步骤做出强调或警示的地方用斜体标出，以引起学生注意。

How to Make an Origami Crane

For this project you will need 1 square piece of paper (preferably origami paper), and nimble fingers.

Step 1: X fold

The first step is to fold the square diagonally, corner to corner. Repeat the same process again so that it looks like an X on your paper. *Make sure that you properly align the edges* or else your crane won't fold as well. *Make sure it is as perfect as possible.*

Step 2: + fold

The second step is to flip the paper over and fold the paper in half horizontally. Repeat this process again so that your paper looks like a + and a X on top of each other. *Make sure it is perfect just like with the X. Making sure your folds are aligned perfectly* is a key part of this.

Step 3: Accordion fold

Open the square up, keeping the colored side down. Turn the square so that one of the corners is pointing at you. Bring the two side corners in to meet the corner on the table that's pointing at you. Take the top corner that's still sticking up and press it down to join the other corners, creating an accordion folded square.

Step 4: Superman fold

With the "flap" corners still facing you, take the top right hand corner of the square and fold it into the center diagonal line of the square. The result of your folds will look a bit like the Superman logo shape. Repeat this with the left top corner.

Once both parts are folded in, pull the top part down and press the crease.

Step 5: Frog mouth to diamond fold

After you have both halves of the triangle pulled in, pull them back out and lift up the top piece of paper. Next, lift up the top front corner and hold down the other three front corners. Pull the top corner up. It should look like a frog's mouth. *The next part is a bit tricky.* Pull the top corner all the up and back so that the top piece lies flat. *Carefully press all the folds down so that you end up with a diamond shape on top of the bottom diagonal square.*

Step 6: Press repeat

Flip the paper over and repeat Steps 4 −6 to the other side.

Step 7: Skinny kite fold

Next, fold the right top corner of the diamond in to meet the center line. Press down that fold. Repeat this for the left top corner. Flip the paper over and repeat the above steps for the other side. You'll end up with something that looks a bit like a skinny kite shape.

Step 8: Wolf's head fold

Now, lift up the top right side and press it over to the other side, like turning a page in a book. Press down the middle fold. Flip the paper over and repeat this in the same direction, right to left, on the other side. You will end up with a very elongated "wolf's head" shape.

Step 9: Snout flip fold

Lift up the wolf's snout and fold it so it meets with the tips of the ears. Press that new fold down. Flip the paper over and repeat on the other side.

Step 10: Book fold

Like you did in Step 7, fold the right side top layer of the paper in a book fold, from right to left. Flip the paper over and repeat on the other side.

Step 11: Heads & Tail fold

Next, you pull out the long pieces of paper (the head/neck & tail). Pull them both out so that they line up with the angle of the body fold. Bend the top of one side down to make the head.

Step 12: Flap fold

Fold both wings down where two different angles meet on the wing flaps. Press the folds.

Step 13: Puff it up

You can also try blowing into the hole on the bottom as you pull out the wings to make sure your crane's body is puffed out. *Be careful to not pull out the wings too much or they'll rip.* If the wings rip you will have to restart your crane with a new piece of paper. To finish off the crane and make it able to stand, gently pull the wings apart where they're folded. Then turn the crane upside down and gently pull the opposite corners apart to finish opening up the body.

Now you are done!

Process Analysis 说明文写作范文 2

版本 2：使用复数第一人称 we。

How to Make an Origami Crane

What You'll Need

Origami Paper and Optional Folding Tools

The Body of the Crane

We take our piece of paper, our six inch red and we fold it point to point. We now have a triangle shape. Set your crease. Open this and fold your other point. Open it again and now we fold it in half this way. Open it up and fold it in half again. Open it up and now we have this shape, if you hold the points as I am doing.

This will collapse into a diamond shape. We are going to take this edge and fold it into the center line, setting your crease. We take the other side and bring that edge to the middle, and we now have this.

We turn this over and bring this edge into the center just as we did on the other side. Set our crease. Bring this edge into the center and set our crease. The next step is to go to the top and along the line here, we're going to fold it like this. It looks like an ice cream cone, and we're going to bring it up, turn the paper and then we're going to fold it the other way.

This is pre-setting creases for a few steps down the road. And we now have this shape.

Origami Wings

The next step is to open these flaps, slide your thumb inside and this will begin to come up like this and using the crease lines we have set, it takes this shape, which we fold down.

Turning it over, we repeat the sequence. The next step is to take the top flap, bring it up, turn it over. Take the other flap and bring it up. The next step is to take this edge and fold it into the center. We go to the other side and repeat that. Then we turn it over and repeat those steps on this side. The next step is to take these legs and fold them up like this and fold them the other way to set the crease in both directions and we do an inside reverse fold and it comes up like this.

Create Origami Crane Head

The next step is to give our crane a head. Slide your finger up on one side or the other and just bend it over and our crane now has a head. The next step is to give our crane a shape and we do this by taking these tips which are the wings and we gently begin to pull it out like this. And now we have the traditional origami crane.

参考文献

Ashwell, T. Patterns of teacher response to student writing in a multiple-draft composition classroom: Is contentfeedback followed by form feedback the best method?[J]. *Journal of Second Language Writing*, 2000(9):227-258.

Attali, Y. Exploring the feedback and revision features of criterion. Paper presented at the National Council on Measurement in Education (NCME), 2004.

Attali, Y. & Burstein, J. Automated essay scoring with e-rater?[J]. *Journal of Technology, Learning, and Assessment*. 2006,4(3):1-30.

Attali, Y. et al. Scoring with the computer: Alternative procedures for improving the reliability of holistic essay scoring[J]. *Language Testing*, 2013,30(1):125-141.

Atwell, N. *In the Middle: Writing, Reading, and Learning with Adolescents*[M]. Portsmouth: Heinemann, 1987.

Bhatia, V. K. *Worlds of Written Discourse: A Genre-based View*[M]. New York: Continuum, 2008.

Berger, V. The effects of peer and self-feedback[J]. *CATESOL Journal*, 1990(3):21-35.

Berg, E. C. Preparing ESL students for peer response[J]. *TESOL Journal*, 1999a,8(2):20-25.

Berg, E. C. The effects of trained peer response on ESL students' revision types and writing quality[J]. *Journal of Second Language Writing*,1999b,8(3):215-241.

Bitchener, J. Evidence in support of written corrective feedback[J]. *Journal of Second Language Writing*,2008,17(2):102-118.

Bitchener, J. et al. The effect of different types of corrective feedback on ESL student writing[J]. *Journal of Second Language Writing*, 2005,14(3):191-205.

Bitchener, J. & Knoch, U. The value of written corrective feedback for migrant and international students[J]. *Language Teaching Research*, 2008, 12(3): 409 – 431.

Bitchener, J. & Knoch, U. The contribution of written corrective feedback to language development: A ten-month investigation[J]. *Applied Linguistics*, 2009, 31(2): 193 – 214.

Burgess, Amy. "I don't want to become a China Buff": Temporal dimensions of the discoursal construction of writer identity[J]. *Linguistics and Education*, 2012, 23(3): 223 – 234.

Burgess, A. & Ivanic, R. Writing and being written: Issues of identity across timescales[J]. *Written Communication*, 2010, 27(2): 228 – 255.

Buzick, H. et al. Comparing human and automated essay scoring for prospective graduate students with learning disabilities and/or ADHD[J]. *Applied Measurement in Education*, 2016, 29(3): 161 – 172.

Chandler, J. The efficacy of various kinds of error feedback for improvement in the accuracy and fluency of L2 student writing[J]. *Journal of Second Language Writing*, 2003, 12(3): 267 – 296.

Coughlan, S. Harvard plans to boldly go with "Spocs". [EB/OL]. Retrieved from http://www.bbc.co.uk/news/business-24166247, 2013-09-24/2018-07-06.

Cremin, T. & Baker, S. Exploring teacher-writer identities in the classroom: Conceptualising the struggle[J]. *English Teaching: Practice & Critique*, 2010(3): 8 – 25.

Cremin, T. & Baker, S. Exploring the discursively constructed identities of a teacher-writer teaching writing[J]. *English Teaching: Practice and Critique*, 2014(3): 30 – 55.

Dillenbourg, P. Introduction: What do you mean by "collaborative learning"? [A]. In P. Dillenbourg (ed.), *Collaborative Learning: Cognitive and Computational Approaches*[C]. Amsterdam: Pergamon, 1999: 1 – 19.

Draper, M. C. et al. Reading and writing habits of pre-service teachers[J]. *Reading Horizons*, 2000, 40(3): 185 – 203.

du Gay, P. et al. *Identity: A Reader*[M]. London: Sage, 2000.

El Ebyary, K. & Windeatt, S. The impact of computer-based feedback on students' written work? [J]. *International Journal of English Studies* (*IJES*), 2010,10(2):121-142.

Elliot, S. Intellimetric: From here to validity [A]. In M. D. Shermis & J. Burstein (eds.), *Automated Essay Scoring: A Cross-disciplinary Perspective* [C]. Mahwah, NJ:Lawerence Erlbaum Associates, Inc., 2003:71-86.

Ellis, R. Corrective feedback and teacher development [J]. *L2 Journal*, 2009,1(1):3-18.

Ellis, R. et al. The effects of focused and unfocused written corrective feedback in English as a foreign language context [J]. *System*, 2008(36):353-371.

Ellis, R. A framework for investigating oral and written corrective feedback: Epilogue [J]. *Studies in Second Language Acquisition*, 2010(32):335-349.

Evgenia, Vassilaki. Reflective writing, reflecting on identities: The construction of writer identity in student teachers' reflections [J]. *Linguistics and Education*, 2017(6):43-52.

Fang Y. Perceptions of the computer-assisted writing programamong EFL college learners [J]. *Educational Technology & Society*, 2010(3):246-256.

Ferris, D. R. Student reactions to teacher response in multiple-draft composition classrooms [J]. *TESOL Quarterly*, 1995,29(1):33-53.

Ferris, D. R. The case for grammar correction in L2 writing classes: A response to Truscott (1996) [J]. *Journal of Second Language Writing*, 1999,8(1):1-10.

Ferris, D. R. *Treatment of Error in Second Language Student Writing* [M]. Ann Arbor, MI: University of Michigan Press,2002.

Ferris, D. R. *Response to Student Writing: Implications for Second Language Students* [M]. Mahwah, NJ: Lawrence Erlbaum, 2003.

Ferris, D. R. The "grammar correction" debate in L2 writing:Where are we, and where do we go from here? (and what do we do in the meantime …?) [J]. *Journal of Second Language Writing*, 2004(13):49-62.

Ferris, D. R. Does error feedback help student writers? New evidence on the short- and long-term effects of written errorcorrection [A]. In K. Hyland & F. Hyland (eds.), *Feedback in Second Language Writing: Context and Issues* [C]. Cambridge: Cambridge University Press, 2006:81-104.

Ferris, D. R. Second language writing research and written corrective feedback in SLA: Intersections and practical applications [J]. *Studies in Second Language Acquisition*, 2010(32):181-201.

Ferris, D. & Hedgcock, J. *Teaching ESL Composition: Purpose, Process, and Practice* (2nd ed.)[M]. NJ: Mahwah, 2005.

Ferris, D. R. & Roberts, B. Error feedback in L2 writing classes: How explicit does it need to be? [J]. *Journal of Second Language Writing*, 2001,10(3):161-184.

Foltz, P. W. et al. Implementation and applications of the intelligent essay assessor [A]. In M. D. Shermis & J. Burstein (eds.), *Handbook of Automated Essay Evaluation*[C]. New York: Routledge, 2013:66-88.

Freeman, J. B. & Ambady, N. A dynamic interactive theory of person construal [J]. *Psychological Review*, 2011,118(2):247-79.

Gardner, Paul. Writing and writer identity: The poor relation and the search for voice in "personal literacy"[J]. *Literacy*, 2018(1):11-19.

Grimes, D. Assessing automated assessment: Essay evaluation software in the classroom. Paper presented at the computers and writing conference, 2005.

Grainger, B. *Introduction to MOOCs: Avalanche, Illusion or Augmentation?* [M]. Moscow: UNESCO Institute for Information Technologies in Education, 2013.

Grainger, T. et al. *Creativity and Writing: Developing Voice and Verve in the Classroom*[M]. London: Routledge, 2005.

Hansen, J. G. & Liu, J. Guiding principles for effective peer response[J]. *ELT Journal*, 2005(1):31-38.

Hislop, J. & Stracke, E. ESL students in peer review: An action research study in a university English for Academic Purposes course [J]. *University of Sydney Papers in TESOL*, 2017(12):9-44.

Huang, Shin-Ying. Revising identities as writers and readers through critical language awareness [J]. *English Teaching: Practice and Critique*, 2013(3):65-86.

Hyland, F. ESL writers and feedback: Giving more autonomy to students[J]. *Language Teaching Research*, 2000,4(1):33-54.

Hyland, K. Authority and invisibility—authorial identity in academic writing[J].

Journal of pragmatics, 2002,34(8):1091-1112.

Hyland, K. *Teaching and Researching Writing*[M]. Beijing: Foreign Language Teaching and Research Press, 2005.

Hyland, K. & Hyland, F. Contexts and issues in feedback on L2 writing: An introduction[A]. In K. Hyland & F. Hyland (eds.), *Feedback in Second Language Writing: Contexts and Issues* [C]. Cambridge: Cambridge University Press, 2006:1-20.

Hyland, K. Genre, discipline and identity[J]. *Journal of English for Academic Purposes*, 2015(19):32-43.

Hu, G. Using peer review with Chinese ESL student writers[J]. *Language Teaching Research*, 2005,9(3):321-342.

Ivanic, R. Writer identity[J]. *Prospect*, 1995(10):8-31.

Ivanic, R. *Writing and Identity: The Discoursal Construction of Identity in Academic Writing* [M]. Amsterdam: John Benjamins Publishing Company, 1998.

Ivanic, R. Language, learning and identity[A]. In R. Kiely et al. (eds.), *Language, Culture and Identity in Applied Linguistics*[C]. London: BAAL/ Equinox, 2006.

Kajee, L. "The road is never straight": Emerging teachers negotiating language and identity[J]. *South African Journal of Higher Education*, 2015,29(5):201-213.

Kellogg, R. T. et al. Does automated feedback help students learn to write?[J] *Journal of Educational Computing Research*, 2010,42(2):173-196.

Krashen, S. D. We acquire vocabulary and spelling by reading: Additional evidence for the input hypothesis[J]. *Modern Language Journal*, 1989(3):440-464.

Koh, Won-Young. Effective applications of automated writing feedback in process-based writing instruction[J]. *English Teaching*, 2017,72(3):91-117.

Kynell, Teresa & Tebeaux, Elizabeth. The association of teachers of technical writing: The emergence of professional identity[J]. *Technical Communication Quarterly*, 2009(2):107-141.

Lai, Y. H. Which do students prefer to evaluate their essays: Peers or computer program? [J]. *British Journal of Educational Technology*, 2010,41(3):432-454.

Lam, R. A peer review training workshop: Coaching students to give and evaluate peer feedback[J]. *TESL Canada Journal*, 2010, 27(2):114 – 127.

Lee, I. Error correction in L2 secondary writing classrooms: The case for Hong Kong[J]. *Journal of Second Language Writing*, 2004, 13(4):285 – 312.

Lee, I. Feedback in Hong Kong secondary writing classrooms: Assessment for learning orassessment of learning?[J]. *Assessing Writing*, 2007, 12(3):180 – 198.

Lemke, J. Across the scales of time: Artifacts, activities and meanings in ecosocial systems[J]. *Mind, Culture and Activity*, 2000, 7(4):273 – 290.

Lemke, J. Language development and identity: Multiple times cales in the social ecology of learning[A]. In C. Kramsch (ed.), *Language Acquisition and Language Socialisation: Ecological Perspectives*[C]. New York: Continuum, 2002:68 – 87.

Lennon, P. Error: Some problems of definition and identification[J]. *Applied Linguistic*, 1991, 12(2):180 – 195.

Li, J. et al. Rethinking the role of automated writing evaluation (AWE) feedback in ESL writing instruction[J]. *Journal of Second Language Writing*, 2015, 27:1 – 18.

Liu, J. & Hansen, J. *Peer Response in Second Language Writing Classrooms* [M]. Ann Arbor, MI: University of Michigan Press, 2002.

Long, M. The role of the linguistic environment in second language acquisition [A]. In Ritchie W. C. & Bhatia T. K. (eds.), *Handbook of Language Acquisition*[C]. New York: Academic Press, 1996:413 – 468.

Lundstroms, K. & Baker, W. To give is better than to receive: The benefits of peer review to the reviewers own writing[J]. *Journal of Second Language Writing*, 2009(18):30 – 43.

Lv, Xiaoxiao. A study on the application of automatic scoring and feedback system in college English writing[J]. *International Journal of Emerging Technologies in Learning*, 2018, 13(3):188 – 196.

Mangelsdorf, K. Peer reviews in the ESL composition classroom: What do students think?[J]. *ELT Journal*, 1992, 46(3):274 – 284.

Masse, R. E. Theory and practice of writing processes for technical writers[J]. *IEEE Transactions on Professional Communication*, 2013, 27(4):185 – 192.

Min, H. T. The effects of trained peer review on EFL students' revision types and writing[J]. *Journal of Second Language Writing*, 2006, 15(2):118 – 141.

Moon, Y. I. & Pae, J. K. Short-term effects of automated writing feedback and users' evaluation of criterion? [J]. *Korean Journal of Applied Linguistics*, 2011, 27(4):125 – 150.

Monje, E. M. Integration of Web 2.0 tools in a VLE to improve the EFL Spanish university entrance examination results: A quasi-experimental study [J]. *CALICO Journal*, 2014(1):26 – 42.

Muncie J. Using written teacher feedback in EFL composition classes[J]. *ELT Journal*, 2000, 54(1):47 – 53.

Norton B. *Identity and Language Learning: Gender, Ethnicity, and Educational Change* [M]. London: Longman, 2000.

Paulus, T. M. The effect of peer and teacher feedback onstudent writing [J]. *Journal of Second Language Writing*, 1999, 8(3):265 – 289.

Polio, C. et al. "If only I had more time": ESL learners' changes in linguistic accuracy on essay revisions[J]. *Journal of Second Language Writing*, 1998(7):43 – 68.

Rahimi, M. Is training student reviewers worth its while? A study of how training influences the quality of students' feedback and writing [J]. *Language Teaching Research*, 2013, 17(1):67 – 89.

Ramineni, C. & Williamson, D. M. Automated essay scoring: Psychometric guidelines and practices[J]. *Assessing Writing*, 2013, 18(1):25 – 39.

Reilly, E. D. et al. Evaluating the validity and applicability of automated essay scoring in two massive open online courses [J]. *International Review of Research in Open and Distance Learning*, 2014, 15(5):83 – 98.

Rollinson, P. Using peer feedback in the ESL writing class[J]. *ELT Journal*, 2005(59):23 – 30.

Rouhi, A. & Azizian, E. Peer review: Is giving corrective feedback better than receiving it in L2 writing? [J]. *Procedia—Social and Behavioral Sciences*, 2013(93):1349 – 1354.

Russell, J. & Spada, N. The effectiveness of corrective feedback for second language acquisition: A meta-analysis of the research[A]. In J. Norris & L. Ortega(eds.), *Synthesizing Research on Language Learning and Teaching*

[C]. Amsterdam: Benjamins, 2006:131-164.

Schwind, C. & Siegel, P. A modal logic for hypothesis theory[J]. *Fundamenta Informaticae*, 1994,21(1):89-102.

Sfard, A. & Prusak, A. Telling identities: In search of an analytic tool for investigating learning as a culturally shaped activity[J]. *Educational Researcher*, 2005,34(4):14-22.

Shand, Jennifer & Konza, Deslea. Creating the student writer: A study of writing identities in non-academic senior English classes[J]. *Australian Journal of Language & Literacy*, 2016(2):149-161.

Sheen, Y. The effect of focused written corrective feedback and language aptitude on ESL learners' acquisitionof articles[J]. *TESOL Quarterly*,2007(41):255-283.

Shermis, M. D. & Hamner, B. Contrasting state-of-the-art automated scoring of essays[A]. In M. D. Shermis & J. Burstein (eds.), *Handbook of Automated Essay Evaluation: Current Applications and New Directions*[C]. New York: Routledge, 2013:313-346.

Shintani, N. et al. Effects of written feedback and revision on learners' accuracy in using two English grammatical structures[J]. *Language Learning*, 2014(64):103-131.

Stefanou, C. & Revesz, A. Direct written corrective feedback, learner differences, and the acquisition of second language article use for generic and specific plural reference[J]. *Modern Language Journal*, 2015(99):263-282.

Swain, M. The output hypothesis: Just speaking and writing aren't enough[J]. *The Canadian Modern Language Review*, 1993,50(1):158-164.

Truscott, J. The case against grammar correction in L2 writing classes[J]. *Language Learning*, 1996,46:327-369.

Truscott, J. The case for "the case for grammar correction in L2 writing classes": A response to Ferris[J]. *Journal of Second Language Writing*,1999(8):111-122.

Truscott, J. Dialogue: Evidence and conjecture on the effects of correction: A response to Chandler[J]. *Journal of Second Language Writing*, 2004(13):337-343.

Truscott, J. The effect of error correction on learners' ability to write accurately [J]. *Journal of Second Language Writing*, 2007(16):1-18.

Tsui, A. B. & Ng, M. Do secondary L2 writers benefit from peer comments? [J]. *Journal of Second Language Writing*, 2000(2):147-170.

Viktor, M. S. & Kenneth, C. *Big Data: A Revolution That Will Transform How We Live, Work and Think*[M]. London: Hodder Export, 2013.

Villamil, O. S. & Guerrero, M. C. M. D. Peer revision in the L2 classroom: Social-cognitive activities, mediating strategies, and aspects of social behavior [J]. *Journal of Second Language Writing*, 1996(5):51-76.

Vojak C. et al. New spaces and old places: An analysis of writing assessment software[J]. *Computersand Composition*, 2011(2):97-111.

Warden, C. A. EFL business writing behaviors in differing feedback environments [J]. *Language Learning*, 2000, 50(4):573-616.

Ware, P. & Warschauer, M. Electronic feedback and second language writing[A]. In K. Hyland & F. Hyland (eds.), *Feedback in Second Language Writing: Contexts and Issues*[C]. New York: Cambridge University Press, 2006:105-122.

Weigle, S. C. English language learners and automated scoring of essays: Critical considerations[J]. *Assessing Writing*, 2013, 18(1):85-99.

Wilson, J. & Czik, A. Automated essay evaluation software in English Language Arts classrooms: Effects on teacher feedback, student motivation, and writing quality[J]. *Computers & Education*, 2016, 100(C):94-109.

Yılmaz, Y. Relative effects of explicit and implicit feedback: The role of working memory capacity and language analytic ability [J]. *Applied Linguistics*, 2013, 34(3):344-368.

Zhang, Z. Student engagement with computer-generated feedback: A case study [J]. *ELT Journal*, 2017, 71(3):317-328.

Zhang, Zhe & Hyland, K. Student engagement with teacher and automated feedback on L2 writing[J]. *Assessing Writing*, 2018(36):90-102.

白云,王俊菊.反馈方式对写作修改过程及质量的影响研究[J].东北师范大学学报(哲学社会科学版),2018(2):137—142.

蔡基刚.中国大学生英语写作在线同伴反馈和教师反馈对比研究[J].外语界,2011(2):65—72.

常俊跃,赵永青.学生视角下的英语专业基础阶段"内容·语言"融合的课程体系[J].外语与外语教学,2010(1):13—17.

陈冰冰. MOOCs课程模式：贡献和困境[J]. 外语电化教学, 2014(3)：38—43.

陈坚林. 大数据时代的慕课与外语教学研究——挑战与机遇[J]. 外语电化教学, 2015(1)：2—8,16.

陈娟文, 王娜. 基于数字化学习资源的英语写作能力培养[J]. 现代教育技术, 2016,26(5)：70—76.

程云艳. 直面挑战"翻转"自我——新教育范式下大学外语教师的机遇与挑战[J]. 外语电化教学, 2014(3)：44—47.

陈晓湘, 李会娜. 教师书面修正性反馈对学生英语写作的影响[J]. 外语教学与研究, 2009(5)：351—358.

陈庆斌. 大数据时代的大学英语写作教学模式重构[J]. 外语学刊, 2016(3)：129—132.

邓鹂鸣, 岑粤. 同伴互评反馈机制对中国学生二语写作能力发展的功效研究[J]. 外语教学, 2010(1)：59—62.

丁往道, 吴冰. 英语写作基础教程(第三版)[M]. 北京：高等教育出版社, 2011.

何旭良. 句酷批改网英语作文评分的信度和效度研究[J]. 现代教育技术, 2013,23(5)：64—67.

胡茶娟, 张迎春. 基于移动学习的大学英语写作反馈模式构建要素分析[J]. 现代教育技术, 2014(7)：71—78.

胡加圣, 靳琰. 教育技术与外语课程融合的理论与实践研究[J]. 中国电化教育, 2015(4)：114—120.

黄慧, 王海. 对基于建构主义理论的我国外语教学研究的调查与思考[J]. 外语与外语教学, 2007(6)：21—24.

黄静, 张文霞. 多元反馈对大学生英语作文修改的影响研究[J]. 中国外语, 2014(1)：51—56.

黄礼珍. 对大学生使用作文自动评分系统写作的调查[J]. 江苏外语教学研究, 2017(4)：18—21.

金晓宏. 非英语专业大学生对不同形式英语写作评改反馈的接受程度研究[J]. 外语研究, 2016(5)：58—62.

蒋艳, 马武林. 中国英语写作教学智能导师系统：成就与挑战——以句酷批改网为例[J]. 电化教育研究, 2013(7)：76—81.

柯清超. 大数据与智慧教育[J]. 中国教育信息化, 2013(12)：8—11.

李航,刘儒德.基于网络平台的英语协作写作模式效果研究[J].电化教育研究,2011(7):67—72.

李书影.大数据时代英语写作教学的创新路径——以"2016年百万同题英语写作"为例[J].外语电化教学,2017(2):3—8.

李奕华.基于动态评估理论的英语写作反馈方式比较研究[J].外语界,2015(3):59—67.

李竞.中国学生英语写作中教师书面反馈特征与学生反应的案例研究[J].外语界,2011(6):30—39.

李战子.身份理论和应用语言学研究[J].外国语言文学,2005(4):234—241.

李志雪,李绍山.对国内英语写作研究现状的思考——对八种外语类核心期刊十年(1993—2002)的统计分析[J].外语界,2003(6):55—60,78.

梁茂成,文秋芳.国外作文自动评分系统评述及启示[J].外语电化教学,2007(5):18—24.

刘润清.大数据时代的外语教育科研[J].当代外语研究,2014(7):1—6.

柳淑芬.中英文论文摘要中作者的自称语与身份构建[J].当代修辞学,2011(4):85—88.

刘奕,王小兰.论基于Blog的英语写作教学中的多元反馈模式[J].外语教学,2010(4):70—72.

刘豫钧,鬲淑芳.移动学习——国外研究现状之综述[J].现代教育技术,2004(3):12—16.

罗凌.大学生移动英语写作学习行为研究[J].外语电化教学,2017(4):33—39.

马武林,胡加圣.国际MOOCs对我国大学英语课程的冲击与重构[J].外语电化教学,2014(3):48—54.

倪清泉.网络环境下基于写作学习的大学英语写作教学研究[J].外语电化教学,2009(3):63—68.

欧阳护华,唐适宜.中国大学生英语议论文写作中的作者身份[J].解放军外国语学院学报,2006,29(2):49—53.

秦秀白.体裁教学法述评[J].外语教学与研究,2000(1):42—46.

秦朝霞.国内大学英语写作研究现状及发展趋势分析[J].现代外语,2009,32(2):195—204.

邵春燕.社会文化视角下英语专业写作教学的多角色参与模式[J].外语界,2016(2):79—87.

石晓玲. 在线写作自动评改系统在大学英语写作教学中的应用研究——以句酷批改网为例[J]. 现代教育技术, 2012(10): 67—71.

唐芳, 许明武. 英语写作者身份研究: 回顾与展望[J]. 外语界, 2015(3): 41—50.

唐锦兰, 吴一安. 在线英语写作自动评价系统应用研究述评[J]. 外语教学与研究, 2011(2): 273—282.

王保健等. 数字信息化环境下大学英语过程写作教学模式研究[J]. 黑龙江教育: 高校研究与评估, 2017(11): 15—18.

王勃然等. 自动写作评价研究与实践五十年——从单一、合作到交互[J]. 外语研究, 2015(5): 50—56.

王海啸. 大数据时代的大学英语写作教学改革[J]. 现代远程教育研究, 2014(3): 66—72.

王立非. 我国英语写作实证研究: 现状与思考[J]. 中国外语, 2005(1): 54—59.

王娜. 创新写作教学, 体验数字写作——来自北京科技大学"信息技术与英语写作课程整合研究"的报告[J]. 中国外语, 2014(2): 68—73.

王娜等. 大学英语SPOC翻转课堂: 一种有效学习模式建构[J]. 外语电化教学, 2016(3): 52—57.

王颖, 刘振前. 教师反馈对英语写作准确性、流利性、复杂性和总体质量作用的研究[J]. 外语教学, 2012(6): 49—53.

吴格奇. 学术论文作者自称与身份构建——一项基于语料库的英汉对比研究[J]. 解放军外国语学院学报, 2013, 36(3): 6—11.

徐昉. 中国学生英语学术写作中身份语块的语料库研究[J]. 外语研究, 2011(3): 57—63.

徐昉. 中国学习者英语学术词块的使用及发展特征研究[J]. 中国外语, 2012(4): 51—56.

徐昉. 国际发表与中国外语教学研究者的职业身份建构[J]. 外语与外语教学, 2017(1): 26—32.

徐昉. 英语写作教学与研究[M]. 北京: 外语教学与研究出版社, 2012.

杨晓琼, 戴运财. 基于批改网的大学英语自主写作教学模式实践研究[J]. 外语电化教学, 2015(2): 17—23.

杨现民等. 我国智慧教育发展战略与路径选择[J]. 现代教育技术, 2014(1): 12—19.

杨欣然. 二语学术写作中的自我指称与作者身份建构[J]. 外语与外语教学, 2015(4): 50—56.

杨永林. 写作教学, 十大视角——从经典修辞学到数字化写作[J]. 当代外语研究, 2012(3): 131—136.

杨永林等. 从"慕课"到"小微课", 看大数据在教学中的应用[J]. 现代教育技术, 2014(12): 45—51.

杨永林, 丁韬. 资源化与智能化视角下的大学英语写作教学研究[J], 外语电化教学, 2017(5): 9—14.

俞婷. 基于Wiki协作式写作系统的大学英语写作教学实证研究[J]. 电化教育研究, 2010(3): 71—82.

曾永红, 梁玥. 不同类型同伴互评对大学生写作的影响实证研究[J]. 外语研究, 2017(4): 53—57.

翟芳, 武永平. 基于微信技术的移动学习设计与实现——以"英语写作"课程为例[J]. 中国教育信息化, 2015(8): 74—77.

赵俊峰等. 大学英语写作研究现状调查[J]. 外语学刊, 2010(6): 98—100.

张之材. 2008—2016年国内大学英语写作研究述评——基于8种外语类核心期刊的统计分析[J]. 当代教育理论与实践, 2018(1): 127—131.

中国教育. 国家中长期教育改革和发展规划纲要(2010—2020年)[EB/OL]. http://www.edu.cn/html/e/2009/gangyao/. 2018-07-10.

朱岩岩. 对我国英语写作研究发展的调查和思考——基于我国外语类核心期刊统计分析(1980—2010)[J]. 外语界, 2011(6): 56—62.

朱岩岩. 国内二语写作评估反馈研究调查(2000—2013)[J]. 北京交通大学学报(社会科学版), 2014(2): 123—128.